# Bullying

## A Complete Guide to
## The Support Group Method

A Lucky Duck Book

# Bullying
## A Complete Guide to
## The Support Group Method

Incorporating a new edition of the bestselling book
*Crying for Help*

George Robinson
Barbara Maines

Los Angeles • London • New Delhi • Singapore

First published 2008

Incorporating a new edition of *Crying for Help* © 1997, 1998, 2000, 2003, 2006

SAGE Publications Ltd
1 Oliver's Yard
55 City Road
London EC1Y 1SP

SAGE Publications Inc.
2455 Teller Road
Thousand Oaks, California 91320

SAGE Publications India Pvt Ltd
B 1/I 1 Mohan Cooperative Industrial Area
Mathura Road, Post Bag 7
New Delhi 110 044

SAGE Publications Asia-Pacific Pte Ltd
33 Pekin Street #02-01
Far East Square
Singapore 048763

www.luckyduck.co.uk

**Library of Congress Control Number: 2007939403**

**British Library Cataloguing in Publication data**

A catalogue record for this book is available from the British Library

ISBN 978-1-4129-3536-4

Typeset by C&M Digitals (P) Ltd, Chennai, India
Printed on paper from sustainable resources
Printed in India by Replika Press Pvt Ltd

# Contents

# Acknowledgements

Since we began writing about Bullying and The Support Group Method we have suffered from unreasonably hostile criticism from a few professionals and politicians.

This hurt has been greatly healed by the tremendous encouragement, support and warmth from so many dear and valued colleagues and friends in the UK and around the world.

We would like to make a special mention of the support and encouragement we have had from Esther Rantzen who has understood and spoken up for our work and featured it in *That's Life* in 1993 and *Esther* in 2001. We are also grateful to the BBC for allowing the transcript of her live interview with Mark and Jamie (shown in *Esther*) to be reproduced in this publication.

Thank you.

# Foreword

Barbara Maines and George Robinson have made a major contribution to 'the field of bullying in schools' with their No Blame Approach in particular and with the myriad of other publishing and training opportunities provided by the resources assembled under the banner of Lucky Duck Publishing. Specifically, since the creation of the No Blame Approach, either in using it themselves to solve bullying problems in schools or in teaching others how to use this anti-bullying programme, Barbara and George have been directly and indirectly responsible for the cessation of bullying in the lives of many children and young people. In some areas designed to help human beings, like medicine for instance, you can see clear and identifiable results when a patient recovers from a serious illness after a doctor's intervention. In relation to anti-bullying programmes, however, is difficult to determine, whether students have enjoyed marginal, adequate or massively improved qualities of life as a result of an effective intervention. You also do not know how many boys or girls did not take that final sad act of commiting suicide because of such an intervention. I am convinced that since the inception of the No Blame Approach, if it were possible to create a table of statistics, we would produce a tangible mass of successes that would enable us to credit George and Barbara for their anti-bullying efforts. Unfortunately, we have no statistics for what was prevented! I would like, therefore, to take this opportunity to acknowledge and thank them for their work and achievements and to welcome the Support Group Approach as an addition to their excellent corpus of work.

In their introduction to The Support Group Approach, George and Barbara describe how they and the No Blame Approach have been under siege for some time as a result of ongoing attacks by Michele Elliott and her Kidscape colleagues, and more recently by Former Prime Minister Tony Blair. In the latter instance, based on inadequate information and a flawed argument, resulted in the withdrawal of significant financial support for the use of the No Blame programme in the Bristol area. Robinson and Maines also express their disappointment in a lack of support from the academic anti-bullying community in the UK when this attack took place. Here, it was assumed that these individuals suspected that by publicly supporting the No Blame Approach (and thereby showing themselves suspect of unsound judgement), their own funding would be under threat. Unsurprisingly, this unpleasant experience seems to contain several elements of bullying as follows:

- there was a process of continuous harrassment;
- the presence of a powerful individual who both misuses his power, and does not expect that there will be an effective retaliation or consequences for his actions;
- bystanders who are afraid/lack the courage to get involved and do not rally the power they could generate as a group (that could allow them to challenge the bullying).

Funnily enough, this situation is (dynamically at least) not unlike those encountered in the much less complex world of the school. Situations that the Support Group Approach deals with effectively all of the time!

In recent years, there have been a number of useful anti-bullying programmes that have been developed around the world. I consider the Support Group Approach to be in the best of these for the following reasons:

- **It is straight forward and unambiguous**  The programme comes with a set of clear instructions and a definite and straightforward path from conflict to resolution.
- **It is designed by practitioners for practitioners**  When you have been a teacher or practicing psychologist (like George and Barbara) and you have a developed insider-knowledge of the ins and outs of the school context, you learn about the importance of being clear, direct and practical in anything you design and to make it make sense to those who have to use it.
- **It deals with complex situation simply**  Although on first appearance a bullying situation may seem complex and very difficult, having a useful, practical and well-designed tool allows an unraveling and simplification that leads to a potentially constructive solution for all participants.
- **There is no need for extensive investigations**  Extensive investigation can cause individuals to lie themselves into corners and as a result feel resentment, antagonism and a need for revenge. This programme avoids this initial and destructive process and concentrates on finding a solution to the bullying that both allows the perpetrators to take responsibility for their actions but also supports them to become part of the solution.

- **Students see bullying addressed in a constructive and non-threatening way** What is anticipated with some nervousness is turned into a positive and constructive solution for all involved.
- **It brings about change quickly** When the programme is put into effect, the actions are practical and a timeline is created that provides for resolution in a relatively short period of time.
- **It is easy to use** The programme provides a logical, straightforward and easy to follow format. It is pragmatic and very accessible.
- **It works** I have seen and heard of numerous situations in which this approach has been found to be a useful way of solving a problem that in the first instance has seemed irresolvable – it works.
- **It is educative** It can show students that effective and practical solutions can be found in issues of conflict. It also provides a model for resolving conflict for all parties.
- **It is humane and hopeful approach to dealing with bullying** This is a refreshing programme. The approach engenders a sense of trust in the participants to be able to act sensibly and find a just solution. Philosphically, there is an underpinning that human beings are essentially well-intended and that given the opportunity can act humanely, ethically and with integrity.

Although Sue Young has carried out research to show that the No Blame Approach works I would not place too much emphasis on the concept of 'proof' in this context. Several years ago, I was speaking with the international anti-bullying expert, Ken Rigby. Ken was concerned because he had introduced an anti-bullying programme in a school setting and although it had seemed at first glance that the programme had caused a reduction of bullying, the post-programme evaluation suggested this wasn't the case. A closer inspection of these situations shows that in such contexts a number of issues come into play that muddy the waters. For instance, as a result of addressing the issue of bullying, people become aware of:

a. that bullying occurs in a wider range of ways than people had understood to be the case (for example, bullying is not only a physical act but can be verbal and exclusionary – very common with girls);
b. with the awareness raising that accompanies the introduction of an anti-bullying programme, pupils become aware of their rights in relation to bullying; and as a result;
c. more bullying is identified and reported.

In other words, in the cut and thrust of a school community with all of its complexities, results that suggest a failure need to be treated with caution. In the above situation, it seems that contrary to the measurement process created by the post-test that suggested a failed attempt of a bullying programme, in fact a process was underway that was starting to create a safer school (and it was starting to work). In other words, is it possible that pre- and post-programme tests about the effectiveness of anti-bullying programmes lack depth and meaning in the 'real world' of the school.

I would argue that the issue of proof of effectiveness for the Support Group Method is not one which should be of major concern. When teachers in schools use such tools, they learn to adapt the method from situation to situation and understand that in order to use it effectively requires skill, practice and concentration. In other words, in abstract terms the programme is excellent in its own right. In practical terms, it is only as good as the practitioner and his or her ability to adapt and change and grow with each situation.

In conclusion, I would like to state that I think the Support Group Method is an excellent tool for dealing with the difficult problem of bullying in schools. I recommend it most highly to you.

Congratulations to George Robinson and Barbara Maines.

*Keith Sullivan PhD*
*Professor and Head of the Department of Education*
*National University of Ireland, Galway*

# Finding your way around this book

## Part One

Writing in 2007, this book is probably the final piece of substantive writing we will publish about our anti-bullying work which started in 1990. Some of you will come to this with little knowledge about our particular way of working and you will be most interested in Part One where you will find a detailed description of the method, the way it started and how it has been refined during the years. From this reading you will have enough information to be confident to try it for yourself. For further training and in order to pass it on to colleagues you might want to acquire the linked training pack (Maines and Robinson, 2008).

## Part Two

Perhaps you will find Part One inspiring and need no further information, but the work is counter-intuitive and advises against the simplistic but commonly held view that the behaviour of bullies can be 'stopped' by punishment. If you are one of the many readers who have some doubts, then in Part Two you will find supporting evidence, overviews of research and accounts from other professionals in the UK and overseas, some of whom began from a position of scepticism. They offer their own experiences, which might encourage you or give you the confidence to try it out for yourself.

## Part Three

In Part Three you can read in detail how our work has been criticised or undermined in many ways, including:

- a persistent campaign of hostility from Michele Elliot and other Kidscape colleagues,
- an attack by the Prime Minister Tony Blair in question time November 2005,
- a silence from eminent colleagues who feared that funding would be withdrawn if they voiced support for our work in the face of government and DfES opposition.

This campaign of criticism has mobilised tremendous support for the work, both in the UK and overseas, and we now rely on the promotion of the work through these channels – our professional colleagues who find it a safe and effective intervention. If you are to become one of these supporters, then we want you to know what happened to us so that you can consider how you will protect yourself from similar consequences.

## Part One
# What is The Support Group Method?

# Introduction

If you are already familiar with our work, you might be confused to see the authors of 'The No Blame Approach' writing a book with 'The Support Group Method' in the title. No – we have not devised yet another method for dealing with bullying. One has been difficult enough. The No Blame Approach will continue to be respected overseas, but in the UK it has become a political football and we have decided to change the name, which was probably ill-advised in the first place, and now use a name that describes what the intervention does. When referring to recent work we use the new name, but where we include previous writing or include contributions from other colleagues we have left the name as it was used at that time.

In this publication, which updates *Crying for Help* (Robinson and Maines, 1997), the recent developments, both educational and political, are fully explained. There is new research and up-to-date case studies are included in this edition.

In policy development, staff with management responsibility for an establishment with a duty of care towards young people, staff, clients, visitors should consider two elements of the policy:

1. Prevention – standards of behaviour and activities that reduce the frequency of bullying incidents.
2. Intervention – safe actions to take when an incident happens.

This publication is about the second and describes a particular method in detail.

Any intervention planned when a bullying incident is reported should have two aims:

1. The duty of care falling on the responsible adult is, firstly, to keep the target safe.
2. There is also a responsibility to act in the best interests of the bullies – to change the pattern of harmful behaviour.

Some of the controversy surrounding this work arises from some misunderstandings – that it 'lets the bully off' or that it requires the bully to apologise to the victim.

The method is a structured, seven-step procedure and the results depend upon several particular elements. This is described in detail below but as an initial starting point it is worth remembering, as you read on, that The Support Group Method:

- does not get bully and victim together to resolve the conflict,
- does not let the bully shirk the responsibility for his or her actions,
- is better researched and validated than punitive methods,
- WORKS most of the time.

# How it all began

Before 1990 our area of interest and expertise was in the field of behaviour management and we had not sought or developed a particular interest in bullying. It was when teachers asked us for help that we extended our work into this field but carried forward the non-punitive, solution-focused approach to behaviour change that we had already established.

Andrew's story is an account of the first time the method was used. A colleague and friend approached us in a state of great anxiety and distress following a meeting with parents of a sixth-form student. Their account of Andrew's distress was a shock and our friend was asking advice on how to intervene. Acting on the suggestion we made, she subsequently wrote the case study below.

## CASE STUDY

### Andrew's story as told by his year head – Spring 1991

The phone call from Andrew's parents requesting a meeting was not totally unexpected. I had been aware for a few months that he had an apt and rather uncomplimentary nickname and in class he seemed rather isolated.

I understood from the teacher who had accompanied a group of students on a field trip that the nickname had been used frequently on that trip and that several students had been spoken to about using the nickname and upsetting Andrew.

When the meeting took place with Andrew and his parents it was apparent that he and they were very distressed. He had been taunted with the name until two o'clock in the morning on the field course, cars drove into their cul-de-sac and students called out the nickname and Andrew had also been taunted when the family was showing a visitor from abroad a local place of interest. Andrew had wanted to return home early from the field course – only the support of another sympathetic student had kept him there – and he was considering abandoning his A level course.

I saw Andrew on his own, having first asked him to write down exactly how he felt. He told me he felt upset, unhappy and pursued in every part of his life. He had tried to ignore the name-calling but it didn't go away, it simply became more persistent. He said he 'felt like beating their heads in, like running away, quite unable to cope'. I found out the names of the students who were the ring-leaders and saw them as a group. I explained to them exactly how Andrew was feeling and that he was considering leaving school. I told them that this was a real problem to us all and we must think about what we could do about it. At this point one boy spoke up and told the group that he had also been a victim of teasing during the previous year. There seemed to be a feeling of concern and I left the matter there, arranging to meet with each member of the group individually a week later.

When I talked to them alone I discovered that they had all apologised to Andrew and that they were also going to intervene when other students used the nickname.

Head of Sixth Form

When Andrew's teacher contacted us for help, we advised her to follow the seven-step procedure which we later named the No Blame Approach. We were very pleased that it worked so well and began to suggest it with increasing confidence as reports came back from teachers, parents and young people that the method was effective in stopping bullying. By the end of the year we were offering workshops and speaking at conferences, and early in 1992 the training video was published. In June 1992 a day conference was held at which teachers who had used the No Blame Approach met the press and completed questionnaires in order to assess the effectiveness of the method. The results were very positive.

At a time (the early 1990s) when little was known about bullying in British schools, when few staff had any training and when the most popular movements in behaviour management focused on rewards, punishments and targets, the emergence of our method seems unexpected. It is, however, firmly rooted in a background of non-punitive and restorative intervention that we had already established while working together as head and educational psychologist in a school for young people with emotional and behavioural difficulties. The students at Woodstock School in Bristol had experienced all the usual attempts made by parents and teachers to improve their behaviour – detentions, suspensions, admonishments – and if these had proved successful, then the young people would have remained in mainstream schools. As it was they had not responded as hoped, so we decided that we should try different approaches. 'If you always do what you always did, you will always get what you always got.' We have written elsewhere about the ethos of the school and the range of strategies we adopted, but a note here will help to explain why we developed this plan for anti-bullying interventions.

Most interactions employed by staff when dealing with young people after an incident of unacceptable behaviour indicate disapproval of the behaviour and include some or all of the following:

- angry words, tone of voice, facial expression and body language,
- public display of disapproval in front of peers,
- inquiry into why the behaviour happened,
- punishment,
- exclusion.

If these worked, then society wouldn't have a problem – we could apply them to wrongdoers, they would not re-offend and others would learn by example not to repeat the undesirable behaviour. Unfortunately, it does not work like that. Many children grow up wanting the approval of significant others and develop mainly pro-social behaviours without frequent punishment. Some are punished over and over again and continue to repeat the offence.

Understanding something about the process of alienation and knowing many young people who believed themselves to be 'bad', 'useless', 'stupid', we recognised that the one thing they believed that they could be good at was getting into trouble and they protected their self-esteem by appearing not to care. We decided that if we wanted these young people to behave like valued and respected members of society, we must value and respect them.

We developed a whole-school approach for students, staff, parents and colleagues based on building self-esteem, behaving politely and appreciating effort. As a foundation for this work, we discarded 'punishment' systems and introduced a restorative approach, supporting young people in appreciating the effects of their actions, taking responsibility and putting it right or making amends.

There are no magic wands in this business, but we were pleased to observe that the behaviour of the young people improved and that the school was highly regarded by the local education authority (LEA) and professional visitors. When we were asked to help staff manage bullying, we applied the same principles – that punishment and negative criticism would not be the best way to support improved behaviour. We decided to apply what we had learned at Woodstock School to our anti-bullying intervention.

# Bullying – what is it and who is involved?

There are many different forms of aggressive or harmful behaviours enacted between people who learn, work, play or live together and not all are bullying. Some are conflict, some are random aggression, and all should be taken seriously. There are many varied definitions of bullying and the one below is taken from the Statement of Purpose of the Anti-Bullying Alliance (www.anti-bullyingalliance. org.uk):

> Bullying is a subjective experience and can take many forms. Accounts of children and young people, backed up by research, identify bullying as any behaviour that is:
>
> - harmful, carried out by an individual or a group
> - repetitive, wilful or persistent
> - an imbalance of power, leaving the person being bullied feeling defenceless.

Managing our social relationships is a difficult skill – for many a life-long learning opportunity. Children come into school too young to manage the complex processes of sharing, taking turns. Some soon learn that dominance works and in many walks of life it is rewarded and admired. Friendships and identities are strengthened by the formation of groups, teams and clubs, and these 'organisations' define themselves by barriers of exclusion. It is not so important who belongs but is more significant to identify who does not belong. After all, if everyone belonged then it would not be a group.

Combine the lead dominance and the nature of group process and it is easy to see how bullying begins by identifying a target who is excluded and harmed by a range of behaviours.

It is our assertion that bullies are ordinary, dominant and often quite popular people who behave in a way that is intended to cause harm in order to establish high status. Throughout history it is evident that it has always been much easier to rally the troops to cause harm than to do good.

> Contrary to popular opinion, school bullies do not suffer from low self-esteem and are often popular and considered 'cool' by their classmates, a new study has found.
>
> 'Bullies are psychologically strong,' said Jaana Juvonen, Professor of Developmental Psychology at the University of California, Los Angeles, and lead author of the study.
>
> Dr Juvonen's research found that bullies were admired by their peers, and thus felt good about themselves. Bullies are popular because their dominance earns them respect among the general student population who tend not to sympathise with the victims, the study found.
>
> 'They don't show any signs whatsoever of depression, loneliness or anxiety,' Dr Juvonen said. 'They look even healthier than the socially adjusted kids who are not involved in the bullying.'
>
> Boys are twice as likely as girls to be bullies, and almost twice as likely to be victims of bullies. Boys are also three times as likely to be in both categories.
>
> Most anti-bullying programs in schools were based on the belief that bullies picked on others because they had low self-esteem, Dr Juvonen said. Attention should focus on how to discourage support for bullying behaviour by other students, she said.
>
> Unless we do something about this peer support and encouragement, we're probably not going to make much headway.
>
> We need to be addressing bullying not only at the level of individual, aggressive kids, but at the level of the whole social collective. How can we get the other kids to be less supportive of the bully and more supportive of the victim? (Jaana Juvonen, 2003: 1232)

A social group defines itself by including its members. It then recognises those who are not members as outsiders and excludes them. This process strengthens the identity of the group members as being 'in' but might involve hurtful, damaging acts towards those who are 'out', thus creating victims.

Victims lack power, victims are hurting, victims live in fear of the next encounter and victims want it to stop. Bullying is so common that almost everyone, maybe everyone, knows what it is like to be a victim.

An article by Jack Straw, published in the *Daily Mirror* (18/1/95), is reproduced below with his permission. In it he gives an account of his own involvement in school bullying – in a group of ordinary boys picking on one of their number, for no obvious reason, and making his life a misery.

### Burdened by memories of bullying

Member of Parliament Jack Straw reveals the shame of his school days:

Eight lads aged 11 and 12 in one dormitory – all living together morning, noon and night. It was always likely to happen. It does in zoos. It does in the wild. And, unless you are very careful, or very lucky, it does in schools too. I'm talking about bullying – that dreadfully cruel process by which a group instinctively picks on the weakest of its members and dumps on that individual all the anxieties and fears of the group. It's 37 years ago that I was one of those lads in a boarding house at Brentwood School in Essex. We never thought of it as bullying at the time. And in the two years that it went on, no adult seriously remonstrated with us for our behaviour.

Indeed, it never occurred to me until eight or nine years ago, when I got involved in education policy, that our behaviour then could be classed as bullying. It was only when I started reading about the mounting problem of bullying in our schools that I realised that's what it was. But for those two years at school, seven of us made life a misery for the eighth – Paul, I'll call him.

It wasn't classic bullying. There was no single big lad beating up a smaller one. Indeed, very little of the bullying was physical at all. It was verbal, psychological, insidious and, in many ways, the worse for that.

Paul had been 'chosen' as the odd one out. I've no idea how the rest of us made that choice. Certainly, it was never a conscious decision. But the rest of us – each of whom, I guess, also found the frugal atmosphere of a fifties boarding school quite hard to bear – picked on

Paul. He smelt – but didn't we all? With only one bath and one shirt a week, who wouldn't? He was stupid – though his academic results were the same as the rest of us. He didn't join in – we made sure of that. Above all, he was different. I cannot for the life of me remember why or how, except that we had to make him different. And we did.

And besides all this, he had to put up with the sense of isolation – that he was, literally, not 'one of us'. For, as I now understand, we had defined our group by reference to him. In the end, Paul could stand it no longer. He stopped boarding and, as he did not live too far away, became a day boy. He survived, at least, and recently he wrote me a pleasant letter from America, where he now lives, about the good times we had at school together. Not a word about the bad ones – which says more about him than it does the rest of us. But I still feel a sense of shame about my part in all this – and how we might have tipped him over the edge.

Of course, bullying can be a worse problem at boarding school because there are so few chances of escape. And, in those days, there was remarkably little adult supervision of boarding houses. That was left to senior boys, who'd often been through the same situation themselves. But bullying in day school in the nineties is still a huge problem that causes misery to thousands of pupils – and can sometimes lead to very much worse. Crime Concern has recently estimated that over two-thirds of children are victims of bullying at some time in their lives. They also found out that young people often did not tell an adult when they were a victim of a personal attack of some sort – whether it was bullying, a physical attack or racial or sexual harassment ... Above all, we've got to recognise the scale of the problem and how and why it happens. That's why I hope the story of my school days may help. For, if we'd been told that what we were doing was bullying, effective action could have been taken and we'd all have been helped – not just Paul.

Jack Straw MP

Here is the voice of a 'bully' who is a successful public figure, not the kind of deviant that some writers suggested bullies become. The article provides anecdotal evidence to support some of our arguments:

1. Bullying is a group process, not a unique relationship between the bully and victim.

   - A group instinctively picks on the weakest.
   - He was, literally, not one of us. We defined our group by reference to him.

2. Victims are not different – the group decides on the difference.

- Paul had been chosen as the odd one out.
- Above all, he was different, I cannot for the life of me remember why or how, except that we had to make him different. And we did.

3. Bullies often don't know the effect they have on victims, but if they are told then their behaviour can change.

- We never thought of it as bullying.
- I still feel a sense of shame about my part in all of this.
- If we'd been told that what we were doing was bullying, effective action could have been taken and we'd all have been helped – not just Paul.

4. Bullying is, unfortunately, normal behaviour.

Given these figures from Crime Concern, and the fact that bullies can become victims, victims can become bullies and that bullying is a group process, it is clear that most young people are involved in some way in bullying. This does not mean that we should see it as acceptable behaviour. What this book does is to describe positive interventions that will not only stop bullying but will also educate those involved to the damage that bullying can cause and the part that they can play in both prevention and support.

In the next story a teacher looks back to the time when he was a pupil and joined in, or at least colluded, with awful behaviour, even though he didn't like it.

Gillian was the leader of the 'gang', which consisted of about eight people, both male and female. All were in the top stream of a large comprehensive school on a south-east London estate. I don't know why Gillian was the leader. She was more precocious than the rest of us, and she had a sharp tongue that nobody wanted to feel.

Joan was a new girl. She had moved from New Cross, and had decided that our estate was soft. She was intelligent and attractive to many of the young males. Maybe Gillian saw her as a threat. Joan wanted to join the gang. Diane, who was one of the more verbal members, thought it would be OK. Several of us nodded in agreement, but Gillian decided that Joan would have to earn her place in the group, so she was told to meet with us during the break. We met in the sheds, eight with the one. We formed a circle around Joan and Gillian suggested that if Joan was going to be in, she would have to prove that she was tough. We all egged her on. Then from her bag Gillian drew a bunch of three daffodils. To earn her place Joan was going to have to eat them!

This was just a laugh, I thought, but it's OK – she won't do it. Joan said she wouldn't. Then somebody said 'Chicken!', and Gillian said 'Are you in or out?' All of a sudden Gillian had Joan down on a chair, and was forcing a daffodil into her mouth.

I looked on in horror – who knew what the daffodil would do to Joan? Who knew what chemicals the plant contained? I knew it was wrong, but I didn't step in. I can't really remember now but I expect I laughed, though inside I knew that it was wrong and dangerous.

Why didn't I step in? I felt shame afterwards and always made a point of trying to be friendly and supportive to Joan in all our future dealings. There were three other boys beside me there, and yet none of us raised a finger. We just waited until Joan had eaten the flower, then we withdrew. All I know is that we never spoke about the incident.

Twenty years later I was reminiscing with Diane on the telephone. 'Do you remember Joan?', I asked. 'Oh, she was the one that Gillian made eat the daffodil.' Obviously the event stuck with Diane as well. I know that now I would step in, I would have told Gillian she was wrong, but I didn't and I still carry the shame with me.

This account, written 25 years after the event, like Jack Straw's, supports another of our key assumptions: the power of the group forces many young people to condone bullying even though they do not like what is happening. Changing the group dynamics can empower young people to behave in the way they know is right.

- I knew it was wrong but I didn't step in.
- I can't really remember now, but I expect I laughed, though inside I knew it was wrong and dangerous.
- I felt shame afterwards.
- I know that now I would step in.

In summary, we think these stories illustrate the point that the characterisitics of victims and bullies are unimportant and that it is the social dynamics that require our consideration when identifying and managing bullying situations.

For those very few individuals whose behaviour is persistently harmful to others, regardless of peer approval, and who seem unable to experience and respond to empathic understanding of victim plight, we suggest that another term be used to differentiate them from 'normal' bullies. The vast majority of people involved in bullying are not disturbed or deviant individuals in need of intensive treatment programmes. Our work deals with this vast majority.

# Our approach to bullying – the rationale

In spite of the change of name from 'The No Blame Approach' to 'The Support Group Method', the steps remain the same – sometimes slightly refined by our experience.

Not every act of aggression or nastiness is bullying and it is important to define the particular behaviours and processes before planning helpful interventions.

Bullying:

- is a social behaviour, often involving groups,
- takes place repeatedly, over time,
- involves an imbalance of power,
- meets the needs of those holding the power,
- causes harm to those who are powerless to stop it,
- can take many forms: verbal, physical, psychological.

Occasional acts of aggression would not be described as bullying unless there was a continuing fear or torment for the victims. It is also important to differentiate bullying from 'warlike' behaviours where opposing groups confront each other because they have different belief systems or territorial claims. These values may be strongly held through generations and are very resistant to change.

We do not differentiate between the 'bullying – by an individual' and 'mobbing – by a group' discussed by Anatol Pikas (1989). This is because we are describing situations in which, even if the bully is operating solo, her behaviour is usually witnessed in some way by others. If the witness supports the bully, however passive that support might be, then the behaviour is in some way owned by the whole group and the strengths of the group can be drawn on in order to confront the behaviour. Where the bullying occurs in complete secrecy, unknown to any witness other than the victim, then there will be no opportunities for intervention unless the victim reports the behaviour.

We have been to several workshops and heard accounts of incidents that have served to confirm our worry about the scale and seriousness of bullying at a group and institutional level. This book sets a challenge to its readers. We believe that effective interventions, which really combat bullying in schools, demand much more from us than just trying to convey to bullies that their behaviour is unacceptable.

## Defining the terms

Our definitions are:

Bully – a person or group behaving in a way which meets needs for excitement, status or material gain and which does not recognise or meet the needs and rights of the others who are harmed by the behaviour.

Victim – a person or group that is harmed by the behaviour of others and who does not have the resources, status, skill or ability to counteract or stop the harmful behaviour.

The bully and victim are in a 'relationship' which persists over time and is characterised by the continuing fear that the victim feels, even when the bully is not there. In this way, bullying differs from chance or random acts of aggression.

## Bullying is 'normal'

Many of those reading this book will have had some close relationship with a very young baby at some time in their lives and they will remember the self-centred and relentlessly demanding behaviour exhibited by that tiny, dependent human being. If babies were big and parents small, then parents would undoubtedly be bullied! You may also remember, if you are a parent or have had close relationships with young children, the first time that a particular child was upset or cried because of sadness or hurt felt on behalf of another person or creature (rather than because some need or demand of their own was unmet). This emergence of 'empathy' is a complex step in social and emotional development and is the basis for kind and unselfish behaviour.

We believe that it is not helpful to regard bullying as abnormal or evil. Many of us will remember standing back and at least colluding with, if not participating in, some hurtful behaviour towards another person because it increased our own sense of belonging, or made us feel relieved that we were not the one being rejected. Parents and teachers will often observe very nice kids behaving in a very nasty way when the need to belong to a group of peers is an overriding factor. Today's young people in affluent countries are subjected to strong pressures by the manufacturers of trendy clothes and toys. Wearing the right trainers is all-important, but they are only the right trainers if someone else isn't wearing them!

A willingness to step outside the peer group, and stand alongside someone who is rejected and harmed, takes strength and courage. It puts the 'rescuer' at risk of rejection herself and the success of her stand is likely to depend upon her social or physical status. We are likely to take this risk only when we identify strongly with the distress of the victim and when we feel that our intervention is likely to bring about some change – when we feel involved and powerful.

Witnesses of bullying, or those who care for the victims, might have very strong feelings of anger and feel a need to punish the perpetrators. If an adult who is in a position of power uses her authority to stop the bullying, then it may have a short-term effect upon that particular situation, but it is unlikely to change the status or identity of the bully and victim. There may well be a risk of further harm to the victim because the bully was thwarted ... 'I will get you later!'

We suggest, therefore, that the primary focus of any plan to reduce bullying must be to change the behaviour of the bully and those who collude or stand by and do nothing. By involving the peer group it is possible to enhance the empathic responses of healthy members of the group. This in turn has an effect on the behaviour of the bully, who might also have an empathic response and wish to change, but if she resists, she no longer has the group's consent to behave in a bullying manner.

## Whole-school approaches

Bullying in British schools is now recognised as requiring effective policy and is referred to in the school inspection procedures. However, most teachers have not had an opportunity to attend a training programme and not all schools would choose bullying as a priority among all the curriculum pressures put upon them.

Most school policies state that:

- bullying is taken seriously,
- bullying will not be tolerated,
- victims and parents are encouraged to report bullying.

Some parents take this advice and seek an opportunity to report bullying but are often told:

- there is no evidence for the bullying,
- the victim is at fault,
- the matter has been dealt with by a 'talking-to' or some sanction such as detention.

The change to non-punitive methods is not, in our experience, happening without the impact of persuasive, attitude-changing forces within the school. During our in-service training days most teachers are easily convinced by the logic and ethics of The Support Group Method and cannot wait to try it. Some teachers are reluctant to put aside traditional and apparently common-sense methods in favour of what appears to be a radical and different process. They also worry about the impact of non-punitive interventions on the 'discipline policy'. From these teachers, all we ask is that they give The Support Group Method a try; this will allow them to discover for themselves that it is safe and positive.

At the same time, some schools still have structures which might promote bullying. Teams and houses create the identity of groups. The members will belong only because others do not, and they will support the identity of the group by strengthening the boundary around it. Are we expecting too much when we ask a young person to discriminate between winning on the sports field through superior strength and using the same strategy to win power or possession in the playground? The very language of success – 'I beat her, thrashed her, wiped the floor with her' – is applauded if it refers to a 'game' and punished if it refers to a 'fight'.

## The challenge to common practice

Many of the strategies in common use do not have a long-term effect on the behaviour of bullies. Inevitably, we approach bullying with strong feelings of anger and frustration towards bullies and sympathy for their victims. We have a responsibility to the students and their parents to respond effectively and the success of our intervention has to be measured by the degree to which it stops the bullying. Some of the responses often made by teachers are not successful in achieving this and we discuss them below. Please try to set aside any feelings of retribution towards the bully, and concentrate on the aim of changing the bully's behaviour, thus achieving the best outcome for the victim.

## The 'serious' trap

In training sessions we use two short video excerpts for discussion. In one, a teenage girl is teased by her friends and tormented about her clothing. During the painful episode, she tries to belong by joining in the laughter against her and protesting that she will be at the party. In the second excerpt, a teenage girl walking with a boy is pushed aside by a group of three girls, forced to her knees and asked to drink from a can of drink which has been spat into. At this point, her friend goes for help and the group scatter.

The second incident is more violent and disgusting. When discussing suitable interventions, participants often choose to do nothing about the first incident, suggesting that it is best to monitor the situation and that almost any course of action might make things worse. However, after watching the second scene, there is always a strong and often punitive response. Participants suggest:

- a full investigation,
- parental involvement,
- comfort for the victim,
- punishment of the bullies.

At the beginning of the training, we make a very strong teaching point which we believe is vital to the establishment of safety in schools:

> The seriousness of bullying can only be measured by the effects that are experienced by the victim. (Besag, 1989)

Although people often agree readily with this point, in the training session the second incident is nearly always taken as much the more serious, even though the girl in question has a friend who helps her. When we point out to the participants that the girl in the first scenario is probably much more at risk, we often find great resistance. It seems that it is very hard for observing adults to make judgements based on a victim's suffering and to set aside their own response to the behaviour. A pupil is often suspended for fighting, even when the confrontation is playful, the protagonists are evenly matched and nobody comes to any harm. No action can be taken against a pupil who gives a 'look', even when it is a sign of repeated and violent aggression.

Similarly, the original DfE document *Bullying: Don't Suffer in Silence* (1994) offered confusing and unhelpful advice by stating:

> Dealing with minor incidents: Mild sanctions can be useful in responding to one-off incidents of bullying which do not result in actual physical harm. (p. 18)

Dealing with serious incidents: For bullying which results in damage to property or person, a serious response should be considered. (p. 19)

Firstly, bullying is not an appropriate label for one-off acts of aggression. Secondly, there is no evidence that physical assault is more serious than verbal or psychological bullying. It is probable that the reverse is often true. A broken arm, a bloody nose or torn clothing is very visible and the recipient is likely to be treated with kindness and pity. Name-calling and teasing are often dismissed by adults as not serious, but these behaviours, especially common among girls, can cause great suffering and lead to tragic consequences.

A new approach to teacher intervention is required, in which adults always respond to the distress of a victim, regardless of their own views about how the pain was caused and whether it is justified.

## Dangers of labelling

Although we use the terms 'bully' and 'victim' in this and other publications and training, we do not think it is helpful to use them as labels in school. We know that to call a young person by a negative name can affect her self-image, and must be difficult to accept for the parents, with whom we want to work cooperatively. We have even seen a video in which a teacher explains the system in use at her school, where bullies are required to wear a badge saying, 'I am a bully!' Is such a label likely to decrease or increase the bullying behaviour?

## Getting to the bottom of it

It seems like common sense to question students about facts and reasons when bad behaviour is brought to our attention. When we talk to the young people, they often report that they give teachers the answers they want – the answers that will let them out of the room as soon as possible.

When you question young people about the facts, they will give their own perspectives. These are often contradictory, especially when a bully is trying to extract herself from blame. You may then be distracted from effective action in your quest for the truth.

Since 1991, we have been encouraging teachers to set aside the need to gather information as though this were, in itself, an effective intervention. Imagine a typical scenario in which teachers separate the 'witnesses' and either ask them to write down their accounts or subject them to a sequence of probing questions.

Often the teachers' plan is to start with the young people considered to be 'reliable' or 'innocent' so that by the time the 'main culprit' is questioned a good case has been built against her. If bullying is not a one-off incident but a sequence of behaviour over time, then how many events can be investigated in this way? How much time will be wasted before something is done to make things better? How much hostility and resentment will be provoked towards the victim during the investigations? The process is negative, unreliable and unlikely to pave the way for positive teaching of better behaviour.

This has been among the most controversial of our teaching points and has often provoked hostility from course participants where schools have used investigation as a cornerstone of the anti-bullying policy. It is only very recently that other writers have begun to recognise this issue, so it is gratifying to read, in *Bullying in Schools and What To Do About It* (Rigby, 1996: 191), that our approach is supported:

> Sooner or later, as the evidence accumulates and is sifted, there is a temptation to really 'get down to the bottom of it' – to discover the truth, the whole truth and nothing but the truth. This can set into motion an increasingly complex process of examinations, cross-examinations, heavy documentation, etc. The temptation is strong, and for some teachers, irresistible. ... We should ask ourselves whether we are going to spend precious time in tracing the origins of peer conflict and precisely and judiciously attributing blame, or alternatively using the time to resolve the problem and bring about a lasting reconciliation between two or more students. What we need to know, basically, is whether a person has been victimised and who may be responsible.

Even less helpful is to ask students to explain why they behave in a certain way. It is very hard to explain our actions, and perhaps impossible to do so in a way which will satisfy a teacher. We were recently told about a small pupil who undid the safety bolts on a climbing frame. His teacher asked him why he had done it, and his predictable reply was 'Don't know, Miss'. The teacher became frustrated and we asked her why she thought he had done it. 'Because he is disturbed and attention-seeking,' she replied. Was the teacher really expecting the boy to reply, 'Well, Miss, it is because I am disturbed...'?

An alternative to the 'Don't know...' is a justification for the behaviour. After all, this seems to be what the teacher wants: 'He took my pencil!' 'She wouldn't play with me.' 'He said my mother was dead.' We are unlikely to get an insightful and useful reply: 'I have very little tolerance of this person and I show off to my peers by abusing her. This makes me feel popular and powerful and I learned this because in my last school it happened to me'.

Does the question 'Why did you do it?' call for a reason, an explanation or an excuse?

## Changing the victim

Over and over again, we hear from victims that they have been advised or urged by parents, teachers or a group to change their behaviour in some way. They try to 'stand up for themselves', 'hit back', 'walk away', 'pretend they don't care', and each time their failure to act in a way which ends their misery just makes it worse.

Margaret Attwood's novel, *Cat's Eye* (1990), illustrates this very vividly in its account of the relationships among the members of a group of teenage girls:

> 'You have to learn how to stand up for yourself,' says my mother. 'Don't let them push you around. Don't be spineless. You have to have more backbone.'

> I think of sardines and their backbones. You can eat their backbones. The bones crumble between your teeth in one touch and they fall apart. This must be what my own backbone is like – hardly there at all. What is happening to me is my own fault, for not having more backbone.

They feel it is their own fault that this is happening to them. It is not. Whatever their own inadequacy or difficulty, it is not their fault and it is not their responsibility to stop it. It is our responsibility and we must give them that message loud and clear if we are not to compound their unhappiness.

There is nothing wrong with assertiveness training for everyone. Social skills programmes can help many students who are having difficulties in making relationships. However, these interventions should not be linked directly with the victim's plight but with more general developmental work.

## Punishment

Perhaps the biggest challenge for us is to advise teachers to abandon punishment as a response to bullying. This can be addressed from two points of view: pragmatic and ethical.

If punishment systems worked in society, then unwanted behaviour would simply be stopped in the miscreants and others would be deterred by example. Unfortunately, it is not as simple as that. The aversive learning process does not seem to work well for impulsive people with an 'external locus of control', and no amount of anticipated punishment seems to deter them at the point of immediate satisfaction. This point comes across very forcibly in our work with young people in special schools for children with behaviour difficulties – if punishment had worked, they would still be in their mainstream schools. Our starting point, long before we began working on bullying, was to find alternatives to punishment for these young people. The criminal justice system provides evidence that, in many cases, the less punitive the sentence, the more likely it is that some rehabilitation can take place.

Social behaviours are learned, and the learning process is nurtured by encouragement, good teaching and experiences of success. There is no evidence that punishing a bully ever turned that person into a kind and helpful friend.

Punishment of a bully does not make life safer for the victim; in fact, it will often make things worse when the bully takes revenge.

If you want to encourage disclosure and to work positively with bullies, then everyone in a school must know that effective action will be taken, but that it will not lead to punishment. We cannot agree with the view put forward by Eric Jones in *Bullying: A Practical Guide to Coping for Schools* (1991: 23):

> **Punish bullies. Record punishment and the reasons for it. Show him what you are putting on file and make him pay for whatever time it cost you to sort it out.**

Bullying is an anti-social behaviour resorted to by young people when their social skills are inappropriate, and we must respond in a way that will help them to learn better behaviour. Increasing their anxiety and alienation from us is not likely to do this.

The emergence of desirable social behaviours can start quite early, when toddlers are encouraged to understand their own feelings and the feelings of others. For example, sharing is a behaviour expected in families, pre-school and early school environments. But sharing is not a natural strategy. It is natural to eat all the sweets oneself. In order to gain satisfaction from sharing the child has to:

- understand and empathise with the feelings of a child who has no sweets,
- experience praise from adults who reward the sharing with something more valuable than sweets: love,
- establish a self-image as a child who shares and thus adopts this behaviour into her repertoire.

The important elements of social behaviours to be learnt are:

- empathy – the ability to 'feel for another',
- altruism – the sense of self as doing good,
- reintegrative shame – the sense of shame experienced when the behaviour causes pain to those who love the perpetrator (very different from stigmatising shame where the perpetrator learns that she is a bad or rejected person).

Some traditional justice systems achieve great success using these influences – for example, the Navajo Peace Courts and Maori Family Conferencing. For an inspirational account of the introduction of the latter into the South Australian criminal justice system, see Braithwaite (1989).

The United Nations Convention on the Rights of the Child (1989) gives schools the responsibility to ensure that:

> In all actions concerning children ... the best interests of the child shall be a primary consideration. (Article 3)

It is hard to justify punishment as anything other than a traditional expedient. It is not in the best interests of either the bully or the victim.

## The use of power

Bullying seems to be a clash between the powerful and the powerless, but power is an acceptable feature of many aspects of human behaviour. Bullying can be viewed as part of a normal process of socialisation, in which the group establishes its identity, which is reinforced by the exclusion of others. The strength of the group lies in its sense of cohesion; without somebody being out-grouped – that is, visibly outside the group – the boundaries are hard to define.

The use of power can be seen in the way the bully dominates, but the possible reasons for this – genetic, family background, learned behaviours, gender differences – are not discussed here. Whatever the reason, we take the view that we have bullies and victims in school, and that this is not a healthy situation. We need to provide a safe environment for all, and we need to question our solutions to the problem. The use of power to stop the bully may confirm to the bully how power can be used to intimidate the weak, and to suggest to victims that they need to be more powerful may leave them feeling even more powerless. The crucial element that we feel is overlooked in much of the research is the potentially proactive role of those who observe and collude.

## Colluders and observers

Most intervention for bullies and victims concentrates on the relationship between them and pays little attention to the part played by the peer group. Even when the bully and victim have a one-to-one relationship, we have found that the peers know what is happening and are, therefore, colluding. A failure to intervene gives consent for the behaviour to continue. Often 'innocent' friends will join in to establish their credibility with the leader, to be safe, to have fun. The victim, who might be in great distress, often tries to hide the pain, fearing that a display of misery will be seen as weakness and provoke even more extreme attacks. Thus the process continues. There is a need to make these pupils aware of the important role of a witness and to allow them to devise and practise safe interventions that they might make.

If we take the view that bullying is an interaction which establishes group identity, dominance and status at the expense of another, then it is only by the development of 'higher values', such as empathy, consideration, and unselfishness, that the bully is likely to relinquish her behaviour and function differently in a social setting. By empowering colluders, observers and potential rescuers, consent for the bullying behaviour is withdrawn and change happens – the bullying stops.

# The Support Group Method – step-by-step

When bullying has been observed or reported, then The Support Group Method offers a simple seven-step procedure which can be used by a teacher or other facilitator. However, it does rely upon the 'discovery' of an incident and all institutions should concentrate on openness and an ethos that supports peers in seeking help for targets without suffering the stigma of 'telling'.

Note that each step has been carefully planned as a single part of the whole and variations may undermine the success of the method. The word 'target' has been used as it is less stigmatising than 'victim' and is congruent with our suggestion that a target can be 'anyone'.

## Step one – talk with and listen to the target

The aims of this step:

1. To understand the pain experienced by the target.
2. To explain the method and gain permission to proceed.
3. To discuss who will make up The Support Group.
4. To agree what will be recounted to the group.

When the facilitator finds out that bullying has happened, she starts by talking to the target. During this conversation the listener encourages the target to describe how he feels with reflective comments such as, 'That must be very hard for you ... So you have felt really upset'. The purpose is not to discover factual evidence about this or other events; if the target wants to include evidence in the account this is always reframed to establish the resulting distress. For example, a comment like 'They have all been ignoring me, nobody will talk to me' might be replied to with a response like 'So you felt really lonely and you were upset that you had nobody to talk to'. At this point the facilitator will have enough of the picture to be able to recount a story which will illustrate the harm experienced by the target.

It is important that the target understands and gives consent to the process. Sometimes there may be a fear that it could lead to further torment, but when the non-punitive aspect is fully explained the target usually feels safe and relieved that something is being done. He may want the perpetrators to understand how much distress has been caused. Talking to someone else who has been through the experience might give further reassurance.

The target will help the facilitator to select the group members by asking who has been causing the harm and subsequently inquiring for names of colluders, observers and potential rescuers. The questions might be:

- Who has been doing this to you?
- Who else joined in?
- Who watched and knows this is happening but did not join in?
- Who is a friend or somebody really popular who would want to help?

It is very important to build the group to include all these roles.

The facilitator should end the meeting by:

- checking that nothing confidential has been discussed which should not be disclosed to the group,
- inviting the target to produce a piece of writing or a picture which will illustrate his unhappiness,
- offering the target an opportunity to talk again at any time during the procedure if things are not going well. This could be arranged by ensuring some easy contact point at the same time each day or by agreeing how a message could be delivered. It is important that, although no meeting is planned until the follow-up, the target does have access should something go wrong in the intervening period.

The target is not invited to join the group to present his own account as it is possible that he will make accusations, provoke denial or justification and undermine the problem-solving approach. It is up to the facilitator to act as the advocate for the target.

## Step two – convene a meeting with the people involved

The facilitator arranges to meet with the group of pupils who have been involved and suggested by the target. A group of six to eight young people works well. This is an opportunity for the facilitator to use her judgement to balance the group so that helpful and reliable young people are included alongside those whose behaviour has been causing distress. The aim is to use the strengths of group members to bring about the best outcome.

In order to establish a welcoming atmosphere the meeting should be arranged in school time in a comfortable room, and the facilitator should greet the participants and thank them for coming. Refreshments can be offered to emphasis that this group is important.

## Step three – explain the problem

The facilitator starts by telling the group that she has a problem – she is worried about 'John', who is having a very hard time at the moment. By asking the group to listen to her worries she can divert some suspicion or irritation which might be directed towards the target. She has a duty of care and this meeting is called to help her fulfil that duty.

She recounts the story of the target's unhappiness and uses the piece of writing or a drawing to emphasise his distress. At no time does she discuss the details of the incidents or allocate blame to the group.

## Step four – share responsibility

When the account is finished, the listeners may look downcast or uncomfortable and be uncertain about the reason for the meeting. Some may be anxious about possible punishment. The facilitator makes a change in the mood here by stating explicitly that:

- no one is in trouble or is going to be punished,
- it is her responsibility to help John to be happy and safe but she cannot do it without their help,
- the group has been convened to help solve the problem.

## Step five – ask the group members for their ideas

Group members are usually genuinely moved by the account of John's distress and relieved that they are not in trouble. No one has been pushed into a defensive corner by accusations and the power of the group has shifted from the 'bully leader' to the group as a whole, whose members withdraw consent for the behaviour to continue.

Each member of the group is then encouraged to suggest a way in which the target could be helped to feel happier. These ideas are stated in the 'I' language of intention: 'I will walk to school with him.' 'I will ask him to sit with me at dinner.' Ideas are owned by the group members and not imposed by the facilitator. She makes positive responses but she does not go on to extract a promise of improved behaviour.

In the original version we stressed that the contributions should not be recorded as a contract that could be 'checked up on'. However, in her use of the method Sue Young (1998) does record the ideas in order to validate the efforts made by the group members. This has some merit so we now suggest that the facilitator, if wanting to provide a written record of the contributions, might go into the meeting with some prepared certificates that record appreciation of each group member and allow for a space to record the suggestion.

> Thank you to _____ _____ for joining a group to
> help support a peer who is unhappy,
> and making the suggestion:
>
> 'I could ..................'

## Step six – leave it up to them

The facilitator ends the meeting by passing over the responsibility to the group to solve the problem. No written record is kept by the facilitator – it is left as a matter of trust. She thanks them, expresses confidence in a positive outcome and arranges to meet with them again to see how things are going.

## Step seven – meet them again

About a week later, the facilitator discusses with each student, including the target, how things have been going. This allows her to monitor the bullying and keeps the young people involved in the process.

These meetings are with one group member at a time so that each can give a statement about his contribution without creating a competitive atmosphere. It does not matter if everyone has not kept to his intention, as long as the bullying has stopped. The target does not have to become the most popular person in school, just to be safe and happy.

The entire process showing the seven steps is available as a training video (Maines and Robinson, 1992, 2008).

# Accounts from a practitioner

Jane, one of our colleagues, has been using the No Blame Approach since 1992. Below she describes some strategies that she has found helpful. As with all documented methods of dealing with incidents of unacceptable behaviour, we have to be prepared to modify the approach to meet the needs of the individual situation.

ooooo

Only about half of the cases of bullying I have handled, using the method, have followed the procedure as explained previously. Many require adaptation or, in a few cases, a repeat meeting. I hope that I can provide you with some of the tricks of the trade and guidelines for incidents that do not follow the normal pattern of events.

The advice has been broken down into the stages involved in the No Blame Approach, followed by some specific case studies and adaptations.

## Meeting with the victim

Regardless of how you have come to hear about the bullying behaviour, you will need to speak to the victim – either alone or with a friend or parent. Allow enough time for this interview. If the need is not immediate, then arrange a time that is convenient for all involved.

Ask if you can take notes during the meeting, as they will help you later when you meet with the group. Check whether there are any details that the victim does not wish to be shared. Remember that students who are unable to express themselves clearly may find it easier to do a drawing or tell a story.

## How does the victim choose the group?

This needs to be done carefully so that there are equal numbers of bullies, watchers and friends of the victim. For 'isolated' victims, the group should include those with whom the victim would like to be friends (see case study 1). If the group is multicultural, ensure that the numbers of bullies, friends and watchers are balanced. The watchers should be popular and respected students who can influence their peers in a positive way.

In discussion with the victim, establish how quickly you need to convene the group. Is it essential, for the safety of the victim, that you meet immediately, or can it wait until you do not need to get cover for your lesson?

How do you establish communication with the victim so that you know that the meeting has been successful?

For the victim's, and your, reassurance there needs to be regular feedback so you know that the behaviour has stopped. You must agree that the victim will tell you immediately if things are not going well after the meeting with the group.

Many students readily communicate their happiness that things are much better for them, or that there is still room for improvement. In a larger school, you may not see the student in a situation where you can ask without peers being present. I have established a signing system. We identify a 'raised eyebrow' or 'thumbs up' sign so I can know whether further intervention is required or things are going well. These messages can be conveyed to me as I walk around the school and peers need not be aware. 'Are you OK?' is not the right question to ask people who need to build their self-esteem or confidence. An agreed sign, though, can be read quickly and enables a meeting to be arranged if necessary.

## Contacting parents

If parents are not aware that their son or daughter is being bullied, then it is at this point that you may contact them to explain what you are doing to help alleviate the problem. I feel that a meeting or telephone call is easier than a letter. Remember that if they are unaware what the No Blame Approach is, you will have to explain to them what you will be doing to help.

## The meeting with the students

After you have carefully chosen the group, they need to be told of the meeting. If you collect the group yourself, ensure that no explanation is given of why you are meeting until you are together. If messages are sent via the registers, check that all the students you need are in school; the key characters must be present.

When I first started using the No Blame Approach I was the only member of staff who used it and if I called for students they immediately knew why. I recommend that several staff should be trained, so that you do not get labelled!

## How do you start the meeting?

'We are here to help X who is feeling ...'. Remember to stick to feelings that you agreed could be shared. As you start explaining the victim's feelings I can guarantee that nine times out of ten someone will say, 'But it wasn't me!' or 'She did it to me first!' At this point, you need to say that you have not said that anyone did anything to anyone else, and no blame has been apportioned to anyone. Repeat that you have asked them to come along as you are sure that they can help X feel a lot happier.

Common responses are:

'But he/she is so annoying' – see case study 1.

'We did not realise...' – see case study 2.

'He/she does not seem to mind' – explain that the person does mind and may have been covering it up well, but we still need to help so they can feel happier.

'He/she did it to me first' – remind the group that we are not here to discuss actions but feelings. You can talk to that student afterwards, if you suspect that he or she, too, may be suffering from bullying.

## Solutions

These are usually incredibly simple. Students may need prompting, but once they have some ideas from you they will soon come up with ideas of their own. For example:

'Ask X to sit with us.'

'Walk to school with X.'

'Ask my friends to stop being nasty to X.'

'Ignore X's annoying habits.'

'Ask X to join in with our games.'

'Just not speak to X.'

Check that they know what they are going to do, but do not record their responses. Arrange a time for individual meetings so that you can see how things are going.

## What if they do not offer solutions?

I have never experienced a complete refusal to offer ideas, but there is sometimes reluctance, especially if the victim has annoying habits or is, in some way, provoking the hostile behaviour. You must reiterate that you need to help the victim feel happier, which may lead to a change in the victim's behaviour. As a group they can help, as they have the support of each other. (See case study 1.)

As an alternative, you can ask if anyone in the group has been bullied, or take them back to PSE (Personal and Social Education) work you have done on bullying and the effects it can have on people. Try to raise the empathy of the group.

If the ideas have been slow in coming forward, I recommend an early meeting with the victim to ensure that the behaviours have stopped. If there is still a problem, then a second group may need to be convened with different students.

## Who needs to know that you have had the meeting?

Parents have already been contacted, so you now need to inform tutors or class teachers. If the bullying was occurring at breaktimes, then ask duty staff in the playground, or dinner supervisors, to keep a watch, too.

## Feedback

During the intervening time you will have seen the students around school and established how things are going. If the behaviour has improved, then the feedback discussion with individuals need only be brief. Remember to thank the group for helping. If things are not any better, then you will probably have heard by now! If there is partial improvement, then encourage the students to keep their offers of help going and enrol some other students into the group. If there is no change, then a second meeting must be called and further suggestions put forward. A change of group members could help.

# CASE STUDY 1

## An isolated student

Laura was in Year 7 and had extreme difficulties settling in at secondary school. She had not attended much during the primary years and had not moved up to secondary school with any particular friends. She found it difficult to work in groups and was feeling very left-out and unhappy.

Her mother contacted me and I met with Laura to discuss the problem. She acknowledged that she found if difficult having to share and work with others. She appreciated that she had some annoying habits and wanted to know what they were so she could change as well as the group having to accept her.

I taught the group but did not know them very well, as it was near to the beginning of the school year. The group included all the confident girls with whom Laura wanted to become friends. We met and ideas were put forward. They also responded to Laura's question as to what her annoying habits were. I explained that many of these were due to the fact that she had been taught at home and was not used to working in a group. We established some strategies that they could all use.

For a few days, things went well but it did not last for long and Laura slowly became isolated again. At our second meeting I explained to Laura, who was not convinced that this approach was going to work, that I thought we had not chosen the right group. It was instinct that led Laura to the popular group in the class rather than the more unassuming girls who would fit in with her character and interests more readily. I asked Laura who she would invite to a party if she were to have one so she would choose a different group.

When I met with the second group one of the girls asked why Laura had chosen them. I explained about the suggestion of who she would invite to a party. At this Sarah responded, 'Oh, isn't that nice!' and the meeting went extremely well and a picnic and sleepover were already being planned as we left the room.

Laura, now in year 9, is one of the more confident students and her attendance and academic progress have improved dramatically.

### Hint:
In cases of isolation, choose the students who would relate well to the victim and not necessarily the ones that the victim would, ideally, like to be friends with.

# CASE STUDY 2

## 'We did not realise'

The incident involved a girl in Year 8 who was very attractive, able, musical and gave the impression that everything was all right. However, unbeknown to the staff and her peers, this was far from the case.

Eventually Nadine's parents contacted the school and explained that she was extremely unhappy at home and was beginning to say that she was too unwell to come to school. Nadine explained to me how unhappy she was; although the girls were trying to include her, she felt that she was always the odd one out. We chose the group carefully and I met with them.

The response was one of shock, 'But Nadine is always so confident and good at everything – we had no idea she felt like this.' It is cases like this that contradict the stereotypical view of 'victims' and 'bullies'. The ideas were spontaneous and easy to implement, and other suggestions were put forward to help Nadine. Within a few weeks, she had a large circle of friends.

**Hint:**
Do not assume that the confident students, who may appear not to want friends, are happy with their situations. Some students do not show their unhappiness at school but it manifests itself in different behaviours at home. If parents contact you about uncharacteristic behaviour that they are seeing, speak to the student and establish whether bullying could be the problem.

## The victim does not want to do anything about it

If students insist that what happens is not, in their eyes, serious bullying, establish that if there is any repeat of the behaviour, then you need to know immediately. Tell the students that you will inform their parents and watch carefully to ensure that things are all right.

If a student obviously needs help, but is not happy about revealing names because, even after reassurance, he is frightened of retribution, ask him to speak to someone you have helped previously. I have a few students in school who have offered to speak to other victims in situations like these. A peer telling them that it does work is often a greater influence than a teacher.

I have recently dealt with a student who was very unhappy about me revealing his name. He experienced lots of name-calling and took a long time to tell anyone. The group involved are known for their verbal unpleasantness to several students and to each other. We decided to honour his request as it was not only David who was experiencing the verbal abuse. He gave me a list of individuals and the year head and tutor added to it. As part of the PSE programme, I always ask students to complete an evaluation sheet. This checks up on their understanding and helps me to gauge how confident they are with the No Blame Approach. The questions are structured to enable me to talk to individuals or groups and discuss their responses. By referring to the students' replies I was able to start the group off by recalling their answers, in general terms, not specifically. The discussion went extremely well and led to questions as to whether certain behaviours could be construed as bullying. Knowing how David was feeling, I was able to put forward his point of view, anonymously, and use that as the basis to decide whether the bullying behaviour was bullying in the eyes of the receiver or giver. The group went on to discuss the possibilities of having a 'name-calling box', like a swear box. The tutor is still working on that one! Paul told me that he was being picked on, but felt that it was not serious enough to warrant a meeting; he did, however, want it to stop. Again, he was one of several victims of name-calling and minor harassment. We discussed the possibilities and, as it was very soon after the evaluation sheet had been completed, we decided to ask a few of the main protagonists to meet with me to discuss their responses to the questions. I met with the group, who all felt that the PSE input had had a very good effect on them and that they were definitely not hurting or insulting anyone by calling them names. I praised them for their positive approach and asked them to make sure that it continued and to let me know if they felt that anyone in the group needed a reminder about the effect of name-calling. Paul happily came to see me saying that all the unpleasant behaviours had stopped.

## The victim wants to attend the meeting

Ranjit insisted on attending the meeting. As we talked to the group, the differences began to manifest themselves again. We returned to the issues of feelings but personal grievances continued to recur. After a long session the group agreed on behaviours that could be modified and stopped. During the follow-up meetings, one of The Support Group, Linda, explained how she did not think the approach was very successful. The victim was much happier, however, and had re-established friendships with all the groups, including the girl who was not convinced with the approach. A few months later Linda asked if I could help her as she was being bullied by a group of boys. We worked together with a successful outcome. When I spoke to her afterwards I mentioned that she had not been convinced earlier. Linda explained that her friendship with Ranjit was now stronger and that maybe her initial response had been wrong.

## Just involving two students

A Year 11 boy, Michael, hit out at another student, Earl. When questioned, Michael explained that Earl had been calling him gay for months. Other students were involved, but he was the main perpetrator. The teacher dealing with the situation decided just to talk to the two boys individually. Michael explained that he needed to wear glasses, as his eyesight was extremely poor. After games lessons, when he had not yet collected his glasses from the PE teacher, he had to establish where all his clothes were in the changing rooms. In order to do this, he needed to grope around and had, on occasion, touched other people. This had been misconstrued as him being gay. It was only by talking to Michael that his view of the situation could be understood. The member of staff next talked to Earl, who appreciated Michael's predicament. After I had spoken to the two boys separately, they were asked to meet together so the reason could be explained. Earl and Michael shook hands and Earl promised to tell the other lads and arranged to help Michael sort out his clothes after PE lessons.

### The main group have sorted it out, but the hangers-on miss their fun

I am sure you are familiar with this scenario: Two good friends, A and B, have an argument and walk off in a huff. A goes up to classmate C and has a bit of a moan about B. C meets D (the class stirrer) and says that A and B have had an argument and, 'you should hear what A is saying about B', elaborating on the story to make it sound more interesting.

In the meantime A and B have got back together again

Later, D goes up to B and says that A has been saying horrible things about him/her and he/she should have nothing to do with A. B and A then fall out and A is bullied by the three of them. You can play this situation in several different ways. I usually get the two friends, A and B, together and establish how much trust there is between them. The other two are then included in the group and it is explained to them how much their behaviour has affected A and B. This is such a common situation that I endeavour to get some role-play activities in PSE or assemblies so the students can see how upsetting and futile their attempts at breaking up friendships can be.

### When those on the periphery really cause the problems

Boy and girl friend, Rhys and Natalie, split up. Their 'friends' got involved and kept claiming that Natalie was saying horrible things about Rhys, then they wrote nasty letters and made telephone calls. Similar reports came back to Natalie about Rhys. They tried to ignore it but eventually they challenged each other and Rhys ended up physically abusing Natalie. The situation then involved teachers who, up until then, had been unaware of the problem.

I used the No Blame Approach very successfully with the students in this case, despite Rhys having been suspended for a couple of days because of the attack. Both of them had been the victims of bullying by their peers and so I spoke to them individually and then met with some of their friends to explain the situation and ask for their help. Rhys and Natalie, although not boy and girl friend, still respected each other and did not wish the behaviour of others to impinge on their relationship. For a few days, things went quite well, Rhys and Natalie getting on together and close friends being supportive.

Some of those on the periphery were obviously missing the entertainment they had had at the others' expense and pointed them out to each other: 'That's Natalie, who was hit by Rhys', and other such provocative comments. Natalie and her mother came to see me, feeling that the No Blame Approach had not worked as far as the wider group was concerned. Natalie did not wish further meetings to be held but did want something to be done, so we negotiated an assembly. I was to talk to the students about bullying generally and the effects it had on people, and would mention the No Blame Approach and how successful it was with those directly involved. However, we, as onlookers, were to remember that we too had a role and ensure that we should not incite further unpleasantness by getting involved in something that is not pertinent to us or by rekindling past unpleasantness that has been resolved. For Natalie and Rhys, the comments stopped. I did not mention any names or incidents in assembly but the impact that the initial incident had had on the group was sufficient for them all to know what my message meant.

The last two incidents illustrate the need for regular input, using assembly, tutorial time, PSE, on the rights of the student. This will emphasise the importance of feelings and empathy for those directly involved in any incident. The role of the bystanders is so important and yet with most other ways of dealing with bullying they are not considered to be significant enough to play a part in helping.

Contributed by Jane Sleigh, 1997

# What makes the process work?

## Empathy and altruism

When we first developed our approach, we were looking for a process that would bring about an empathic response in the bully and the rest of the group. In the majority of cases this happens, and we have often heard words such as these:

> 'I knew we weren't being very nice but I never realised just how much it was affecting Michael.'

In some cases the bully may not have any concern for the target, but if some of the group understand the target's pain, they often provide supportive strategies. It may only take one or two people to be friendly to stop the feeling of isolation and pain of the target.

---

**CASE STUDY**

**Just one friend**

Before taking his life, the boy wrote a message in the class diary, a portion of which I quote.

> I decided to kill myself because day after day I go to school and only bad things happen. Nothing good ever happens to me. If the kids in my class could be in my shoes they would understand how I feel. If only they knew how I feel every day. Even in my dreams there are nothing but bad things. The only one I can talk to is the hamster, but the hamster can't speak back. Maybe my being born was a mistake. ... I can't stop the tears now. There was one, only one thing I wanted while I was alive, a friend I could talk to, really talk to from the heart. Just one friend like that, only one, was all I wanted. (Yoshio, 1985: 409)

---

## Shame

The perpetrators are not identified but they know who is responsible for the target's distress. There is no stigmatising shame to make them likely to seek revenge but an internalised shame that is likely to help them change their behaviour.

## Power

The intervention alters the dynamics of the group. Even if the bully does not want to change behaviour patterns, the rest of the group, with their statements of good intent, take the power away from the bully. He finds it very difficult to continue with the hurtful behaviour in the light of the supportive strategies provided by the rest of the group.

## 'I'-language of intent

Normal patterns of teacher language that are used to deal with inappropriate behaviour are described by Gordon (1974) as 'you' language:

'If you do this again.'
'Why did you behave like that?'
'Do you realise how serious this is?'
'If this goes on you will be in serious trouble.'

The pupils' helpful suggestions are stated in what we describe as the 'I'-language of intent. They own the solution and there seems to be a significant shift in locus of control from external to internal.

'I will sit next to him in history.'
'I'll invite him to my house.'
'I will play football at breaktime with him.'

By offering suggestions, creating images of some positive interactions and owning the idea, a new 'pattern' is established. It works a bit like a mental rehearsal similar to the technique of positive self-talk. This internal instruction is far more likely to ensure that the strategies are implemented.

## Problem-solving

The approach moves very quickly into problem-solving. By involving the young people in the process, it creates a more positive atmosphere than the traditional investigatory and adversarial methods. Positive comments can be made about the suggestions as they are put forward, and the group can be thanked at the end of the meeting for their help.

## The power of group process

The composition of the healthy group brings the problem out into the open; many more people have a knowledge of the problem and a commitment to do something about it. The decision to see all those involved at the final stage changes the initial group into a series of individuals, all with their own responsibilities. Their unique contributions can be recognised, and they can leave feeling proud of this.

The case study below was a very problematic one because it was presented only after other punitive interventions had been tried and the lead bullies were already hostile and alienated. However, it does demonstrate the elements of the method at its best.

---

### CASE STUDY

### Teenage boys

One of the criticisms of the approach has been that it works for mild 'falling out' but not for 'serious' bullying. This was one of the most widespread and longest-running examples that I have encountered, led by two boys who were regarded as extremely challenging.

While working as a behaviour support teacher I was approached by one of my colleagues. He was supporting a 14 year-old boy who was referred because he was friendless, isolated and seemed to be unhappy at school. Pete, an experienced colleague, had been seeing Sam for several weeks and decided to shadow him around the school to in order to find out for himself whether Sam's account of his difficulties was accurate. Pete was shocked at what he saw – the bullying was 'led' by two popular boys in his year group. They had school-wide influence on their peers and it seemed that everyone felt that it was acceptable to insult, tease, jostle and torment Sam. The abuse was constant and Sam would run along various quiet outdoor routes between lessons in an attempt to avoid crowded corridors. In fact he avoided contact with other students as much as possible. Sam also reported that this sort of behaviour was happening outside school and that he never went out into the community, preferring to stay safe in his own home. Pete was very worried about Sam and asked me to join him in school to facilitate a Support Group intervention.

---

On my first visit to the school I was concerned to learn that the lead bullies, Mark and Jamie, had already been identified as 'bullies' and had previously been disciplined and suspended for their behaviour. I met Sam and listened to his story about his very difficult time in school. He had survived school life by avoiding encounters with other young people and enduring what he could not avoid. This suffering had been going on since he was about seven and nobody had been effective in their attempts to make him safe. Sam was invited to draw a piture to illustrate his experience in school and the image he drew was of a small person represented like a football being kicked around by a group of big boys towering above him. Sam gave his agreement to a Support Group intervention and helped us build the group:

- Mark – bright, challenging student who was underachieving. He only attended school for maths lessons and had been out on a work experience at a car tyre centre for several months.
- Jamie – best friends with Mark, often in trouble but more successful in lessons.
- Twin girls who adored Mark and Jamie and actively joined in with their bullying.
- A very popular girl who had considerable influence among her peers and had been kind to Sam.
- A strong girl who presented as a boy, Jim, and hoped to become civil rights lawyer.
- Two other boys who had joined in with the bullying but were not active in initiating incidents.

The day for the meeting was arranged and all eight participants invited during lesson time. We booked a pleasant room and arranged for tea, coffee, juice and biscuits to be available. Pete joined as an observer and I greeted and shook hands with everyone as they arrived. Refreshements were served and I began to explain my worries about Sam. From the start of the meeting Mark asserted himself and argued with everything I said – he made himself the centre of attention and turned my worries around to make a joke, performing in front of the group. Ten minutes into the interview my heart was sinking and I saw no way that I would engage the group in an empathic response. At that point the school ran a fire drill and everyone left the room … I didn't even expect them to return. This was the most resistant group I had ever worked with and the failure was to be in front of a colleague!

After the fire drill the group did return, explaining that it was 'better than lessons'. At this point I had a stroke of luck that raised my credibility. Mark told the group that he hoped to join the police force. George and I had recently trained the Avon and Somerset force and when I revealed this Mark saw me in a different light. I turned the conversation around and suggested to the group members that they are confident and highly regarded individuals in school but when they go into the workplace they will find themselves as new and less significant – that they might be the target of fun or even unpleasantness from workmates. This gave me the chance to use Sam's picture and explain how he felt … it was a breakthrough!

*(Continued)*

*(Continued)*

Mark and Jamie completely changed their behaviour and became Sam's protector, ensuring he came to no harm in school. Within a short time he felt safe and began to make his own friends.

A few months later, December 2000, I was telephoned by Esther Rantzen with a request to appear on her BBC programme and bring along reformed 'bullies'. I am very reluctant to expose young people to this sort of publicity and warned them of the risks. They were confident that none of their friends watched the programme and they were very keen to be on TV.

I will let Mark and Jamie explain in their own words why they changed.

(Transcript of interview with Esther from the BBC programme *Esther* broadcast in Spring 2001)

Esther:   I'm talking to people who have been bullies. Tell us about what it was like when you were a bully.

Mark:    Everyone was just doing it so I thought that I'd be one of the bullies so I started hitting the kid but it don't make nothing more of you. It's just horrible at the end of the day.

Esther:   But you didn't realise it was horrible at the time?

Mark:    No.

Esther:   Do bullies get a buzz out of it?

Mark:    It's like a buzz, yeah.

Esther:   It's like a buzz. OK, so what changed you?

Mark:    This lady Barbara come in. She never told us off. She didn't say, 'Don't hit him, don't have a go at him, don't do nothing like that.' She just spoke to us on our terms and then we were, in our way, we were changed. We didn't bully the kid anymore.

Esther:   What did you understand then? What made a difference?

Jamie:   The way the actual boy felt that we were bullying.

Esther:   You hadn't realised what it felt like for him?

Jamie:   No, but then once you think about how he's feeling it makes you think and you understand.

Esther: But what convinced you? How did you understand what he was feeling?

Jamie: In the meeting, they got the actually boy to draw a picture about how he felt and it was shocking really, how he did feel.

Esther: How did he feel?

Jamie: On the picture there were, like, all these big people and then in the corner there was, like, this little boy and this was representing him and all the bullies around. There were just a load of things like that really.

Esther: It's interesting isn't it, because people can talk about low self-esteem and how bullying saps your confidence, but for a young person to describe it to another young person in this vivid way, in a picture… Was this news to you? Was this something that you hadn't realised before?

Mark: Yeah. It was shocking to see it.

Jamie: It really changed our mind about the whole point.

Esther: Did you actually stop bullying then?

Jamie: Yeah, we don't do it no more. This boy, I don't think he even gets bullied now. I think he's got a load more friends now.

Esther: I have heard about this before. This is a project, which I used to know as the No Blame Approach. Which doesn't actually let young people off. You see, these young people were very involved. How did you feel when you actually realised how much pain you caused this boy?

Mark: I felt smaller than him in that picture. I thought I was nothing. He was so brave to come back to the school each day to get bullied even more. I couldn't have done it myself. I reckon he's a strong willed person. I wouldn't have done it.

Esther: What people often don't realise is that it took this moment, when you looked at the picture, for you to understand it. You really hadn't appreciated. Did you know that bullying was wrong?

Mark: Yeah, but I don't really listen to the teachers cos they just shouted at you. They don't explain it properly.

Jamie: And when the teachers get mad at you that just makes you want to go back and do it even more but when Barbara actually came in and spoke to us like a normal person rather than someone higher than you shouting at you.

*(Continued)*

*(Continued)*

Esther: What this is about is taking a group of young people and not saying, 'You're bad,' but asking the child who is suffering to find some way, a drawing, a poem, an essay explaining what it feels like and then for the first time they recognise that cruelty really does cause pain of this kind.

At this point Esther approaches a teacher to talk about other pupil-based approaches. Later in the programme she returns to Mark and Jamie, contrasting The Support Group Method with work being done in schools by 'Britain's Strongest Man'. She subtly picks out the difference between his attempts to make bullies feel ashamed and The Support Group Method where the shame arises only from the experience of empathy with the target and not from criticism or humiliation.

Esther holds up a poster of Strong Man saying, 'No to bullying!'

Esther: Is that a message to the children who are being bullied?

Strong Man: Yes, because the biggest message that I take to the school is confidence and talk, talk, talk.

Esther: To whom?

Strong Man: To the whole school. Because when I'm addressing the school I don't know if there are bullies there but if there are bullies there I'll make them feel the lowest of the low while I'm there.

Esther turns again to Mark and Jamie.

Esther: But these ones said they felt the lowest of the low, didn't you?

Mark: Yeah.

Esther: But it was a little subtler with these young people because it wasn't someone telling them to feel bad, was it … ?

Mark: No. It was me, myself. I felt bad in myself for doing it. I can't believe that I was actually that stupid to do it. I think that I was one of the thickest … I think it would have ruined my life if that person wouldn't have come in cos I'd have been a bully all my life.

Jamie: It made me feel ashamed, like, as I was walking through the corridor and I'd see him it made me feel ashamed of what I've done in the past.

Esther:      God, aren't they amazing!

Strong Man:  Absolutely.

Esther:      Sorry [*tears in her eyes*], I find you very moving.

Strong Man:  But that's another form of confidence, though.

Esther:      I don't know why you do this to me but you do. I think it's their courage, actually sitting here on television saying how ashamed you were. Sorry [*reaching out for tissue, crying*], I've gone.

Esther shakes hands with both young men and congratulates them. Round of applause.

# Questions people ask

## You are not seen to be taking strong action – what will parents, pupils and colleagues think?

A school which has a clear written policy which sets out its anti-bullying procedures is not likely to incur disapproval from the community. In our experience, dissatisfaction arises when teachers do not take parental complaints seriously or when they respond by blaming the victim: 'It's six of one and half a dozen of the other', 'She doesn't do much to help herself.' We have explained The Support Group Method at several parents' meetings, and reactions have been very positive. Parents of victims do sometimes feel angry, or want revenge, but when they are confident that action will be taken, we find that they agree that the most important thing is to stop the bullying.

## What do you do if there is a serious incident of violence?

When a pupil is seriously assaulted by another then the usual sanctions must be applied, even calling the police if that is appropriate. The Support Group Method can still be used as well, since there is no need to discuss the particular incident of violence. What should be addressed is the misery of the victim and how that might be alleviated.

## Surely you need to know exactly what went on?

It is only necessary to know that bullying is happening and to have the names of the young people involved. Any attempts to take accurate accounts about the events are likely to stir up further disputes, to increase hostility towards the victims and to waste a lot of time, because the 'truth' may be hard to find and may vary from one person's perspective to another's. Bullying is a complex process and you are not likely to discover all the ramifications, and certainly not all the causes, by questioning the participants.

## What if only one bully is involved?

We believe that it is very rare that bullying takes place in real isolation – there is nearly always some knowledge and even consent from a group, even if they disapprove and refuse to join in. Secret bullying of one person by another is rare and hard to discover, but if it is revealed, then The Support Group Method might still be tried. A peer group can be given the opportunity to help put things right, even if they have not been involved in the unhappiness.

It might be worth considering whether the kinds of intervention used on child-protection programmes would be helpful for these situations, since they may apply to abuse of an individual by another who is not a member of the peer group.

## What if the bully is seriously disturbed?

Pupils with seriously maladaptive behaviours should be helped in the usual ways. The Support Group Method is a method that can be used to stop bullying, not to treat pathology. Any individual who is involved in this process may be offered other additional interventions or be referred for specialist advice as necessary.

## What about victims who provoke bullying? Why can't we help the victim directly?

Some victims may display behaviours which appear to encourage bullying from their peers. Young people who have poor social and friendship skills, or who are very unassertive, can be offered help and support in order to learn appropriate social interaction – although this should not be taken to imply that they are responsible for dealing with the bullying by themselves.

When the group convenes to discuss the plight of the victim, someone may suggest that he or she is encouraged to behave in a different way. 'We could ask her to stop...'. That is fine as long as the group takes the responsibility to help her, and the changes are within her ability.

## What do we tell the parents?

If anyone is hurting more than the victim, it is likely to be the parents who may present, initially, as angry, blameful and needing revenge. When they are allowed to express these feelings, without denial or resistance on the part of the listener, we have almost always found that it is possible to reach agreement about the first priority... everyone wants the bullying to stop. In all but two cases from a collection of hundreds of accounts, the parents have at least agreed that the school could try The Support Group Method.

We suggest that:

- Parents/carers and pupils all receive and understand the school policy.
- Parents/carers are told that, when incidents are reported or observed, The Support Group Method will be used.
- Not every incident will be reported to all parents/carers, just as not every incident of other 'difficulties', such as lateness or forgetting homework, is reported. However, if a student is in difficulty or if she is invited to join a support group, then this can be noted on her records. If a pattern emerges that this student is frequently involved or matters have not been resolved, then parents/carers should be involved.
- The school will always contact parents/carers if there are significant concerns about behaviour or well-being.
- Parents/carers are encouraged to discuss any worries they might have, with a promise that they will be heard.

## Record keeping

There is good reason to keep records other than to collect data about individual students. It would be wise for the person with responsibility for the management of the anti-bullying policy to collect data about all incidents and give details about how the incident was managed and what was the outcome. This is a record of the success of establishment policy.

# Comparisons with the work of Pikas

Almost all advice on the management of bullying incidents includes some action to be taken to show both the bullies and the rest of the community that there is a negative consequence. Sometimes this punitive response is graded according to the seriousness of the incident, as perceived by the adults with a duty of care.

In 1992 we enjoyed a meeting with Anatol Pikas, author of another non-punitive intervention, the Method of Common (or Shared) Concern (Pikas, 1989 and 2002). An excellent summary of the Pikas method prepared by Ken Rigby can be found at: http://www.education.unisa.edu.au/bullying/concern.html

Some confusion has arisen because, since these are two non-punitive methods, they must be the same, or, even worse, the accusation is made that The Support Group Method plagiarised the Method of Shared Concern.

> It was brought into this country by George Robinson and Barbara Maines. It was bastardised—that is the best word I can use—to the point that it became totally ineffective. (Oral evidence to the House of Commons Select Committee, Michele Elliot, Kidscape, 10 May 2006)

The two approaches have several features in common, but there are also some significant differences:

1. Pikas speaks first to the bullies in order to protect the victim from further damage in revenge for 'telling'. We have found it worthwhile to take this risk on behalf of the victim, in exchange for the powerful influence that the victim's story will have on the group.

2. Pikas speaks separately to each member of the bullying group. We suggest that the first meeting should be with all those who are involved in the bullying, or who know about it, even if they were colluding only by failing to intervene. The group can also include friends of the victim.

3. We share with Pikas his approach of identifying a 'Common Concern' which leads on to problem-solving. However, we place more emphasis on heightening the concern by telling the bullies and the rest of the group how the victim feels.

4. Pikas aims to create a partnership between the bully and the therapist in a shared common concern. We work much more with group dynamics to change behaviour.

5. By the very nature of Pikas' interviews with the bullies, and his second step (of getting agreement from individuals that the bullying has happened), he is attaching a bully label. Our approach never publicly attaches any label – the bullies are just members of the group.

## An educational psychologist who uses two methods

### Pragmatics versus therapy: the No Blame Approach and the Method of Shared Concern

Methods of resolving bullying situations that do not seek to apportion blame, find the truth or exact a punishment are rapidly finding favour among teachers and educational psychologists. The simple reason is that in the majority of cases the specific situation of bullying is stopped. The two main non-punitive methods are the No Blame Approach and the Pikas Method of Shared Concern. At first glance there appears to be very little significant difference between these approaches. Both explicitly warn the practitioner against seeking out the 'truth' of the situation. Both encourage the victims to voice their feelings about the bullying situation. Finally, both methods accept that bullying is part of a normal range of behaviours and, in the majority of cases, it is both inappropriate and unproductive to punish those who are doing the bullying.

There are, however, more subtle differences between the two methods other than the order in which one sees bullies and victims. I believe that the main strength of the No Blame Approach is that it is a pragmatic method that makes it very clear to those who are doing the bullying that their activities have been 'rumbled'. Without apportioning any blame, it gives those involved a chance to make amends without losing face in front of their peer group. My experience is that when the bullies are encouraged to give suggestions as to how they can change and resolve the situation, they often make grand and too friendly suggestions as how they can help the victim. Suggestions such as 'I will share my sweets with him' or 'I will call for him on the way to school' are common. In reality, such suggestions are seldom followed through, but the bullies generally leave the victim alone to the obvious relief of the victim and his or her parents. It is unlikely that any psychological transformation has taken place on the part of the bullies, and in few cases has the victim been encouraged to consider the effects of their own behaviour. Neither of these factors should be seen as a criticism of the No Blame Approach, as, in my experience, and in that of many of my colleagues, the approach has been extremely successful. Both teachers and psychologists find its uncomplicated process and philosophy appealing, and its effectiveness can be demonstrated in all but the most complex of bullying situations.

So, is there really a need for another similar non-punitive, non-blaming approach to tackling bullying, especially when the author of this approach generally recommends its use by only those who have some experience of counselling or therapeutic work with children? Perhaps there would be a need if one approach claimed a greater degree of effectiveness or stated that there were certain types of bullying situation that only responded to one particular method of intervention. My understanding is that neither of the approaches makes such extravagant claims and it is likely that many of those practitioners who are aware of both are happy to interchange between the two approaches.

As I have gained more experience as a facilitator in the resolution of bullying situations, I have begun to realise that I do tend to favour the more overtly therapeutic Method of Shared Concern when dealing with an all too common but potentially very difficult situation, that of the 'provocative victim'. The majority of classroom teachers are able to readily identify such children – those who appear to go out of their way to provoke hostility both in adults and in other children. Many provocative victims continue to associate with a group even though they are often the butt of jokes, name-calling and even physical aggression. In such cases I feel that it is necessary to mediate a change in the victim's behaviour as well as demonstrating to the bullying group that they can be part of the solution to a problem that they see is not entirely of their making.

In both the No Blame Approach and in the Method of Shared Concern, it is essential to put from one's mind the notion that one party in the bullying situation is wholly guilty and one is wholly innocent. This is particularly true in the case of the provocative victim. In this situation, the teacher or psychologist is not merely attempting to show the bullies that activities are now known to adults and that they have the chance to make amends without being punished. They also need to help the victim to explore how his behaviour is contributing to the unhappy state of affairs while at the same time demonstrating to the bullies, without condoning their activities, that they are justified in feeling annoyed at the victim for seeking out their attention even when they have made it clear that his behaviour is irritating. Interviews with both the bullies and victim demand considerable listening skills and demonstrations of empathy to both sides. One also needs to be highly attuned to when to move the discussion forward to suggestions of how both parties can change their behaviour to a position of mutual tolerance.

The Method of Shared Concern highlights the necessity of the final meeting. This meeting is potentially the most difficult part of the process but is essential where a provocative victim is involved. It is extremely important to prepare both the bullies and victim carefully, and it should be stressed that the meeting is a way of cementing the positive actions that have arisen from the earlier meetings. Of equal importance, however, is the need to allow both sides the freedom to express their annoyance and frustration at the other party's behaviour. This final session is often daunting for inexperienced practitioners and can sometimes appear to be an arena for the airing of old quarrels and rancour. It is, however, an essential part of the 'therapeutic' process and can demand counselling skills of the highest order from the practitioner. It is, of course, essential that both the victim and bullies are guided from the stage of recriminations towards the idea that both parties can live together and then on to a shared understanding of the practicalities of making this happen.

Perhaps these different approaches to dealing with the problems of bullying should be seen as parts of a tool-kit and the decision as to which is the appropriate tool for that particular problem should be left to the individual. My own anecdotal evidence suggests that both methods work well in most cases. The straightforward nature of the No Blame Approach allows it to be readily passed on to colleagues in many different professions whereas the Method of Shared Concern demands a greater awareness of the psychological processes occurring between the bully, victim and 'therapist'. Some teachers feel uncomfortable working in such areas and are happier to pass on the more complex difficulties to those with greater experience and training. I hope that those who have this experience and training continue to be allowed the time to work with children and families caught up in the misery of bullying.

Contributed by Richard Gilham, 1997

# Conclusion

Bullying is a serious problem, which spoils the lives and learning of a significant number of young people in schools. It is time to stop collecting data on its frequency. It occurs in all schools. Preventative approaches will reduce it, but it will still happen and teachers need to know how to deal with it when it does.

The Support Group Method seems almost too simple and it may be hard for some teachers to let go of the traditional ways of dealing with bullying, such as interrogation and punishment. However, the students and parents tell us that what they care about is that the behaviour stops. The Support Group Method achieves just that.

# Part Two

# A Broader Perspective: Colleague Evidence

# A selection of practitioners' experiences

Our approach has achieved its wide implementation because practitioners around the world have found it to be an effective intervention. In *Crying for Help* (Robinson and Maines, 1997), we asked for participant voices as valid data to support the work in schools. After the political interference during 2005 many practitioners wrote again to support us and our method.

> When people fully understand what the No Blame Approach to bullying is all about, they soon see that it isn't a soft option and that it works. It is very sad that all the good work that George and Barbara are doing through the Anti-Bullying Alliance might have to stop because their messages have been misunderstood by parts of the press, by politicians and by those who advise politicians. I hope that they will be given an opportunity to set the record straight and get on with what they have both spent their lives doing – making the world a safer place for children. (Jean Gross, psychologist and writer)

Some of those who contacted us to support the work and contribute to this new book were introduced to The Support Group Method on a training day.

ooooo

I am Headteacher of a school on one of Europe's most disadvantaged estates. Our free school meals profile is almost 70%, our SEN register over 30%, 30 pupils out of our 308 receive one-to-one support mainly for social or emotional needs. We also have a very high profile nationally, working as we have with DfES over some years to promote a wider response to need through integrated services – now recognised as Extended Schools.

When in my last Headship I attended training courses run by George Robinson – in fact I attended a programme that ran over two years and it was a privilege to work with someone with such commitment, enthusiasm, knowledge and skills for addressing behaviour through a positive approach.

When I began my current post as Headteacher at North Prospect Community School it was 'the place from hell'. Nobody wanted the Headship, I was advised not to accept the post – some referred to it as professional suicide. The behaviour of pupils was as bad as it gets! My entire day would be taken up dealing with incidents of bullying and anger. Over ten years on I am still here and George and Barbara have to take some of the credit for that. My time with George gave me heart that things could change.

It was by using strategies such as the 'No Blame Approach' to bullying that I was able to turn around the behaviour of a significant number of pupils and begin to build an ethos in which children could flourish. In a disadvantaged community how would punitive measures sit alongside the principles and values that were needed to create an appropriate learning organisation?

When we appoint staff they are asked about their approach to pupil management and if they can't offer a positive response we do not appoint. All of our staff have classroom strategies based on reinforcing positive behaviour and playing down the negative.

At an emotional level, there can be no logic in making a child feel that they are the problem, particularly in a community where the culture has been to apportion blame. By separating the child from the behaviour we can help the child reflect and accept that something needs to change and it is at this point that progress can be made without ripping apart the child's emotions and creating self-fulflling prophecies.

I certainly won't be changing our approach and I don't believe that George and Barbara will be deflected from a pathway that their experience proves is a successful one.

Stay lucky duck!

Contributed by Chris Watts, Headteacher, 2006

Following is another contribution from a principal psychologist who was concerned by the controversy and provided an account of the 'evidence' he could quote in the face of biased criticism.

ooooo

Dear Barbara

You may remember that we met some years ago when you did some training for our County Psychological Service on the No Blame Approach to bullying. I was then, and am still, convinced that the No Blame Approach should be one of the measures that schools can use to combat bullying.

The key question is 'Does it work or not?' I have no better access to research evidence than you have, but I have searched the DfES's own websites carefully and find instances where the DfES itself has supported your approach. For example:

The No Blame Approach is mentioned positively and recently by the Primary National Strategy: http://bandapilot.org.uk/pages/seal/downloads/books/pns_seal134305_bullying_pur.pdf

It is commended on The Research Informed Practice Site [*sic*] which is part of the DfES Standards site: http://www.standards.dfes.gov.uk/research/themes/inclusion/ThuMar25102 1012004/674405

And also on the Teachernet site, recommended as a strategy for supply teachers: http://www.teachernet.gov.uk/supplyteachers/detail.cfm?&vid=4&cid=17&sid=111&ssid=4030903&opt=5

Additionally, with the right search terms typed into Google, you can access an impressive number of inspection reports which comment favourably on the use of the No Blame Approach in schools. Some of these are Ofsted reports, and others come from the Independent Schools Inspectorate. LEA schools and independent schools use the approach and inspectors, for the most part, say it works.

I was therefore perplexed and saddened to learn that the No Blame Approach has fallen out of favour with the DfES. Scotland, where I now work, takes a different view and rather likes the No Blame Approach. Try, for example, a visit the website of the Anti-Bullying Network (funded incidentally by the Scottish Executive and based with the University of Edinburgh). This is at http://www.antibullying.net/index.html

In brief:

If the No Blame Approach works in Scotland,
If it worked for the DfES in 2000 [Bullying: don't suffer in silence, DfES 0064/2000],
If it works now for the Primary National Strategy,
If Ofsted's inspectors find it works, and if it works in independent schools,
If it's recommended by the DfES for supply teachers, and

If, as the DfES tells us, this is 'research informed practice' ... what conclusion can I draw?

Is this an attempt to re-write history, to ignore the evidence of what actually works, in order to score political points?

Or have we been misguided all these years?

Best wishes

Contributed by Douglas Thomson, 2006

This next contribution comes from an Australian educational psychologist who has worked in Switzerland for many years and has tried and tested the No Blame Approach since 1995. His resistance to the criticism is expressed in his refusal to change the name. He has never found it to be a problem.

ooooo

## Implementing The Support Group Method in Switzerland

Since 1995 I've conducted countless school-based and other professional development workshops for teachers, educational psychologists and school social workers in Switzerland and have talked to many groups of parents about bullying in schools. For the past six years, I've also been directly intervening in bullying situations in the school in which I now work as a trouble shooter. During this time, I've learned a lot about bullying, about victims, about bullies and about bystanders ('enablers').

My message in these workshops and lectures is simple: (1) Bullying occurs in this school; (2) Bullying is distressing, especially for the victim; and (3) Bullying situations can (and must) be resolved. Through my workshops, lectures and direct interventions, I challenge the capitulation and helplessness that too often accompanies the bullying dynamic. (My psychologist colleague, Jacqueline Schmid, has been engaging in similar work over the same period.)

Although the necessity for systematic violence prevention initiatives in Swiss schools has been recognized since the 1990s and a new word 'mobbing' has been found to describe what English speakers have always known as 'bullying', many adults who work in schools are unsure about whether (and how) they should (and can) deal with bullying behaviour amongst their pupils. I still detect a tendency in some places to blame the victim for his or her predicament ('If he didn't behave so strangely, this wouldn't happen!') or to believe that learning to deal with bullying is a necessary developmental stage that we all pass through ('She just has to learn to assert herself better!'). And this from teachers as well as pupils!

Two important initiatives have helped, however, to raise awareness about bullying and it effects in Swiss schools. The leading Swiss bullying researcher, Professor Françoise Alsaker (Psychology Department at the University of Berne), and the film maker, Ruedi Welten, have produced a very moving documentary film 'Bullying Is Not Child's Play' ('Mobbing ist kein Kinderspiel') in which children and adolescents (bullies, victims and bystanders) explain their motivations and actions. The Swiss Teachers' Union arranged the translation into German of a wonderful Australian children's poster 'Bullying: Spotting It, Stopping It' (from the Australian Psychological Society) and has distributed more than 20,000 copies free of charge to its members and other interested people. This poster is now also being distributed in Germany by Detlef Beck and Heike Blum, who also maintain the website www.no-blame-approach.de. A training video, in which a teacher, Lydia Sidler, demonstrates her resolution of a bullying situation in her class of quite difficult adolescents, has added to the credibility of the 'No Blame Approach'/ 'Support Group Method' amongst teachers.

The film, poster and video contribute to a heightened empathy in our Swiss audiences and thus fuel their desire to intervene effectively in bullying situations. Being a somewhat pragmatic folk, the Swiss are then keen to hear about and implement practical techniques to achieve their goals. The 'No Blame Approach'/ 'Support Group Method', with its simple steps and focused language, is well received. The feedback that we get during the workshops and then later about successful interventions is very encouraging. But as with most solution-focused interventions (of which I consider the 'Support Group Method' to be one), it is simple, but not easy. The sophistication of the model can be overlooked and indeed misunderstood, which has probably lead to the current controversy in England. In recent personal correspondence with Barbara Maines, I expressed my regret that the 'No Blame Approach' had become the 'Support Group Method'. For me, a 'method' describes more a technique, whereas an 'approach' denotes a way of seeing the world, from which specific actions can then be derived.

Perhaps I write from a Swiss cultural perspective, in which the need to apportion blame and to punish the perpetrators of bullying seems to be less strong here than in England. It doesn't require much to convince Swiss teachers that our prime goal should be to stop the bullying rather than to punish the bully, particularly when this could possibly lead to a worsening of the situation of the victim. Once the bullying stops, the need to punish dissolves. The implications of the difference between 'stopping the bullying' and 'punishing the bully' were first pointed out to me by Barbara Maines and George Robinson in a workshop they conducted in Switzerland a number of years ago. Their ideas found a resonance here then which we continue to feel.

In my experience, it is the combination of the two elements, 'no blame' and 'support group' which are responsible for the good results that we are achieving in Switzerland. The members of The Support Groups (particularly those in the roles of the bully or bystander) are motivated to engage in helpful behaviours (or at least desist from further bullying) when they hear that I intend to assist the person who is feeling distressed ('sad', 'angry' and 'desperate' are the most common feelings experienced by the victims), rather than prove the guilt of the perpetrators. It's a civilised process with civilising results.

'No blame' in Switzerland does not mean 'no responsibility'. On the contrary, it means full responsibility for one's actions in a school context in which physical, verbal or relational violence is by no means condoned. An intervention with the 'No Blame Approach'/'Support Group Method' creates time and space for those involved in the dynamic to reflect on their previously aggressive and destructive behaviours, to 'save face' and to publicly demonstrate restitution. (But without 'naming and shaming'.) This process is carefully supervised by responsible adults who can thus demonstrate that two important principles of violence prevention are being observed: (1) protection of the victim; and (2) undertaking actions which serve to reduce the probability of further assaults. My optimistic world view is continually being confirmed by the willingness of children and adolescents to turn away from their bullying behaviour. These are often very influential children who then learn to use their influence in a socially constructive manner. I watch many of them develop into very fine young adults.

In my experience, it is quite embarassing for pupils involved in a bullying situation to have an adult drawing attention to their behaviour and demanding that this stops, and therefore calls for subtlety on the part of the adult, especially when dealing with the induced shame. Members of The Support Groups with which I have worked often express a strong desire to explain or justify their bullying behaviours, particularly in terms of something that the victim has done wrong. They realise that what they are doing is hurtful, but they argue that their behaviour is justified. Often they are very angry at the victim, also because he or she has reported the bullying. At first, they are often not particulary positively disposed to helping this person.

I overcome this initial resistance by saying to them at the beginning that it is *me* who has the problem and it is *me* who needs their help. My problem is that the victim is suffering and that some of our school rules (e.g. 'All pupils and adults in our school have a right to feel safe and happy' and 'I refrain from verbal and physical violence') are not being adhered to. I need the assistance of the group to solve this problem. Are they willing to help me? In this way, I deal very gently with their shame.

I find that those Support Group members who respect me as a person are willing to actively participate. I offer these a carrot, but I also carry a stick, so to speak. Those who have less respect for me as a person are aware of the possibilities afforded me by my position in the school and are clever enough to realise that this gentle (but firm) intervention of mine is a chance for them to show restitution, otherwise the consequences of further bullying could be more drastic. But this is a perceived threat and remains unstated on my part. The bullies know what I'm saying without me having to say it. The success of the 'No Blame Approach' (or 'Support Group Method') relies on understatement and an engaged, assertive non-verbal style. I do not recommended it for 'softies'!

On the basis of my own experience as well as of those of many course participants over the past decade who have reported on their own work with the 'No Blame Approach'/'Support Group Method' in Switzerland, I can conclude the following:

1. It is my intervention of first choice, although I am prepared to intervene in other ways when the situation calls for it.
2. The victim and his or her parents must receive detailed information (also in written form) about the procedure and then give their consent.
3. The victim is assured that 'we are not going to stop until the bullying stops'.
4. The authority of the person leading The Support Group discussion is respected by the group members.
5. Although one expects success with the intervention, this is not 100 per cent guaranteed and therefore a hierarchy of alternative interventions should be established before one begins.
6. The intervention should be embedded in a comprehensive bullying and violence prevention programme of the school.

There will always be bullying in Swiss schools. Always has been. But with our current information campaigns and our training programmes, I hope we can contribute to a greater sophistication in even more schools, enabling them to encourage the reporting of bullying behaviour and then guarantee the implementation of successful strategies to reduce the damage done. Without this security, the bullied pupils are reluctant to tell.

Unless we come under the same political pressure in Switzerland that is being applied in England, we probably won't allocate the resources to engage in systematic quantitative research to prove the effectiveness of the 'No Blame Approach'/ 'Support Group Method' in Switzerland. That's because we know it already!

Contributed by Christopher Szaday

Another contribution is taken from a highly reputable publication which arises out of a collaboration between a professor at Wellington University and a principal of a high school. In New Zealand, as in Switzerland, the work appears to be controversy-free.

ooooo

## Changing the social dynamic: the No Blame Approach

The No Blame Approach is radical and ameliorative and models a prosocial response to bullying. Whereas a common reaction is to want to punish the bully or to seek revenge, this approach steps outside of the cycle of blame and thus de-escalates reaction, defensiveness, and denial. Instead of focussing on who did what to whom, and why, it focuses on the feelings of the victim and what the social group around the victim (including the bully) can do to make things better. It is inclusive and socially enabling.

Unlike the restorative justice and conflict management models, this approach can proceed without fundamental agreement about events and issues. The truth is that the victim is suffering, and in order to stop this suffering, blame does not have to be apportioned.

Punishment is a common response to wrongdoing and transgression, but it will not bring a halt to bullying. It usually has the opposite effect: the bully is likely to blame the victim for telling, to bring in other people who support the bully's story, and eventually to escalate the bullying. A climate in which punishment is the response just drives bullying underground. The punishment–blame contact is a mutually supportive sustainable environment... the bully will 'punish' the victim even more if they themselves are punished. All that punishment does is to sustain this dynamic; and all that fact-finding missions do is to cause the bully to lie and the victim to be blamed and victimized. Most anti-bullying strategies depend on evidence, inequality, and power, and unlike No Blame they address specific incidents, not relationships.

The No Blame Approach forces everyone in the group to reflect on the impact of the bullying behaviour. Not only does the facilitator ask for everyone's help in solving the problem, all the participants are given a chance to think about what is really happening as a result of the bullying. The process carefully avoids blaming or shaming the bully and supporters, but gives everyone in the group the opportunity to condemn the behaviour. The intention is that the bully, still driven by desire to be a dominant member of the group, will decide to find other more prosocial ways of exhibiting their leadership, or retaining their status. The message that needs to be accessed through the process is clear: the group does not condone bullying.

## Why does it work?

- The first thing that the No Blame Approach does is to focus on how the victim is feeling. By focussing on feelings rather than on what happened, or who did what, attention is drawn away from blame, cause, and sequence and towards empathy, which is the most powerful catalyst for change in this dynamic.
- The No Blame Approach causes the bully and supporters to think about the impact of their behaviour.
- It draws the bystanders and non-involved students into finding a solution to the problem. They are forced to be involved.
- The group members are asked for their help. The teacher involved makes it clear that it is up to them – it is their process.
- It is a non-confrontational, prosocial approach.
- No-one has to hide behind an untrue picture of what happened as no-one is going to be blamed for anything that occurred.

All the participants are given the opportunity to empathize with the victim, the bully perhaps for the first time. The bystanders are given an opening to voice what they may have been thinking but were lacking the confidence to express. This process subtly changes the power structure within the group. The effectiveness of the approach lies somewhere between the encouragement of empathy and the fact that when people do something helpful they usually feel good about it. Bullying relies on an audience for bullying and support from the bystanders. The No Blame Approach erodes the bully's power base, humanizes the victim, and causes the other students to lose interest in or support for the bullying. The intimidation stops (Young, 1998).

## How do teachers feel about it?
The No Blame Approach is popular with teachers and counsellors because:

1. it deals with potentially complex situations in a straightforward way;
2. there is no need for extensive and difficult investigations;
3. students see bullying addressed in a constructive, nonthreatening manner;
4. it brings about change quickly;
5. it is easy to use; and
6. it works.

## Golden rules of the No Blame Approach

- *Students are surprised that they are not going to be punished.* This leads to a more relaxed empathic response and makes problem-solving much more successful.

- *The victim does not have to do anything differently*. If they had the personal skills and resources to deal with the problem, they would have already dealt with it. Often the victim is made to feel more helpless if asked to adopt strategies to counter the bullying. The No Blame Approach takes the onus off the victim.
- *This is a nonreflective process*. It is important not to ask anyone why they behaved as they did. They will be unable to explain, and may become more alienated, demotivated, or antisocial if challenged. The only thing that counts is that empathy levels are raised.
- The participants should not be labelled, as this will reinforce the power imbalance that is an essential part of the bullying relationship. Bullying is about behaviour, not personality.
- Stopping the bullying behaviour must be separated from addressing specific incidents such as assaults. The No Blame Approach deals with bullying behaviour, whereas specific violent acts and minor rule infringements need to be dealt with formally in accordance with the legal system or school behaviour management programme.

From: Sullivan, K., Cleary, M. and Sullivan, G. (2004), *Bullying in Secondary Schools*, pp. 226

Mark Cleary, one of the authors who contributed to the above, also wrote and sent us a case study from his own practice as a deputy principal in a New Zealand High School. This was first printed in *Crying for Help* (Robinson and Maines, 1997).

ooooo

## The No Blame Approach to Bullying at Colenso High School, Napier, New Zealand

Background: Colenso High School is a progressive, co-educational secondary school of 600 students (Years 9–13) in a small provincial city, Napier, on the east coast of the North Island. The school, which emphasises school-wide processes, has developed innovative programmes to support student learning by focusing on self-esteem and providing practical organisational skills. In 1993, using the SCRE anti-bullying pack (1991 and 1993), the school, in collaboration with its community, agreed on an anti-bullying policy supported by a curriculum awareness-raising programme 'Kia Kaha'. The anti-bullying initiative was carefully monitored and its impact measured as part of a post-graduate study.

The results showed a dramatic decrease in the levels of bullying in the school but subsequent monitoring has shown that the impact and efficacy of the programme were limited and both enthusiasm for the programme, and willingness to counter bullying, dwindled during 1994. Concern over this lack of sustained change led the Deputy Principal to apply for and be awarded a Nuffield Foundation Travel Bursary to study British approaches to bullying. February–April 1995 was spent in various parts of Britain looking at successful schemes.

The visit to Britain clearly showed that a Whole-School Approach is the most successful way to reduce the levels of bullying in schools. The success of this approach was clearly demonstrated and reinforced during visits to Sheffield University, the Tayside 'Anti-bullying' Team in Dundee and the Strathclyde Education Authority in Glasgow, as well as many schools. In the bulk of these visits, the school approach was focused on the development of a positive environment where bullying was not tolerated.

While vastly impressed by the commitment and success of these programmes in reducing bullying, there was little emphasis on solving the core problem of what to do with students who bullied.

## No Blame Approach

During my visit to Bristol, I attended a training session at Patchway High School led by Barbara Maines and George Robinson who advocated the 'No Blame Approach' for dealing with the inevitable cases of bullying. Their method filled in the missing element from the other programmes, with its problem-solving approach that dealt with changing the offending behaviour rather than attempting to change victims.

## The application of the No Blame Approach

On my return to New Zealand, I started using the approach in response to reported cases of bullying.

*Case study 1*

A distraught fourth form (Year 10) girl came to my attention as the result of a classroom discipline incident. She let it be known that she was being constantly harassed by several others in her class. The cause was a letter she was accused of writing about a relationship she had developed with a boy in the class. The victim was new to the school and was very unhappy. She denied writing the libellous letter that graphically discussed the activities of several members of the class and the boy.

In consultation with the form teacher, I called a meeting with six of her classmates, including the protagonist. At the meeting I addressed the main issue: 'Rachel, a new member of the school community is very unhappy ... she feels ...'. I then went on to read some of the feelings that Rachel had expressed on paper and placed the problem on the table for discussion. It was generally an unproductive discussion and the protagonist dominated the group by concentrating on what she saw as Rachel's main transgression. The others in the group were unable or unwilling to intervene. I ended the meeting feeling unhappy and disappointed with my first attempt to use the No Blame Approach – generally feeling that perhaps New Zealand children were less susceptible to this fancy British method.

I did, however, maintain my contact with Rachel, who continued to report that she had been accepted back into the mainstream of relationships in the class. I met the group a week later and they all saw the issue as being well past them! Perhaps it did work after all.

### Case study 2

Stefan, aged 13 (first year secondary – Year 9) was brought to my office by a teacher after he had been found kicking the walls in a stairway. He was crying and quite agitated. Stefan had a reputation of being a professional victim with a serious temper problem. The teaching staff had little sympathy for him and believed he was the cause of a lot of his own problems.

After talking to him, it became clear that he had been persistently bullied for the last four years. He had been assaulted immediately before being found by the teacher. Once he had calmed down, I explained the No Blame Approach and asked for his permission to talk to a group of his classmates, including his tormentors. He readily agreed, to my surprise, and undertook to write about his feelings that night. I also telephoned his mother and explained what I was going to do. The next day I held a meeting to discuss the problem with a group of seven of Stefan's class (a cross-section carefully selected in consultation with the form teacher).

The subsequent discussion was absolutely fascinating. After the initial denials of any problem, the group (beginning, I suspect, to trust the No Blame Approach), started to talk sympathetically about Stefan and the bullying problem.

While the main protagonists were flippant, the rest of the group, confronted by Stefan's piece of writing, began to sympathise with his plight. They suggested that he did not have a temper and that he put up with an enormous amount of teasing before reacting. There was a definite change in power within the group as they discussed what happened when Stefan was isolated, teased and assaulted. After about twenty minutes of discussion, I asked for ways we could solve this problem.

The responses went like this:

> 'I could walk home with him after school.'
> 'Stay away from him.'

'Stop calling him Fuller.'

'Ask him to join in with me when we do group work.'

'Sit beside him.'

I thanked them for their excellent and mature approach to the issue and we agreed to meet a week later to see how things were going. That meeting was brief and all agreed that they had tried to solve the problem. They said that Stefan was a much better classmate now that the bullying behaviour had stopped.

Each day for the next three weeks I made a point of seeing Stefan just to keep in touch. He assured me that things were fine. He continued to appear much happier and better behaved in class.

At the time of writing, three months after the first incident, while the physical bullying has stopped, the verbal teasing and goading have started up again. I met with the group last week and they agreed that after the holidays old habits had started up once more. The short meeting has been effective, though, as both staff and students blame Stefan for his problem, until his isolation is addressed he will continue to attract attention.

*Case study 3*

I became aware of Gavin's plight at a parent support evening (a monthly meeting of a group of parents) that was devoted to looking at bullying. During discussion Gavin's father started talking about Gavin's misery.

Gavin had been the victim of some particularly savage verbal rumour-mongering about his father for over a year. There was one main protagonist who had effectively alienated a whole group of Gavin's year group from him. The Dean of third form and the form teacher had, in liaison with some angry parents, taken firm action against the protagonist. They had forced public apologies and had moved the rumour-monger into a different form group. The problem had apparently gone away.

I spoke to Gavin's father, who initially was opposed to the No Blame Approach. He wanted Gavin's tormentors punished and saw the approach as being a weak response. He did, after some time, agree to let me try.

The next day I spoke with Gavin. He agreed readily to write up his feelings and was not at all resistant to the ideas of sharing these with his peers. Gavin explained that he had good friends out of his year group and had tried over the last twelve months to avoid the boys who kept making comments about his father's sexuality. He did, however, admit that he was fundamentally very unhappy, had trouble sleeping and had lost weight since the rumours had started. He observed that, if anything, his troubles had grown after the actions of the Dean and form teacher last year and that the group supporting his tormentor had grown.

I called a meeting of a group of six boys from Gavin's form group. We went through the steps of the approach, identifying the problems, discussing the issues and looking for solutions from within the group. Again, as in Stefan's case, I was enormously impressed by the depth of discussion and the mature approach. The boys realised the gravity of the situation and the impact their behaviour was having on Gavin. By the end of the meeting a range of solutions had been discussed and each boy had given an undertaking to work at it.

The change in Gavin was immediate. He started to look much better, the bags under his eyes went and his father was positively over the moon about the change. I see Gavin at least once a week and he has been almost totally free from any hassle since the first meeting. It all seemed so easy.

The No Blame Approach has been used on at least four other occasions in the last 16 weeks in Years 9 and 10 (Forms 3 and 4). It has been relatively successful in each case. In at least three cases the success has been outstanding, while in the other cases, the bullying has halted, albeit temporarily, and has needed further meetings as the bullying behaviour has moved targets. The message is definitely getting through: if there is bullying, telling the teachers results in positive action. There are several important preconditions that must exist. The school needs to have a firm anti-bullying policy and needs to work hard to develop a 'telling culture'. The students need to have had some exposure to an anti-bullying programme, need to know what bullying is and understand relationship dynamics.

## Conclusion

Colenso High School is a rich and diverse school community. We are committed to excellence in education and believe we achieve this best for all our students in a mixed-ability classroom. Our student population is diverse and each classroom will have the full breadth of New Zealand's economic, social and racial landscape.

Our community has few shared values and the success of the No Blame Approach in this mix is a testimony to the robust nature of the programme. If for nothing else, the experience of discussing, with a group of involved teenagers, the complex relationships that take place in adolescent groups, and being amazed at their mature, sensitive approach, is worth it.

The fact that it works so well is an added bonus.

Contributed by Mark Cleary, 1997

Chris Evans made a contribution to our earlier publications in the 1990s and has prefaced this with an update written in 2006, wanting to explain that his support has lasted through a decade of experience.

ooooo

I spent the first 15 years of my teaching career trying valiantly to deal with instances of bullying, with varying degrees of success. For the past 10 years I have used the 'No Blame Approach' and have had a 100 per cent success rate. The 'No Blame Approach' is the emotionally intelligent way of getting children to understand the impact of their bullying behaviour and for providing a means for them to do something constructive about the damage they have done to indivdual lives. The DfES have spent a lot of time and money developing resources and training for the development of social and emotional learning, partly because our prisons are full of young men who have very limited understanding and control of their own emotions and even less of an understanding of the feelings of others. Applying the 'No Blame Approach' to dealing with bullying not only resolves the bullying issue but provides an exemplar lesson in the development of emotional intelligence.

I am interested in developing the full the potential of children. This involves creating the right sort of environment for children to thrive and sometimes means stamping out instances of bullying. It doesn't mean this has to be done in a confrontational way whereby punishment is meted out, resentment adds fuel to the fire and the positive relationships that previously existed are undermined and eroded. I am sure that my staff would agree that we have had our own 'respect' agenda in school for a long time and have high expectations for how children treat each other. Therefore, I use the 'No Blame Approach' because it works, because it helps children to learn from their mistakes, because it provides a mechanism for supporting the child who has been bullied and because it sets children back on to the path where respect for the rights and feelings of others shape the day-by-day interactions of the school community.

Contributed by Chris Evans, 2006

## Getting rid of blame and punishment – Primary School Deputy Head
Two years ago I was given the responsibility for developing Lakes Primary School's policy for Behaviour, Discipline and Bullying and started to find out more about the issues involved. I was, therefore, quite susceptible to the message coming at me from an unsolicited mailshot that proclaimed, 'Michael's being bullied. Here's what to do.' I had a vague memory of the same message from months earlier when I had quickly grasped the opportunity to reduce my volume of paperwork by throwing the leaflet in the bin. This time my response was more positive.

A few weeks later a colleague and I were heading off to Durham University to spend our Saturday finding out more about the No Blame Approach. As we drove along I reflected on the many hours, over the years, that I had spent trying (with varying degrees of success and failure) to resolve instances of bullying. I was quite intrigued by the title of No Blame and the idea that someone could claim to have the answer to this problem. Previously, I had always tried to impress upon the culprit(s) the seriousness of their actions and the harm they had done to another person. I thought that 'getting to the bottom of it' was essential if I was to ensure that the punishments meted out were fair and deserved. The consequences of getting it wrong were numerous, complicated, time-consuming and usually stressful for all involved. Even when I got it right, though, the process was nearly as stressful, and far from straightforward.

By lunchtime I was beginning to realise how many of my strategies and actions were actually helping to undermine what I was trying to achieve, although there were many teachers on the course who appeared to be much more resistant than I to considering the effectiveness of what they were doing. During the afternoon, the group was presented with the No Blame model and it became crystal clear to me that channelling my efforts into blame and punishment was counterproductive. Taking these two issues out of the process would enable me to deal with a bullying problem in a way that was consistent with how I normally interact with children. It offered me the scope to work in a problem-solving and supportive way.

I drove home full of enthusiasm about how I could work with children in order to resolve bullying, and wondered when I would be able to put the theory to the test. It wasn't a very long wait. Four o'clock on a Friday afternoon: 'Excuse me, Mr. Evans. Can I have a word with you? Our Mark is being bullied and I'd like it stopped.'

I knew exactly what I was going to do and how I was going to do it. In a similar situation a month earlier I would have felt angry that Mark had been bullied and very frustrated that there was next to nothing I could do until Monday morning. Then I would start the week by embarking on a complicated and drawn-out process involving investigation, accusation, counter-accusation, cover-up, punishment and, probably, quite a few emotional meetings with parents. What a way to start the weekend! Instead, I invited Mark's mother into my room and we sat down while I listened to her describe what had happened and then explained how I was going to sort out the problem. I asked her how Mark felt about the situation, and then explained that it would be very helpful if he could come to school with a written account of his feelings about the situation and how it had affected his life. Mark, 8 years old and not really able to express his ideas in writing very well, arrived at school the following Monday with a letter written for him by his aunt. It explained how his best friend was now his tormentor and that some of his other friends were part of the problem. He was isolated, having nightmares and suffering from asthma attacks.

I spent 10 minutes talking to him about this and asked who he thought I should speak to in order to stop the bullying. The group of six children included two who were still 'nice' friends. Mark agreed that I could read his letter to the group. At morning break, I asked the six children to come and see me because there was a serious problem and I needed their help to resolve it. I explained that I was going to read them a letter from Mark. I also explained that the letter named one person and said to that particular boy that he should just listen and remember that he was there, like everyone else, because I needed their help to make Mark's life better.

The response I got as I read the letter was typical of what has happened on nearly every occasion since that time. Half way through reading the letter the 'best friend' bully started crying. He realised and understood the full impact of what he had done to Mark. The rest was very easy (just follow the remaining steps of the No Blame Approach) and Mark has been happy ever since. He still gives me the thumbs up (everything is fine) sign whenever he sees me around school. I continued to try the No Blame Approach for a little longer. As the Deputy Head in the school, parents seemed to come to me with the 'serious' problems. Each time I worked through the seven steps and explained to the class teacher what I was doing and why. The No Blame Approach has helped me to resolve quickly and successfully every instance of bullying that I have been involved with since November 1993.

The next step with the policy development was how to secure a common approach to dealing with bullying. The staff agreed to commit two Professional Development days to working with George Robinson on the issues of raising self-esteem, using punishments positively, the No Blame Approach and how we could create a school environment where misbehaviour and bullying would be minimised. At the end of our two days, the staff were unanimous in adopting the No Blame Approach as our common strategy for dealing with bullying.

We also had a wide range of ideas to minimise bullying behaviour. In pursuit of these ideas, I became more aware of how the school grounds can have quite a dramatic affect upon the behaviour of children. After attending a 'Learning Through Landscapes' conference and discovering how school grounds could be developed, the staff, children and parents became involved in planning for a better playtime.

We now have a plan for the development of the school grounds and have already converted one large quadrangle into a quiet retreat, complete with pond, marshes, log seats, picnic tables, shrubs and flowers. The children demonstrate a proud ownership of the area and are very enthusiastic in watering the plants and weeding the beds. One boy, who was admitted to school a few years ago as a difficult and insular 8 year old, recently spent a busy weekend with his friend baking cakes so that he could pay for an outdoor tap to enable other children to water the plants without sloshing water over the cloakroom floors.

It seems to me that the children have quickly accepted greater responsibility for their own environment. They asked for their own noticeboard to go up in our 'patio' area and there are frequent requests from children for permission to do one thing or the other in order to raise money to continue the developments.

Two years later I know that for me there is no other way. The school is gradually working towards creating the sort of environment that interests and stimulates young children, provides 'safe' areas, and is leading towards a greater use of the school grounds as an outdoor classroom. Meanwhile, the main issue that promoted these changes is still a high priority. Parents have been invited into school so that the No Blame Approach can be presented and explained. From my experience, the only thing that parents are interested in when their child is being bullied is that it is stopped and their child is happy. I have recently asked some parents whose children have been the victims of bullying, to come along and give their impression of the No Blame Approach. Their support has been invaluable.

The most recent instance of bullying came to light when Anne's father asked if he could see me as he had discovered that his daughter had truanted because she had been too frightened to come to school. Anne (aged 11) is conscientious and takes school seriously and had spent the entire day in the local library, as she wanted to be in a safe place. He explained how two girls had threatened his daughter with a knife and that they had used the knife to cut off a small amount of Anne's hair. He had been unable to persuade Anne to come to school. The incident had happened outside of school hours and although one of the girls was in Anne's class, the other attended a different school.

Anne's father was undecided about whether he should go to the police. I explained that I shared his view that this was a serious issue and outlined how I would deal with the problem. I said that he might wish to see how things worked out before deciding to go to the police, but that he should make his own decision on that matter. An hour later he returned with Anne so that we could record her feelings and establish which children I should talk to. They both went home and I met a group of girls at breaktime.

Once again, the bully broke down in tears before I had finished explaining how Anne had been so scared that she had truanted. The group made a number of suggestions as to how they could support Anne. One of the girls suggested they spoke to her over the phone to tell her that everything would be all right. I phoned her father and explained that the girls wanted to talk to Anne and that I thought it would be a good idea. He wasn't so sure but called his daughter to the phone. The first girl told Anne that everything was sorted. The second girl (the bully) took the phone told Anne, 'It's OK, I won't stab you. We all want you back in school.'

Later, Anne's mother told me how her daughter had been adamant about not going to school. However, as soon as Anne had put the phone down Anne had said, 'I want to go school now.' The change in attitude was instant. Anne's mother thought I had waved a magic wand.

Dealing with bullying is no longer a stressful and long drawn-out process but a quick and positive way of resolving problems. Occasionally I think about those resistant teachers I met two years ago in Durham and wonder how they are doing.

Contributed by Chris Evans, 1997

One of the most exciting but also daunting experiences was our collabration with the BBC in making a 50-minute documentary about our work. Although very confident of a high success rate, what if this was just the occasion when things might go wrong and in front of a huge audience. But things went well!

ooooo

A BBC Director/Producer, who was investigating bullying for the BBC 2 Bullying Season (26–31 August 1997), came to discuss our approach. After further research, he asked to observe a training session, and came to Nottingham for a No Blame training day. As a result of this, we were then asked to train the whole staff of one school, and the BBC followed the school's progress made in implementing the approach. The filming culminated in a 40-minute programme (*I just want it to stop* – 27 August 1997), which examined three bullying incidents, all of which had positive outcomes.

Over six months I had to research, direct and produce three films for BBC2's Bullying Season. Taking on what used to be three different roles was a lot of work, but gave me the opportunity to get completely absorbed in the subject matter. It turned out to be a fascinating and rewarding experience. As the programmes were funded by BBC Education, the brief was to produce something which was informative and also helpful, not something you might normally associate with most television.

However, the temptation was to be drawn towards the more dramatic end of the anti-bullying spectrum, bully courts, exclusion etc. on the grounds that this would be good TV. Once I realised how redundant most punishment-based strategies were, I concentrated on 'listening' techniques like Circle Time and No Blame.

What attracted me most to No Blame was, firstly, that it appeared to work and, secondly, that it required most new practitioners to undergo a kind of conversion. Old prejudices had to be abandoned – it was a new way of seeing things which could change all the parties involved. Perhaps most of all it was supportive, an element often sorely lacking in schools.

As a result, our programmes made no attempt to offer a 'balanced' view; we wholeheartedly recommended schools to adopt No Blame and parents to press for its introduction. It was something we never regretted.

Contributed by Ian Pye, BBC TV, 1997

While the method is in itself simple, the underlying rational is complex and the following contribution addresses the question frequently posed: will it work when empathy is not available? We cannot always expect that everyone will experience empathic emotions and that is why it is so important that the group includes a range of participants.

ooooo

## Children who are bullies: Do they understand the feelings of others?

I now work as an Educational Psychologist in Derby City. Before my training as an Educational Psychologist, I worked for 12 years as Deputy Head at the Royal School for the Deaf, Derby. As Head of Pastoral Care in the school, a lot of incidents of bullying came to my attention and required intervention, both in school and residence. Over several years, it became apparent to me that a worryingly high proportion of pupils, often of secondary age, simply did not have a full understanding of the emotions and feelings of their fellow pupils. Consequently, while it was important to stop the bullying and apply consequences, straightforward 'punishment' of the bully was morally questionable and certainly did not develop understanding. A study of pertinent research offers an explanation as to why this is the case.

An inherent difficulty for children with language delay, and in particular for deaf children, is that research clearly shows that many of them are extremely delayed in their 'theory of mind' understanding. Theory of mind is the development of an understanding of how others think and the realisation that they may have thoughts, desires and beliefs different from one's own. Children typically develop this understanding between the ages of 3 and 4 (Wood, 1998). Much of this research has been based on studies of false belief, which assesses a child's ability to predict the behaviour of another person based on (false) information that the child knows the other person believes to be true.

However, autistic children and deaf children are extremely delayed in this area of theory of mind. For example, research studies by Peterson and Siegal (1995), Russell et al. (1998) and my own research (Edmondson, in press), suggest that significant numbers of profoundly deaf children – even at secondary level – have still not attained this fundamental understanding of the thought processes of others.

Why should this be the case? Once again, a perusal of the literature and relevant research studies offers some answers. There is an extensive amount of literature on the importance of early conversation in facilitating the understanding of how others think. Dunn (1995) looked at the social understanding of young children and found that the most important contributor to this was the frequency with which they communicated about feelings and emotions with a parent/carer, siblings or friends.

With deaf children in mind, Crocker and Edwards (2004) point out that far from autistic children being the only ones to have a theory of mind deficit, other children who have impoverished language development and limited communicative opportunities will also have a deficit in their ability to understand that others think and feel differently from themselves. De Villiers (2005) suggests that deaf children provide good evidence for a causal role for language in theory of mind development for all children, as many deaf children have significantly delayed language acquisition, but have age-appropriate non-verbal intelligence and are active socially. Consequently, the effects of language acquisition can be teased out from those of cognitive maturation and social functioning.

Harris (2005), in an exploration of the development of theory of mind, notes that conversation highlights different points of view. He also emphasises the importance of language-rich pretend play, and in particular pretend role-play. He suggests that certain types of conversation help children to imagine the world from the point of view of others and to understand their feelings. He also refers to the world of fiction and discussions about historical characters as helping to develop social understanding. Dunn and Brophy (2005) reiterate that it is through the experience of communication within close dyadic relationships that children begin to understand others' minds.

This convergence of research findings about the development of theory of mind comes at a time when there is increasing concern about many children (not just deaf and autistic children!) being 'entertained' by television, play-stations and computer games and consequently being deprived of adult/carer conversation and focused attention. These children have limited opportunities to develop a level of social understanding that research suggests emanates from close carer/child contact, play and conversation.

We would all agree that protection for the victim of bullying is of paramount importance. However, 'punishment' for such bullies is not helpful at all. They need to be helped to understand thought processes of others, and helped to understand the distress they cause. There is an underlying assumption in the 'punishment' philosophy that the bully is fully aware of the pain and distress they are causing to their victim and so they need to be 'taught a lesson'. However, if the child has not developed theory of mind and an understanding of thoughts and feelings of others, it is a different and genuine lesson that needs to be taught. Assessment, followed as appropriate by education, skilled mediation and explanation, is what is needed. The development of social understanding and awareness in bullies is the way forward if genuine progress is to be made and we are to equip these children to function socially in our society.

Contributed by Peter Edmondson, 2006

In the face of scepticism on a training day, we urge the participant to just try it. Many times the person arguing from the audience has had the grace to contact us later and tell us how well it worked.

ooooo

## No Blame Approach to Bullying: Stockdale Road Primary School

Late last year I attended a Professional Development training day on the No Blame Approach to bullying. At the beginning of the day I became quite defensive as George and Barbara purposefully challenged us to think differently about our approach to dealing with bullying. As the day unfolded I began to agree with their premise that bullying (to an extent) is a normal part of human social behaviour. Any approach to dealing with it in schools should aim to stop bullying when it inevitably occurs, rather than to punish it.

Not surprisingly, my first chance to use the No Blame Approach came on the following Monday when I got back to school. There was some ongoing victimisation of a student in a group of friends.

I followed the No Blame Approach to the letter by first talking to the victim and finding out how she felt and what had happened to her. I asked her to draw or write down the way she felt, which she did very enthusiastically. I explained to her that I was not going to punish anyone, but that I would help to make the bullying stop.

I told her that I was going to talk to the bullies and would she mind if I showed them the drawing she had done. She said she was quite comfortable with me showing them one side of the page, but not the other. I assured her I would do as she requested.

At recess I met with the group responsible for the bullying, as well as two other girls that I had selected from the grade. I knew the latter were astute and had healthy social skills. I told the group that I needed some help to fix a problem for the victim. This is where things strayed from the videos we had seen on the PD day. As soon as I mentioned the victim's name, the girls in the friendship group folded their arms, began to snarl and put their side of the story.

I had to restrain myself from retaliating on the victim's behalf. Instead of defending her position, I made notes and said, 'I will talk to her about that.' I then continued to emphasise that no one was being blamed. We needed to find ways to help the victim with her problem.

Then I showed the group the victim's drawings. That touched a raw nerve. Instead of a guilty silence, the drawings drew floods of tears. Not for the victim's pain, but for their own. Two of the bullies related directly to the feelings represented in the drawings.

I later held individual meetings with the children who were upset. They explained the extreme difficulties that they faced in their family lives. Both were themselves victims in conflict-torn homes. I listened intently to their stories and counselled them as best I could. I offered ongoing support and talked about ways of managing their feelings.

As things hadn't gone completely to plan, I wondered how successful the outcomes would be. To my surprise the victim and the perpetrators came to see me (separately) the following day with looks of relief and happiness on their faces. They expressed gratitude and appreciation for my help. The bullying stopped.

Contributed by Brian Strating, Assistant Principal and Welfare Coordinator, Gippsland, Australia, 2006

In Essex, the Educational Psychology Service and the Behaviour Support Service joined together in each of their four county areas to train with George in The Support Group Method. From this a unified authority approach was delivered, a special booklet printed, and this was promoted to all schools in the authority.

ooooo

Essex has a clear anti-bullying policy and has provided every school with a guidance document written in conjunction with George Robinson. The Support Group Method has been widely and effectively used in Essex for over 10 years.

One of the key aims of Behaviour Support in Essex is to work alongside key school staff to develop a whole-school reward and sanction system as well as an effective anti-bullying policy. During such an intervention, while small groups of children were discussing what was fair and unfair and what rules they needed, one 8 year-old girl, Shelley, asked to speak to a Behaviour Support Worker without the other children being present.

She explained eloquently how sad she felt and how she feared coming to school as the children in her class called her names. The Behaviour Support Worker asked her if she would like to set up a plan to stop the bullying. Initially she was very scared about reprisals, but it was explained to her how The Support Group Method would work and she readily agreed. She was asked to name the children who were the most responsible, those who watched but did nothing to help her and those who supported her or who she would like as her friends, and these were recorded. The teacher of the class was consulted to ensure that we had full information about the children she had named. We know from much experience that if there are two or more children engaging in the bullying we need to implement two groups and divide the main perpetrators. In some instances where there are large numbers of colluders and perpetrators we also increase the balance of the groups by adding more good role models and friends of the targeted child. In this instance it was felt that one group would be sufficient to solve the problem. Shelley's parents were contacted and it was explained to them that Shelley had told staff about some incidents of bullying. She was reassured that the school would deal with it immediately and The Support Group Method was explained as well as the reasons why the perpetrators would not be punished. She agreed to try the method.

Shelley was asked to write or draw a picture of how the situation made her feel.

The following is Shelley's account of the situation which she agreed could be read out to the children chosen to be in The Support Group:

> I don't feel right at this school. It feels like I am different to everybody else and they treat me like I am.

It makes me feel really upset. I feel like I want to cry.

I love school but the way I get treated isn't very nice. I try to make friends but they don't want to know. I say sorry to try to be friends but I don't know what I'm saying sorry for.

I just want to be friends but they just say 'No!' and I get pushed and hit. Sometimes I get kicked – I got kicked in the privates.

I feel like they hate me.

On the way to school I feel upset. I don't feel like I want to come to school anymore.

I try to tell my Mum and Dad but they have a lot to do.

I want to cry but I don't because my younger brother would be upset. When I get upset my belly starts to hurt – even when I stop crying it hurts. I cry in school a lot but I put my hood up so people can't see. They would just go and try and sort it out but that makes it worse 'cos then I get bullied more and I get called a 'grass' and that I am a 'grasshopper' and I get pushed and they say 'Go on, be like one'. I've been pushed to the floor and they wouldn't let me up.

Working with a key member of staff (Mrs B an LSA [Learning Support Assistant]) to model to, the Behaviour Support Worker convened the group. This was very carefully done to ensure that the perpetrators were not immediately identified. When children name the perpetrators it is easy to record all their names at the beginning of the list and then read them out to the class. The names were jumbled to prevent this. A meeting was convened in a safe place in the school. The headteacher's room was avoided as often this is perceived by children as a place where they will be told off. It was agreed that he library would be the most neutral place.

When the eight children were sitting around a large desk, they were told that they had been chosen to help solve a difficult problem in their class. They were also told that the adults had every confidence in them to solve this problem. The Behaviour Support Worker read out Shelley's account *without* mentioning her name. The group were asked if they knew who this could be. They named Shelley immediately. The group were asked to think for a few minutes about what each one of them could do to make Shelley happier in school. Gradually each of them came up with the following ideas:

- If she has a problem – get her friends
- We could let her play with us
- Tell her jokes – make her laugh
- Share our books
- Ask her to my house

- Tell her friends to tell her you're sorry
- Ask her to play
- Help her if she gets hurt
- Ask her to sit next to me at lunch
- Say 'She hasn't done anything wrong to you'
- Stick up for her
- Talk to her – see how she's feeling
- Take care of her – look out for her
- Take her to a Playleader if she's got no one to play with
- Tell them to 'Stop it'
- Don't take the mickey out of her
- Make a big friendship group – share my friends with her.

The Behaviour Support Worker praised the children for their super ideas and then explained carefully and modelled how Mrs B would monitor how things were going over the next few days and weeks. To ensure that the children were not removed from lessons any more than was necessary, a simple thumbs up, thumbs sideways and thumbs down monitoring system was agreed. The children were told that whenever they saw Mrs B around the school and at playtimes they would need to put their thumbs up if all was well, thumbs sideways if they had any concerns and she would find time to meet them, and thumbs down if they needed Mrs B immediately. The children practised and then were asked, 'When do you think you will need to put your ideas into action?' There was a pause and one child said, 'Right now Miss as soon as we get back to our classroom.' The children were thanked again for sharing such great ideas.

Mrs B was advised to record the dates of any monitoring in writing so that Shelley's parents could see that staff were keeping a regular check.

After playtime Mrs B and the Behaviour Support Worker asked Shelley how things had gone. She explained that the children had made the following responses to her:

- If you get upset, ask someone – I'll always be there to play with.
- A —— did a funny dance to make me laugh.
- I'm really sorry if I've done anything wrong.
- Do you want to come and play with us?

Shelley's final comment to staff at the end of the day was: 'They've all been really nice and made me really happy. My life has changed – I'm a new kid!'

The school continued to monitor for a short time and now, over one year later, the bullying has not recurred. Since then the school has set up preventative measures and continue to use The Support Group approach on the rare occasions bullying is reported.

Contributed by Lynne Blount, Behaviour Support Service, 2006

Following is a slightly longer account but we use it to demonstrate that many teachers' responses to bullying are often based on well meaning but perhaps misplaced intentions. It is often hard not to want to punish the bully. The outline of one teacher's initial punitive responses and the movement towards a more problem-solving approach provides an account that may be relevant for many teachers.

○○○○○

## From reaction to bullying to bullying prevention

There is a view that bullies should always be punished or they will not understand that there are consequences to their behaviour. That's what I believed when I first began to work on bullying in my school at the time (1990). This was a multi-ethnic boy's secondary school in the East End of London. Quite tough really: yet, as I discovered, full of young men happy to be given the opportunity to support others in need of help. This understanding, which came through using support groups on the Maines/Robinson model, was, and continues to be, the main inspiration and tool for the work I have since developed on bullying prevention rather than anti-bullying.

Anti-bullying was what I did at first. This is the model 'find a bully, punish a bully', and, among other flaws, it is wholly reactive and can only ever be a 'sticking-plaster' short-term solution. It was pupils at the school who told me that, though they used different words. We (including a multi-agency group I had invited to participate) had put together an anti-bullying strategy, based on contemporary research, with five levels of punitive responses to discovered and evidenced bullying behaviours. We had some successes where the evidence was obvious (which it seldom was) and where bullying was admitted (unusual). Mostly, though, we were dealing with children that bully, rather than bullying itself. We tried to scare the bully into inactivity, essentially bullying the bully, which is not the best role model from adults. We were not challenging the bullying tendency either in our students or ourselves.

Evidence for this failure came from an extensive questionnaire on the anti-bullying strategy, after it had been in place for 18 months, completed by all the pupils in the school. As a school staff, we had set out to:

- devise and implement a whole-school strategy to approach and deal with the problem of bullying.
- heighten the awareness of governors, parents, all staff (including ancillary staff), and pupils about the nature and problem of bullying and its consequences.

- agree on common definitions for the term 'bullying' within a framework of anti-discriminatory practice.
- promote an environment of personal safety and a philosophy of caring in practice.
- provide caring professional support for both victim and bully, but suitable punishment would always be given to the bully as a first response.
- empower the victims of bullying through designated institutional procedures.
- empower the bystander through breaking the 'conspiracy of silence'.

The following quote from the questionnaires indicates the general mood in the student body:

> It's not working sir. It did at first, but they've just got cleverer at hiding it and threatening to beat up anyone who tells. (Pupil at Warwick Boys School, Walthamstow, London, 1992)

It would be dishonest to suggest that this was a surprise to me. I had been receiving similar comments from students, and it was a major reason for the questionnaire. However, there was a secondary, and more personal, reason for my suspicions that the strategy was not working. Coming from a personal history of being bullied at school and home, I knew that I would have been too unsure of the system to have the courage to use it. I would not have told on my bullies in case they found out it was me and beat me up.

Overall, the results of the questionnaire showed me that:

- we hadn't scratched the surface of the conspiracy of silence. The punished bully simply sought revenge.
- we hadn't reached and supported the kind of victim I'd been. There was no end to their isolation.
- we hadn't challenged a 'might is right' ethos. In fact we were role modelling the opposite through using our power over the bully – a thoroughly mixed message reinforced by the number of complaints of bullying in the classroom by teachers. Using punishment was simply a reactive sticking-plaster strategy. If punishment worked in anything but the short term, and even that is doubtful, there wouldn't be new bullies.
- because we hadn't broken the conspiracy of silence we hadn't explored the role of colluders and bystanders in any bullying scenario. Therefore we hadn't changed the way the boys behaved generally towards each other – a key indicator of any successful policy and strategy. We weren't supporting bullies out of their behaviour.

- Sixty-four per cent of pupils, acknowledging they'd been bullied, also bullied others. Sorting out the pecking order: this is what we had left unchallenged. We hadn't challenged that ethos and behaviour by having punishment as the first response. If I was to punish all bullying, I'd end up punishing most boys in school, and when teachers are seen as bullies, who's to do the punishing? In fact punishment was counter-productive because it created even more secrecy, simply leading to more incidents beyond the school gates. Might is right doesn't sit easily with preventing bullying: neither does bullying the bully.
- I was identified by pupils as the only teacher actively dealing with bullying – something that I had become aware of since I was getting a large number of referrals. So much for a whole school policy!

My anti-bullying stance had been quite simple and deeply emotional. I liken it, now, to being the knight on a white charger galloping to the help of the victimised. I was determined to be the teacher, the adult, I'd never had. I was the avenger dispensing punishment to those who hurt others. I admit to taking some enjoyment from watching, deliberately making, evidenced bullies squirm. Now they would begin to understand what it was like for those they preyed on: visceral revenge. How tempting it was to bully the bully.

However, fortunately for anti-bullying work in the school and the plight of the victimised, I was a touch more professional, and emotionally literate, than the above would suggest. Overriding all the emotions was the need to be effective. I had thought that graded punishment was the answer: that was the teacher strategy. It had proved ineffective in turning or preventing bullying behaviours. Students were still using bullying as an expression of personal power. We had labelled and punished some students, but we hadn't begun to do what all victims of bullying want: begin to prevent them from being bullied in the first place.

Looking back, there'd been little rising of the general level of emotional literacy among pupils, and such concerns did not impinge on the classroom and pastoral management of staff. We weren't successful in challenging the bullying tendency among pupils, or ourselves, at the level of daily, casual, interactions: yet it is the casual and sometimes terribly thoughtless interactions that are the seedbed for all bullying behaviours.

We weren't really helping: time for a change of strategy … and philosophy.

## A 'Damascus' moment

I might as well get straight to the point. I'd heard of the No Blame Approach and, probably because of the name, dismissed it immediately. How, I wanted to know, in bullying can you not blame the bully? What an absurd idea! How does that protect, or help, the victim? Stupid…

Actually, I was so angry at what I thought was the idea I decided to go to a No Blame conference and make my protests known. I'm a big gob me.

I listened to Maines and Robinson, and began to allow myself to hear what they were saying. My biggest problem was that they were talking about what my students had been reporting, and what the victim in me had been trying to shout. Threatening to punish the bully stopped the victim, or bystanders, from telling. It kept the victim in isolation and did nothing to counteract bullying behaviours or the bullying tendency. It was actually counter-productive because it allowed adults to believe they were doing something, and, because of success with teacher-discovered bullying, continue to believe so: but we were blinded to what was continuing to happen. Our threat and practice of punishment strategy simply drove bullying further underground. No appropriate support there for the victimised or bullying child/young person. I had no choice but to keep my gob shut!

I can remember sitting there thinking, probably grumpily, 'Ok, how do you suggest solving these problems?' Their answer to that, the use of support groups, was going to change my life and, as a byproduct, the lives of quite a few young people that I knew back in school. I was beginning to have a 'Damascus' moment – though I don't recommend them when driving from Manchester back to London. I know what I thought about on that journey, but remember little of the journey itself … it was hugely enjoyable though!

I knew, having been a child and young person victim of bullying, that you feel isolated. If you are the persistent victim of bullying, and by most around you as I was, fear and depression are constant companions with nobody you can turn to who can either understand, or you can trust. You feel powerless. Frankly, the last thing you need is for those who bully you to think that you've told on them. It really doesn't matter how many reassurances adults give you that they will sort it out. Fear stops you as much as does your mistrust of adults – especially when you're scared of adults too.

As adults we want to charge in – to get it sorted. We will not tolerate bullying! That's the reaction the victimised are scared of … and they are left to pick up the pieces as soon as the adult back is turned, especially when a punishment has been involved. Unfortunately, this is not the place to explore the adult-to-adult, adult-to-student and student-to-adult bullying that co-exists with the student-to-student bullying.

All schools are 'telling' schools now. It's a policy alongside promised punishment for bullies. It's why we rarely scratch the surface of bullying activity. It doesn't (though it intends to) put the victimised and their fears and doubts at the centre of the activity. Support groups do, and they utilise the greatest resource we have in both anti-bullying and bullying prevention – the other students. Support groups are an essential bridge between reactive anti-bullying and bullying prevention, a point I shall return to.

I have a much better understanding now of how support groups can become the centre of a bullying prevention strategy: how they support both the child at the centre of the group and support the group members in their own emotional and communal development. However, I'd only got a glimpse of that on the way back to London.

The first group I formed was remarkably instructive. It was for a year 7 (aged 11) who had arrived late into the year group and was quite shy. We had suspicions he was being bullied, but he'd said nothing. I engineered a meeting with the student. I didn't ask him outright about bullying, but rather enquired how he felt when he had come into school (this) morning. That discussion helped him to open up, especially since I was able to swap experiences with my own school days. I asked him to talk about the bullying, but without him mentioning any names. When it came to names, I assured him I wasn't going to go challenge and punish them. They would have no reason to seek revenge on him. I then talked to him about The Support Group. If he wanted one, we would choose the members together – but he would have the final say. He agreed, and we agreed on the proposed membership. It included two boys he played with sometimes, two boys he thought were ok (they'd never bullied him), one boy of my choice who he didn't object to (a bystander) and the boy who had been bullying him the most.

He was most courageous in allowing this, but I had explained that we would not be talking in the group about bullying but about supporting someone in need of help. I also reflected with him that it might be a way to help the bullying child realise what he was doing to someone else by asking him to be part of a group set up to support someone. No accusations of any sort would be made: no blame. That seemed to be the key for him. He wrote for me a little piece on how he felt coming into school and agreed that I could read it out to the group where I would advocate for him.

We had agreed that he would not attend this meeting. Two reasons: it would place great stress on him to talk about how he felt to a group – that was my job as his advocate; it would also allow the boys to talk freely about him and how to support him. However, I also discussed with him what he thought would help him, what the students could do, and I took that to the meeting.

I called the selected students to the meeting. The only information I gave them before the meeting was:

- They were not in trouble!
- They had been selected because I thought they could help somebody experiencing difficulties in school.
- The meeting (held at lunchtime) wouldn't take up too much of their time.

I began the meeting by explaining that someone they knew was unhappy in school, and that they had been specially chosen by him as the boys whom he would like to help him. They, of course, immediately asked who it was and tried to guess. I told them that before naming him I was going to read out how he felt about coming into school, which I then proceeded to do in a quiet voice. We then had some discussion based on them trying to put themselves in the position of someone so unhappy. What would they want to happen?

I then named the student and asked if they would be prepared to help him enjoy school. Each student was asked individually if they would like to help, and each was given a full and easy opportunity, with obviously no repercussions, to say no. All students, including the bullying boy, expressed their enthusiasm for helping. I was really pleased and told them so.

We then discussed the how of helping, including looking at how he wanted to be supported. It was all simple help that was offered: sit next to him in class; play with him at breaks; eat lunch with him; share toffees with him, etc. The bullying child said he wouldn't hit him any more (we had not discussed bullying and he had not been singled out). We agreed to meet a week down the line to see if we all thought he was enjoying school more – the target we had settled on. I sent them off to do it. During the week I checked daily with the group members that he was being supported. At the next group meeting the students reported on what they had been doing with a certain element of pride. I kept the group in place for another couple of weeks and then disbanded it with the agreement of the, much happier, group members. The story has a happy ending in that the bullying student and his target became the best of friends (though a pain to the teachers with their silly behaviour!).

It was so easy and hardly took any of my time. I'd got partners now.

### Extending the Support Groups

After that initial success, I began to put together more groups and started asking staff to participate. Some did, some didn't! Initially, all groups were on victimised/bullying scenarios, but it didn't take long to realise there was no reason not to use them to help with any issue a student may have. So we set up groups to help with bereavement; classroom disruption; the bullying student; problems at home (with parental approval); literacy or numeracy problems; second language problems; and any new entrant to the school. The actions of the groups were proving very flexible yet each was following the same process – and they were working across the age range. I had groups in year 11 (aged 15–16) as well as year 7. I also had non-teachers facilitating the groups, including ancillary staff. The only qualification for working with a group was, and is, a caring attitude.

I have two small anecdotes to give here that I use when facilitating bullying prevention workshops in schools. The first concerns a year 9 (aged 13–14) student. Teachers generally found him difficult in class, and with other students he had a reputation as a bit of a bully. There were not many who had a good word for him. The image I hold is of him bouncing (he was somewhat overweight) across the playground to ask me if he could form a support group for a student in year 7 who he knew was having difficulties. I agreed but told him I would keep a watch on it. He did it superbly.

The second anecdote comes from a term I spent in a primary school piloting the work (the Support Code). I was just developing on bullying prevention, using The Support Groups as the basis. I had worked with the year 4 class (aged 8–9) on supporting each other, not just via the groups. I simply wanted them to develop a caring and supportive attitude as I believed, and believe, that this is where bullying prevention starts. One day I was coming back to the classroom from lunch. Down the corridor I spotted one of my girls crying. Before I could get to her, three of her classmates got to her and started comforting her. As I approached, one turned to me and said 'It's alright sir. We're helping her.' The children were beginning to group support each other in and outside the classroom. They weren't waiting for me (though I told them I wanted to be kept informed). This is the supportive and caring atmosphere of bullying prevention.

What was using the groups across both the primary and secondary sectors showing me?

- That they work – not only in helping the focus group but also in raising the general level of thoughtfulness in the group participants. This often had an impact on classroom behaviour, and learning, as a by-product.
- That the vast majority of children and young people are enthusiastic in their support for others when asked to help out.
- That they liked being asked, it empowers them to help.
- That they have no shortage of ideas about how to help and they keep to the task.
- That empathy, the discussion of how a person feels, and how they might feel if it were them, is a powerful tool in bullying prevention. It also supports the development of an emotional, literate and healthy community.
- That parents like them.

- That unintentional bullying (essentially thoughtless behaviour lacking in emotional literacy) is the common background for all intentional bullying behaviours, but cannot be prevented through punishment-based anti-bullying which only attempts to deal with the immediate problem when it finds one. Such reactive strategies do not utilise the skills, or make a partnership with, the student body. They don't look ahead. Part of the problem with anti-bullying is that it only comes into play when there is a victim.
- That they are non-hierarchical. A student at the centre of one group may also be a member of another group. Students could both receive and give support at the same time.
- That all students could take part in the groups. Poor behaviour or learning difficulties did not disqualify or exclude.
- That they don't consume vast amounts of time (as in investigating a bullying problem when all and sundry deny any knowledge) but rather (as in the primary classroom example given above) help to release time through the partnership with the students.

Not all the groups worked for the group members; even sometimes with the advice of social workers, etc. (members of the multi-agency group I had formed were actively supporting groups). However, most did (and we never resorted back to punishment where they were bullying-based), and I began to understand how they could be used to form the foundation for bullying prevention. I left teaching to work with schools on developing my ideas on bullying prevention: a very tough decision since I loved the classroom and liked my nice steady salary. It was the right choice though: too many students in too many schools do not get enough support from staff or peers.

Contributed by Dave Brown, 2006

## Conclusion

The contributions from colleagues show that skilled and experienced practitioners have shared our view that punitive interventions do not work. Instead they have used, modified and developed their own Support Group Methods, with confidence and supported by case study evidence.

UK Government policy in 2007 tells us that all bullies should be punished. We hope that our writing and these voices will have some influence in the future.

# Andrew's Postscript, July 1997

We started this book (p. 8) with a story from 1991. We could finish Andrew's story in 1997.

A few years after the events described earlier I received a message to phone Andrew's father. I was surprised, and a little puzzled, as there had been no contact since Andrew had celebrated his 'A'-level success at our presentation evening. When I returned the call I was delighted to hear that Andrew had successfully completed a degree course. Andrew's father wanted to say thank you for the intervention when Andrew was being bullied and to let me know how successful he had been from then on.

Head of Sixth Form

For at least one pupil, the No Blame Approach made a difference for life.

Part Three

# Political Events, Controversy and Research

# Political events

The inclusion of a section on 'political events' in a book about effective methodology might seem unexpected or inappropriate. The justification for this chapter is that no social process can rely solely on accountability. It is embedded into the *Zeitgeist* of the time and can become a political football.

The Support Group Method was launched under the name 'The No Blame Approach' in 1991 with the publication of a training video (Maines and Robinson, 1992). The intervention was a response to a crisis and the name was adopted in haste. While 'No Blame' is an important ingredient, the procedure includes other essential elements:

- encouragement of empathy
- shared responsibility
- problem-solving.

None of these is made explicit in the name and, in this book, we launch the work under a new title, The Support Group Method.

At first it attracted little attention. The major research project funded by the DES in the early 1990s and headed by Professor Peter Smith at Sheffield University was already underway and it was too late to include our work on his research plan. The growth and development of the work depended on the training programme we offered and the feedback we were getting from our own interventions and those of our colleagues who were using the method.

It is acknowledged that:

- the method is counter-intuitive,
- the original name is misleading.

But these points do not adequately explain the attack made on the work and the subsequent fate of its originators.

Michelle Elliot, Director of Kidscape, has criticised the No Blame Approach from its beginnings as a 'soft' and ineffective intervention.

> It seems to me that the No Blame Approach will only reinforce the attitude of joy riders, lager louts, muggers and others like them, who ultimately take no blame or responsibility for the consequences of their actions. (Letter, *Sunday Times*, 21/11/1993)

She claims that she has a large body of critical evidence in the form of letters from parents who tell her that the method did not work. Peter Smith commented on this claim in his presentation at a conference entitled 'Bullying, How to spot it, How to stop it', City University, London, 14 November 2006. He referred to the possibility that the criticisms result from the failure to follow the seven steps: 'My personal opinion is that some of the hostile responses result from misuse of the method.'

Some of this misunderstanding is perpetrated by professionals who oppose the method and frequently describe it as a confrontation between victim and bullies, and also confuse it with a very different process known as the 'Shared Concern Method' developed by Anatol Pikas in Sweden. The similarities and differences between the two methods is discussed in detail earlier in the book (see pp. 53–56).

During the years 1993–2006 it could be argued that the forces of opposition and support surrounding the work took on much more significance than any rational evaluation of its effectiveness. On the one hand, most of those who took part in training events and others who studied the method through publications were convinced, after trying it for themselves, that it was a significantly successful intervention. Many accounts are included in this publication but they represent only a small portion of people who reported success. A significant piece of research carried out by a team of behaviour support teachers in Hull was reported by Sue Young (1998). Her team had used a modified version and established a very high success rate.

The method was not mentioned in the first edition of the government guidelines *Bullying: Don't Suffer in Silence* (DfE, 1994). By 2000, when the second edition was published, Peter Smith was confident that its positive reputation was established and wrote a favourable comment, calling it 'The Support Group Approach', the first time an alternative name was suggested.

# The Anti-Bullying Alliance (ABA)

In 2002 the Anti-Bullying Alliance was founded. Alison O'Brien of the NSPCC and Gill Francis of the National Children's Bureau (NCB) shared a concern about bullying and a commitment to involve a group of 'experts' and experienced professionals. The word spread and soon the organisation had more than 65 members, a constitution, a website (http://www.anti-bullyingalliance.org.uk) and held regular meetings.

We, as publishers and trainers in the field, were members from the beginning, and it was exciting and rewarding to belong to a group of people willing to give time and effort to achieve a shared aim to reduce bullying and create safer environments in which children and young people can live, grow, play and learn.

One of the most successful and popular items in the ABA programme was the establishment of a week in November designated as Anti-Bullying Week. The first one took place in 2004. Organisations in all parts of the country took part in a festival of events and the press and media gave positive and supportive coverage. The blue wrist-bands were introduced and worn by several celebrities who declared their opposition to bullying, some admitting that they had suffered as children. A new level of awareness had been achieved with opportunities for very active participation by all members of the community. It became 'cool' to demonstrate concern about bullying.

The Department for Education and Skills (DfES) allocated money to fund more structured activities and a plan to appoint seven regional coordinators on a one-year contract was agreed with ABA. In the South West, we were the successful candidates, having offered a programme which included meeting and working with representatives from all 16 authorities in the region, policy development, resources for anti-bullying week, and small projects with particular groups (for example, Looked After Children).

We include the detail here in order to make clear that:

- our own work on The Support Group Method was not a feature of the programme, nor did we create any opportunities to offer training or sell publications through the course of our work as regional coordinators.
- from the time of our appointment by the ABA we were on salaries as employees of Sage Publications and no income generated from our roles as regional coordinators, training or book sales was passed to us.

Funding from the DfES was arranged in time-limited chunks, paid to the National Children's Bureau which hosted the administrative and public relations issues associated with ABA. An extension of the initial contract was agreed to the end of 2005. During the Autumn term the news came through that further funding was to be made available until the end of August 2006. We were delighted, confident and proceeded to plan our prgramme of events for the following year.

In November, in time for Anti-Bullying Week, Bristol City Council launched new authority-wide policy guidelines and The No Blame Approach was mentioned as one of the effective methods suggested as useful to Bristol schools. This provided a high-profile opportunity for Dan Norris, a local MP with a longstanding opposition to our work and a close association with Kidscape, to draw attention to his views in Parliament. During Prime Minister's Question Time, he invited Tony Blair to comment on Bristol's policy that 'lets bullies off':

Dan Norris (Wansdyke) *Hansard* source:

> This Friday, as part of anti-bullying week, Lib-Dem controlled Bristol city council will call on its teachers not to punish or blame pupils who bully other pupils. What message does the Prime Minister have for those who adopt a no-blame approach, which, in my view, is dangerous and reckless, does nothing for the victims and does nothing to make bullies change their behaviour?

(The previously Labour-controlled council had supported the work for many years without criticism.)

Tony Blair (Prime Minister) *Hansard* source:

> If what my hon. Friend says is correct about the Liberal Democrats, then it is an extraordinary thing for even them to do and I am shocked by it. [Interruption.] To describe oneself as shocked by the Liberal Democrats is perhaps an oxymoron.
>
> I profoundly disagree with the position taken by the council. Bullying should be punished. Children who bully must be made to understand the harm that they have been doing. New sanctions are available. I am pleased that in the schools White Paper we are giving teachers an unambiguous right to discipline. It is absolutely necessary, and I pay tribute to my hon. Friend's work on that serious problem.

This event was the start of a rapid and damaging series of politically driven events bearing no relation to any new research evidence or to any balanced argument.

# Anti-Bullying Alliance, 2005–2006

During the Autumn term we celebrated the confirmation from the ABA that further funding was available and that our new contracts were in the post. This ensured the continuation of the programme we had planned with colleagues and young people in the South West.

On 16 December we received a phone call from Paul Ennals, Chief Executive of the National Children's Bureau, which hosts the service agreement for the ABA, telling us that our contracts as regional coordinators would not be renewed. He explained that he was under extreme pressure from the Prime Minister's office to end our employment.

During the school holidays (Christmas 2005), the DfES website removed all references to the No Blame Approach.

These events distressed us and outraged many colleagues and professionals around the world. We were inundated with messages of support from people who read or heard about our experience. In spite of the attempt to discredit our work, it is encouraging to report that invitations to provide training increased.

A media centre was set up on our website to provide full information on the events (http://www.luckyduck.co.uk/supportgroup) and space to post supportive contributions from colleagues around the world.

The termination of the contracts shocked our publishing colleagues. The day that we received the news was the occasion when we had provided a training day for the CHIPS (Childline in Partnership with Schools) colleagues. The day was hosted by Sage in their London office and a cheque was presented for the funds raised by Sage staff during Anti-Bullying Week. The directors offered us support in several ways:

- legal advice to protect our position,
- media expertise in preparing media statements and handling press inquiries,
- research and installation of a new link on our website devoted to our anti-bullying work.

An independent research project was funded by Sage to establish the validity of the No Blame Approach. Professor Peter Smith was approached to carry out this research. He was recommended as the most suitable person, and respected as the leading authority on school bullying in the UK. Some of the significant points are mentioned in the section on Research below and the full report is provided in Appendix 1.

# The research evidence

In this section we will:

- provide reference or full accounts of the evaluations and research projects undertaken,
- describe how both the controversy and the opposition to The Support Group Method have included a continuing demand that we provide 'research evidence' to validate this work while some other punitive methods appear to rest on nothing more than intuition,
- refer to the recently published report on bullying from the House of Commons Education and Skills Committee Session 2006–07 (http://www.publications.parliament.uk/pa/cm/cmeduski.htm#reports).

## Background

When the method was published by us in the form of a video training pack (Maines and Robinson, 1992) a book (Robinson and Maines, 1997) and various articles, the established experts in the field, even when open-minded, were understandably cautious in their appraisal. For example, Rigby (1996: 208) writes:

Hard evidence from unbiased evaluators of the method is notably lacking.

Yet this is true of most methods, and many claims of success are made which seem to have no sound statistical basis.

In the same book, Rigby notes that the approach 'is likely to work better with younger children'. He gives no evidence in support of this view, which conflicts with much of the experience reported to us.

It is confusing to read that there is 'insufficient evidence' for our approach, when the Pikas Method of Shared Concern was used by only 12 teachers in the Sheffield research referred to below. Rigby notes some of the critiques of the method, but then goes on to state:

> However, the method is understood best through participation in workshops provided by Pikas himself. During his visit to ... Australia in 1995 the method was explored in some depth in his workshop, and the present account is based, in part, on the experience of attending one of these. (Rigby, 1996: 209)

We greatly admire the pioneering work of Pikas and hold him in the highest esteem, but feel that, if a researcher's participation in a workshop is sufficient to provide evidence in support of a method, then the accounts presented here may also have some validity.

## Practitioner support

While we were surprised and delighted by the accounts of the successful use of the work by practitioners, we recognised a need for some data to account for our claims. With limited resources we were able to carry out two small-scale, unpublished evaluations referred to in *Crying for Help* (Robinson and Maines, 1997). We were looking for success criteria in two aspects:

- Does the distress of the victim reduce after the intervention?
- Do the users, mainly teachers, find the programme easy to use?

These can be found on our website at http://www.luckyduck.co.uk/approach/bullying.

Neither of these studies can be claimed to be independent and we relied upon others to show sufficient interest in the work and provide the valid research. It was therefore a thrill to open our copy of *Educational Psychology in Practice* and read an article by Sue Young in which she gives an account of a very high success rate using The Support Group Method (Young, 1998). She headed up an anti-bullying team in Kingston upon Hull and reported on 55 interventions.

She reports on a two-year project in Kingston upon Hull where the Special Educational Needs Support Service (SENSS) offered schools advice and support for individual referrals for bullying incidents. During the two years the Service dealt with over 80 referrals that required active involvement beyond advice over the phone. She describes the cases as being serious.

By the very nature of the referral process, the complaints tend to be serious – indeed, the police may have been involved, there may have been a medical referral, the problem may have been going on for years and the child may be absent from school.

The intervention used was a No Blame Approach with minor modifications. It was used in 55 cases (over 70 per cent of referrals) and the referrals were predominantly from primary schools. Young (1998) writes:

The approach has been successful in the great majority of cases – to be precise the bullying stopped completely or the victim no longer felt in need of support.

Of the 51 primary cases, there was immediate success in 40 (80 per cent), delayed success in seven (14 per cent), where the intervention had to be continued after the first meeting, and limited success in three cases (6 per cent), where the victim continued to mention incidents that bothered him/her, although there had been considerable improvement. One case was not completed because the child was excluded. Of the four referrals from secondary schools, two were of immediate success and the other two could not be completed as the pupils had left the school. Young (1998) states:

The confidence of Maines and Robinson has been substantiated in our experience, so much so that now SENSS advises the schools to adopt this approach, unless there are compelling and usually obvious reasons why it would not be appropriate.

The publication of this research and a subsequent study by the same author (Young and Holdorf, 2003), facilitated the recognition of the value of the method in the eyes of some esteemed professionals, notably Professor Peter Smith, who sets out his views and indicates his support in an email to Paul Ennals (January 2006), making an attempt to demonstrate the validity of our work:

… I know of two better pieces of more recent research, both by Sue Young using The Support Group approach as a slight variant of NB. The first is from S. Young (1998), The Support Group approach to bullying in schools, *Educational Psychology in Practice*, 14, 32–39. This was an independent evaluation carried out in the Kingston upon Hull Special Educational Needs Support Service (SENSS). Over a two-year period, in 80% of primary school cases treated through the modified No Blame Approach there was an immediate success; in 14% of cases there was a delay, but after 3 to 5 weekly reviews, the bullying stopped or the victims reported that they no longer needed The Support Group; in only

6% of cases did the victim report that the bullying continued, or that he/she was bullied by different pupils. There was a similar outcome in secondary school referrals.

The second is from S. Young & G. Holdorf (2003), Using solution focused brief therapy in individual referrals for bullying, *Educational Psychology in Practice*, 19, 271–282. This was a study of solution based brief therapy as an intervention with individual pupils, these being 118 pupil referrals from both primary and secondary schools. The authors found this procedure more effective in certain cases, but they did use The Support Group approach in 12 cases, 11 of them successful.

These reports suggest a high success rate. The quality of the reports are on a par with most of the better research literature available on anti-bullying work. My main reservation is the very high success rates achieved (around 90%). Given the persistence of bullying in our schools (as we know, it is widely believed to be getting worse, though that is media hype), it is clear there is no 'magic wand' – not yet, anyway. Claims for success rates above 80% – whether for NB/SG, or for bully courts, or whatever – leave me suspecting either that the research is flawed in some way (e.g. social desirability affected responses), or that the findings are not generalisable because this was a special sample group in some way. If we had truly generalisable success rates of over 80%, then our problems really would be nearly over but I doubt we are out of a job yet.

In summary, what evidence there is, is supportive of NB/SG, but there is definitely a need for more research, carried out independently in 'normal' schools that are using the approach. (Email from Peter Smith to Barbara Maines, 7/2/06, quoting excerpts from an earlier email to Paul Ennals and ABA Advisory Group)

In the same email, Peter Smith demonstrated his own commitment to the inclusion of our work as one of the recommended strategies to help schools develop effective policies (DfEE, 2000):

The NB/SG approach was not mentioned much in the first edition of *Don't Suffer in Silence*, simply because the Sheffield Project had got going before we learnt about it, and we were evaluating the somewhat similar Pikas method (similar in philosophy at least). So the first edition has a lot on the Pikas method, and some shorter reference to NB.

When the second edition of *Don't Suffer in Silence* was commissioned in 1999, and was less tied to the specific evaluations of the Sheffield Project, I and others working on it felt that the NB approach should receive more profile, and we wrote more into it. Everything we wrote for that edition was cut back a lot, first by DfES staff (reasonable pruning, basically), and then halved again by David Blunkett, then Minister for Education, who wanted a short and snappy document. He also vetoed mention of the No Blame Approach (so this sensitivity has a long history).

At that time I said I could not have my name associated with the Pack if NB was not mentioned as being one important approach. However a compromise was reached by calling it The Support Group approach. So it is in the second edition, in that form.

This support from the leading and most highly respected authority in the UK on bullying was very important to us, as was his agreement, in the spring of 2006, to undertake a small research project to evaluate the views of schools and local authorities (LAs). The full report is available on our website, www.luckyduck. co.uk/approach/bullying, and in Appendix 1.

## Summary of the research by Smith et al. (2006)

Questionnaires were sent to local authorities and to schools, and were available on a website. The response rate was 38 per cent, which is fairly typical of educational survey work (e.g. Smith and Samara, 2003).

The main points are:

1. Some two-thirds of LAs were supportive of The Support Group Method in general terms, although fewer said they had sufficient evidence to judge effectiveness (from schools, parents, pupils and governors). The modal rating when given was 'satisfactory'.
2. Most schools had used The Support Group Method for one to five years, often across the whole school. Two-thirds received direct training in the method.
3. Over one-half of schools gave a rating of effectiveness, based on teachers, pupils and parents; the modal rating was 'very satisfactory'.
4. A majority of LAs and schools that responded to the survey were satisfied or very satisfied with The Support Group Method.

On 27 March 2007, The House of Commons Select Committee – Education and Skills published its report on bullying. Professor Smith did not choose to refer to his research in his evidence and the report contains little support for the method.

Our evidence presented to the Select Committee is included in Appendix 2, and the full report can be downloaded as a pdf at: http://www.publications.parliament. uk/pa/cm/cmeduski.htm.

We hope that what you have read in this book has provided:

- an account of the development of the work over a period of 15 years,
- a clear explanation of the way it works,
- our hypothesis on why it works,
- case studies and evidence from some of the colleagues who have used, developed and modified the approach.

We do not intend to publish further on this work, but to go on training and eventually leave the reputation of our work in the hands of those who use it and find it an effective and safe intervention.

We want to thank these colleagues and many others who have supported us through the times of criticism and attack.

# Bibliography

Attwood, M. (1990) *Cat's Eye*. London, Virago Press.

Besag, V.E. (1989) *Bullies and Victims in Schools*. Milton Keynes, Open University Press.

Besag, V.E. (1992) We Don't Have Bullies Here. 57, Manor House Road, Newcastle Upon Tyne.

Braithwaite, J. (1989) *Crime, Shame and Reintegration*. Cambridge, Cambridge University Press.

Crocker, S. and Edwards, L. (2004) Deafness and additional difficulties. In S. Austen and S. Crocker (eds) *Deafness in Mind*. London, Whurr Publishers Ltd.

Davies, J.G.V. and Maliphant, R. (1974) Refractory behaviour in school and avoidance learning. *Journal of Child Psychology and Psychiatry*, 15: 23–31.

De Villiers, P.A. (2005) The role of language in theory of mind development: what deaf children tell us. In J.W. Astington and J.A. Baird (eds) *Why Language Matters for Theory of Mind*. Oxford, Oxford University Press.

DfE (1994) *Bullying: Don't Suffer in Silence*. London, HMSO.

DfEE (2000) *Bullying: Don't Suffer in Silence*. London, HMSO.

Dunn, J. (1995) Introduction. In J. Dunn (ed.) *Connections between Emotion and Understanding in Development*. Hove, Lawrence Earlbaum Associates Ltd.

Dunn, J. and Brophy, M. (2005) Communication, relationships and individual differences in children's understanding of mind. In J.W. Astington and J.A. Baird (eds) *Why Language Matters for Theory of Mind*. Oxford, Oxford University Press.

Edmondson, P. (in press) Deaf children's understanding of other people's thought processes. *Educational Psychology in Practice*, 22(2): 159–169.

Elliot, M. (ed.) (1991) *Bullying: A Practical Guide to Coping for Schools*. London, Longman, in association with Kidscape.

Foster, P., Arora, T. and Thompson, D. (1990) An example of one school's approach to the task of developing a whole school policy. *Pastoral Care in Education*, September.

Gordon, T. (1974) *Teacher Effectiveness Training*. New York, Wyden.

Harris, P.L. (2005) Conversation, pretence and theory of mind. In J.W. Astington and J.A. Baird (eds) *Why Language Matters for Theory of Mind*. Oxford, Oxford University Press.

House of Commons Education and Skills Committee (2007) *Bullying: Third Report of Session 2006–2007*. London, HMSO.

Jones, E. (1991) Practical considerations in dealing with bullying in secondary schools. In M. Elliot (ed.) *Bullying: A Practical Guide to Coping for Schools*. London, Longman in association with Kidscape.

Juvonen, J., Graham, S. and Schuster, M.A. (2003) Bullying mong young adolescents: the strong, the weak, and the troubled. *Journal of the American Academy of Pediatrics*, December, as cited in *Pediatrics*, 112(6): 1231–1237.

Maines, B. and Robinson, G. (1990) *You can...You Know You Can*. Bristol, Lucky Duck Publishing.

Maines, B. and Robinson, G. (1991a) *Teacher Talk*. Bristol, Lucky Duck Publishing.

Maines, B. and Robinson, G. (1991b) *Stamp out Bullying*. Bristol, Lucky Duck Publishing.

Maines, B. and Robinson, G. (1991c) *Punishment: The Milder the Better*. Bristol, Lucky Duck Publishing.

Maines, B. and Robinson, G. (1992) The No Blame Approach (video and training booklet). Bristol, Lucky Duck Publishing.

Maines, B. and Robinson, G. (1994) The no blame approach to bullying. A Paper presented to the British Association for the Advancement of Science. 8 September, Loughborough.

Maines, B. and Robinson, G. (2008) *Bullying: The Support Group Method Training Pack*. A Lucky Duck Book. London, Paul Chapman.

Munro, S. (1997) *Overcome Bullying for Parents*. London, Piccadilly Press.

Olweus, D. (1978) *Aggression in the Schools: Bullies and Whipping-boys*. London, Wiley; Halsted Press.

Olweus, D. (1987) Bully/victim problems among school children in Scandinavia. In J. Myklebust and R. Ommundsen (eds) *Psykologprofessionen mot ar 2000*. Oslo, Oslo Universitetsførlaget.

Pearce, J. (1991) What can be done about the bully? In M. Elliot (ed.) *Bullying: A Practical Guide to Coping for Schools*. London, Longman, in association with Kidscape.

Peterson, C. and Siegal, M. (1995) Deafness, conversation and theory of mind. *Journal of Child Psychology and Psychiatry*, 36(3): 459–474.

Pikas, A. (1989) The common concern method for the treatment of mobbing. In E. Roland and E. Munthe (eds) *Bullying: An International Perspective*. London, David Fulton.

Pikas, A. (2002) New developments of the shared concern method. *School Psychology International* 23(3): 307–326.

Rigby, K. (1996) *Bullying in Schools and What To Do About It*. London, Jessica Kingsley.

Robinson, G. and Maines, B. (1997) *Crying for Help*. Bristol, Lucky Duck Publishing.

Robinson, G., Sleigh, J. and Maines, B. (1995) *No Bullying Starts Today*. Bristol, Lucky Duck Publishing.

Roland, E. and Munthe, E. (eds) (1989) *Bullying: An International Perspective*. London, David Fulton.

Russell, P.A., Hosie, J.A., Gray, C.D., Scott, C., Hunter, N., Banks, J.S. and Macauley, M.C. (1998) The development of theory of mind in deaf children. *Journal of child Psychology and Psychiatry*, 29(6): 903–910.

SCRE (1991) *Action against Bullying*. Edinburgh, Scottish Council for Research in Education.

SCRE (1993) *Supporting Schools against Bullying*. Edinburgh, Scottish Council for Research in Education.

Sharp, S. and Smith, P.K. (eds) (1994) *Tackling Bullying in Your School: A Practical Handbook for Teachers*. London, Routledge.

Smith, P.K. and Sharp, S. (eds) (1994) *School Bullying: Insights and Perspectives*. London, Routledge.

Smith, P.K. and Samara, M. (2003) Evaluation of the DfES anti-bullying pack: research brief no: RBX06–03. London, DfES.

Smith, P.K., Howard, S. and Thompson, F. (2006) *A Survey of use of The Support Group Method (or 'No Blame' Approach) in England, and some Evaluations from users*. London, University of London.

Stephenson, P. and Smith, D. (1989) Bullying in the junior school. In D. Tattum and D. Lane (eds) *Bullying in Schools*. Stoke on Trent, Trentham Books Ltd.

Sullivan, K., Cleary, M. and Sullivan, G. (2004) *Bullying in Secondary Schools*. London, Paul Chapman.

Straw, J. (1995) Burdened by memories of bullying. *Daily Mirror*, 18 January.

United Nations (1989) The Convention on the Rights of the Child. Adopted by the General Assembly of the United Nations on 20 November 1989.

Wood, D. (1998) *How Children Think and Learn*. Oxford, Blackwell.

Yates, C. and Smith, P. (1989) Bullying in two English comprehensive schools. In E. Roland and E. Munthe (eds) *Bullying: An International Perspective*. London, David Fulton.

Yoshio, M. (1985) Bullies in the classroom. *Japan Quarterly*, 32: 407–411.

Young, S. (1998) The Support Group Approach to Bullying in Schools. *Educational Psychology in Practice*, 14(1): 32–39.

Young, S. and Holdorf, G. (2003) Using solution focused brief therapy in individual referalls for bullying. *Educational Psychology in Practice*, 19(14), December: 271–282.

# Appendices

## Appendix 1

A Survey of use of the Support Group Method [or 'No Blame' Approach] in England, and some Evaluation from Users

*Peter K. Smith, Sharon Howard and Fran Thompson*

## Appendix 2

Written Evidence for the House of Commons Education and Skills Select Committee. Bullying in Schools and The Support Group Method.

# Appendix 1

# A Survey of Use of The Support Group Method [or 'No Blame' Approach] in England, and Some Evaluation from Users

*Peter K. Smith, Sharon Howard and Fran Thompson*

## Foreword

This survey was carried out in June–August 2006, with the support of Sage Publications.

Although we have had the assistance of Barbara Maines and George Robinson in this survey, and it is funded by their publisher, the findings in this Report are entirely independent. There may of course be bias in terms of which LAs and which schools chose to respond – unavoidable in any survey. However we contacted all LAs in England, and sent inquiries to a very large number of schools (over 2,500).

We believe we have reported our findings fairly; and the full, verbatim transcriptions of comments, and the quantitative figures provided, will enable readers to make their own judgments. We believe any policy decisions must be evidence-based.

Finally, while this survey is an advance on our previous state of ignorance; it clearly has strong limitations. It should only be a beginning to more focussed and dedicated study of the effectiveness of The Support Group Method and indeed of all other anti-bullying interventions.

Unit for School and Family Studies, Goldsmiths College,
University of London, August 2006

# Introduction

The Support Group Method for intervening when bullying has taken place in schools originated as the No Blame Approach with the work of Barbara Maines and George Robinson, in 1991–92. While based in the West of England, the method rapidly achieved recognition as one approach, and is now used quite widely in England. It has influenced approaches in other countries such as Switzerland, Germany, and New Zealand and Australia (e.g. McGrath & Stanley, 2006). Maines and Robinson have disseminated the approach via leaflets, booklets and videos, first through their own publishing (Lame Duck, later renamed Lucky Duck) and latterly through Sage Publications. They have held many training events across the U.K. and internationally. They have also presented at many practitioner and academic conferences.

Philosophically, The Support Group Method is non-punitive, seeking to change the behaviour of children involved in bullying through making them aware of the suffering of the victim, combined with some peer pressure to make a caring or prosocial response. The method has seven stages or steps, and is sometimes known as the Seven Steps approach.

The non-punitive stance has many advocates; and The Support Group Method clearly has many supporters, for example Keith Sullivan and Mark Cleary in New Zealand (Sullivan, Cleary & Sullivan, 2004), and Ken Rigby in Australia (Rigby, 1997). It also has attracted criticism from several quarters. Critics include Dan Olweus, who believes that if bullying children break the school or class rules against bullying, they should be sanctioned in some way (whether such sanctions are 'punitive' becomes a matter of definition – Olweus recommends 'serious talks', telling parents', and 'suspension of privileges', for example). Another prominent critic is Michelle Elliot, Director of Kidscape. She believes that The Support Group Method or No Blame approach is harmful, and has emails and letters from parents saying that its use in their child's school has been detrimental (http://www.kidscape.org.uk/press/131200NoBlameReasons.shtml). The current U.K. government is also critical of the approach, and indeed in December 2005 the contracts for George Robinson and Barbara Maines to continue as regional coordinators for the Anti-Bullying Alliance (which is mainly supported by government funds) were withdrawn because of their association with The Support Group Method.

The Support Group approach used by Sue Young was developed from Maines and Robinson's work, with some small modifications, including making it more explicitly solution focussed. Maines and Robinson see this approach as identical, and also now prefer to use the name 'Support Group Method', acknowledging that Young avoided possible antipathy aroused by the name 'No Blame'.

Another non-punitive approach is the Pikas method, developed in Sweden at about the same time. This method has been used in the U.K. as well, and has also been criticised by Olweus on similar grounds. However the Pikas method is different (involving individual interview with bullying children, and the victim, followed by a group meeting). In our questionnaires we made it clear that we were not evaluating the Pikas method.

Another approach sometimes confused with Support Group Method, is Restorative Justice. Restorative Justice approaches share the philosophy that what is important is to repair damage or hurt rather than to 'punish'. However, it does usually differ from Support Group Method in that the perpetrator(s) or bullies are held responsible for their actions; they are required to acknowledge the hurt they have caused. The reparation or consequence is something decided mutually by all parties concerned. Some advocates of Restorative Justice feel that The Support Group Method is compatible with this, but some others (e.g. Valerie Braithwaite, Eliza Ahmed; personal communications) do not agree with The Support Group Method or No Blame approach in that they feel the bullying children can escape this acknowledgement.

In sum, The Support Group Method has many advocates, and has been widely used; but has many critics. Despite the very public controversy, there is remarkably little evidence. Up to the time of the second edition of *Don't Suffer in Silence* (DfES, 2000), the main source quotable was a survey of teachers who used it, carried out by George Robinson and Barbara Maines and students working with them. This reported a very high success rate: 8 out of 8 in primary, and 47 out of 49 cases in secondary. This is 'soft' evidence as it is produced by the advocates of the method.

Sue Young, using a slight variant of The Support Group Method, has reported two studies. Young (1998) was an independent evaluation carried out in the Kingston upon Hull Special Educational Needs Support Service (SENSS). Over a two-year period, in 80% of primary school cases treated through The Support Group approach there was an immediate success; in 14% of cases there was a delay, but after 3 to 5 weekly reviews, the bullying stopped or the victims reported that they no longer needed The Support Group; in only 6% of cases did the victim report that the bullying continued, or that he/she was bullied by different pupils. There was a similar outcome in secondary school referrals. Young and Holdorf (2003) was a study of solution based brief therapy as an intervention with individual pupils, these being 118 pupil referrals from both primary and secondary schools. The authors found this procedure more effective in certain cases, but they did use The Support Group approach in 12 cases, 11 of them successful.

The other source of evidence comes from two evaluations of the DfES 'Don't Suffer in Silence' Pack (Smith & Madsen, 1997; Smith & Samara, 2003). As part of these evaluations (carried out in 1996 and 2002 respectively), 109 (in 1997) and 148 (in 2002) schools responded on which methods they used and to rate satisfaction with them on a 5-point scale. The proportion of schools using a Support Group Method (this may also have included Pikas method in the compilation used) was 34% in 1996 and 28% in 2002. At both times, mean satisfaction rating was 3.5 (moderately satisfied, and on a par with many other interventions).

In summary, what evidence there is, is supportive of The Support Group Method – but, there is definitely a need for more research, carried out independently and targeting a wide range of schools that are using the approach. This survey is a first step in this direction. It had two main aims:

1.  to attempt to get information from all LAs in England about the use of The Support Group Method in their schools, their support for it (or otherwise), and their evaluation of it if based on evidence.
2.  to get information from a sample of schools across England that have used or do use The Support Group Method, concerning the way it has been used, and their views on it's effectiveness if based on evidence.

# Method

## Procedure

Two questionnaires were designed to investigate the effectiveness of The Support Group Method (SGM) as an anti-bullying strategy: Local Authority (LA) and School. These were designed by the team, checked with Barbara Maines and George Robinson (e.g. for accuracy of types of training), and piloted with colleagues. Initially, direct phone contact was made with 2 LAs who were known to support and use the SGM. [Despite being in the forefront of criticism over the use of the SGM and some initial reservation/defensiveness, one particular LA's anti-bullying officer was a very helpful contact, supplying lists of the relevant people to contact in all Secondary and Special schools.] They completed and gave feedback on the LA questionnaire and one LA recommended a Secondary school in their area that used the SGM and whose Deputy Head subsequently completed and gave feedback on the schools questionnaire.

The final (slightly modified) questionnaires were sent by email and were also available on the Unit for School and Family Studies website: www.goldsmiths. ac.uk/departments/sychology/research/usfs.html.

The study was conducted and data collected during June–July 2006. The term 'Support Group approach' (rather than 'Method') was actually used in the questionnaires, as final terminology had not then been agreed.

## Questionnaires

The LA questionnaire consisted of general demographics (numbers of primary/secondary/special schools) and was prefaced by a definition of the SGM and makes a clear distinction between the SGM and the Pikas method. The 6 following questions were

1. if the LA had any indication of how many schools used the SGM in the last 3 years
2. if the number of schools using the SGM had changed in the last few years and if so, why
3. if the LA supported or discouraged the use of the SGM
4. if the LA provided any financial support for teachers/people to use the SGM in the last 3 years, and if so, which version
5. evidence of the overall effectiveness of the approach and if evidence-based, a satisfaction rating
6. any names and contact details of schools using the SGM.

The questionnaire concluded with a further comments section requesting feedback on the SGM and their experiences of this method.

The School questionnaire also began with general demographics: name; LA or area within England; type of school (primary/middle/secondary/special); school roll and a definition of the SGM (i.e. not to be confused with Pikas). The 8 following questions were:

1. how long the schools had used the approach
2. were they continuing to use it, and if not, then why

3. if the SGM was used across the school or with certain years/groups; and if used in only certain groups/years, which ones and why
4. who generally used the approach with pupils
5. how did the person/s acquire their knowledge of the method
6. to describe their use of the method
7. if their use of the method had changed over time, and if so, how and why
8. if the school had evidence of the overall effectiveness of the SGM in dealing with bullying, and if evidence-based, the sources of feedback, and a satisfaction rating.

The questionnaire concluded with a further comments section requesting feedback on the SGM and their experiences of this method.

## Participants

An initial plan was to contact the Anti-Bullying Alliance (ABA) regional coordinators to get feedback on the questionnaires and hopefully collect contact details. There was, fortuitously, an ABA Meeting in June 2006 in London. However, the DfES representative there objected to any ABA involvement in this research. Contact was made with some ABA coordinators but only through their LA roles; the ABA has not been involved directly in any way in this survey.

**Local Authorities (LAs):** All 150 Local Authorities in England were approached initially by email to identify the person responsible for anti-bullying initiatives/strategies. All 150 responded, identifying individuals ranging from Behaviour Support officers; Outreach officers; Teacher/advisors; Educational Psychologists and Independent advisors.

The speed and progress of collecting data from LAs was varied. Some refused to do the questionnaire at all, citing workload. The political sensitivity of this anti-bullying strategy at this time was a considerable hindrance in collecting data; some individuals were extremely reticent to discuss the SGM or participate in this research. One London LA flatly refused to discuss anything to do with the study.

Some LAs were very efficient, having well established anti-bullying strategies and active engagement with schools. Others had no idea of the strategies used by schools and some were in the process of collecting data, having recently created advisory posts for anti-bullying. Some LAs did not reply at all, despite having received an email with attached questionnaire for over a month and subsequently having had two reminder emails with a deadline. Some LAs commented that there was not enough time to provide us with the information needed and that the deadlines were unrealistic.

Following initial approach and two reminders, a total of 57 completed questionnaires were returned. This was a response rate of 38%, which is fairly typical of educational survey work (e.g. Smith & Samara, 2003).

**Schools:** Very few LAs gave any school contact details. Despite some LAs proving particularly responsive and helpful, it was decided in boroughs/councils/counties that indicated use/support of the SGM, *all* schools would be contacted; this was to avoid selection bias. All email addresses were accessed from LA websites and over 2,500 emails were despatched. Schools that had no email addresses were faxed with questionnaires.

In all 101 schools responded. Of these, 39 schools did not complete the questionnaire: 34 because they did not use SGM (1 of which stated they did not wish to use it); 4 schools through lack of time or no wish to do so and 1 school had returned the questionnaire incomplete, except for filling in their name. Of the remaining 62 usable responses, it was clear in 3 cases that in fact SGM was not being used. 2 Secondary schools filled in the questionnaires on the Restorative Justice strategy to anti-bullying and another defined the 'other' form of SGM training as the 'Lee Cantor video and subsequent training'. This left 59 usable responses on the SGM approach; these came from 17 LAs. A response rate is difficult to calculate, but an estimate would be 3–4%. The low response rate was exacerbated due to time restrictions as the summer holidays approached.

## Results

The completed SGM questionnaires (57 LA and 59 School) were analysed question by question. The quantitative data was collated and processed in SPSS to form the basis of descriptive statistics, percentages and charts. The qualitative data was examined for themes and used to expand on the results and in the discussion.

### Local Authority Questionnaire Analysis

The 57 responding LAs ranged in size from one LA with 6 schools to another with 634.

*Question 1: Do you have an indication of how many primary, and secondary, schools use this approach or have done so in the last 3 years?*

6 LAs (11%) indicated that they did know. In the first, 54% of primary and 41% of secondary schools used SGM; in the second, 79% of primary, 86% of secondary and 100% of special schools; in the third, 47% of primary and 100% of secondary; in the fourth, 40% of primary, 40% of secondary and 33% of special schools; in the fifth, 26% of primary and 5% of secondary; and in the sixth, 9% of primary and 8% of secondary.

The remaining 51 LAs (89%) indicated they did not know.

*Question 2: Has the number changed over the last few years?*

4 LAs (7%) stated that the number of schools using the SGM had changed. 13 LAs (22%) indicated they did not know; and the majority of 40 LAs (70%) gave no rating.

In response to 'why it had changed?', 7 LAs responded. Four of these were basically about increased demand; and 2 reflected a decrease due to negative publicity.

*Question 3: Do you actively support, or discourage, the use of this approach?*

All 57 replied. 12 LAs (21%) strongly supported the use of the SGM; 24 LAs (42%) supported the SGM in general terms; 17 LAs (29%) were neutral; 4 LAs (7%) did not encourage the SGM and no LAs discouraged the use of the SGM.

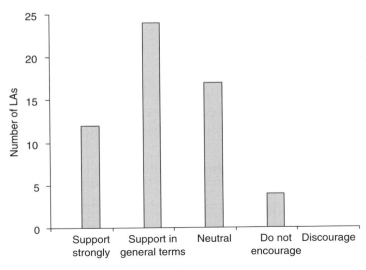

Figure 1    Ratings of LAs demonstrating support of SGM

*Question 4: Do you provide, or support financially, any training for teachers or other persons to use this approach (or have you done so in the last 3 years)?*

16 LAs (28%) indicated that they did financially support training in the SGM and 41 LAs (72%) indicated they did not.

A cross-tabulation of questions 3 and 4 shows that only LAs supportive of the use of SGM also provided or financially supported SGM training; see Table 1.

Table 1    Ratings of support for SGM by financial support for training in SGM

|  | Strongly support | Support in general terms | Neutral· | Do not encourage | Total |
|---|---|---|---|---|---|
| Yes | 7 | 9 | 0 | 0 | 16 |
| No | 5 | 15 | 17 | 4 | 41 |
| Total | 12 | 24 | 17 | 4 | 57 |

In open-ended responses to what version of the method they supported, 15 LAs wrote responses. These usually referred to the Maines & Robinson version, or in 2 cases the Young version. Of these, 12 were purely factual, one added positive comments, two added more qualified comments.

*Question 5: From your experience of the use of the method by schools in your authority, do you have any evidence for the overall effectiveness of the approach in dealing with bullying?*

This was analysed in 3 stages. First, the LAs responded on whether they had evidence from schools in their authority/remit for the efficacy of the SGM: see Table 2. Three did not answer this question.

Second, the LAs identified the sources of feedback on the effectiveness of the SGM.

Table 2   Whether LAs had evidence of overall effectiveness of the SGM

| No | 17 (30%) |
| --- | --- |
| Not enough to give evidence-based opinion | 29 (51%) |
| Yes, based on feedback | 8 (14%) |

9 LAs (16%) stated Schools provided most feedback; 7 LAs (12%) stated parents; 3 LAs (5%) stated governors; 8 LAs stated pupils and 1 (2%) stated other sources, but not specifying how they had collected their information; see Figure 2.

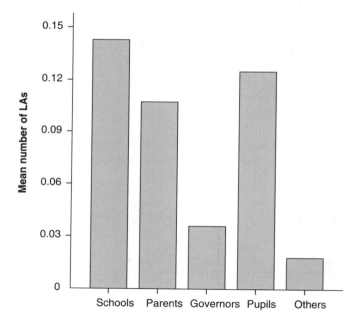

Figure 2   Sources of SGM feedback identified by LAs

Third, although a majority of 46 LAs did not provide a rating, of the 11 that did (8 with evidence of the effectiveness of the SGM plus 3 more), 2 rated the SGM as very satisfactory; 5 as satisfactory; 2 were neutral and 2 as rather unsatisfactory; there were no ratings of very unsatisfactory (see Figure 3).

In response to an invitation to add further comments, 32 LAs did so. Of these, 6 could be classified as very positive, and another 9 as generally positive; 5 were positive but qualified in some significant way; 9 were neutral; and 3 could be classed as negative.

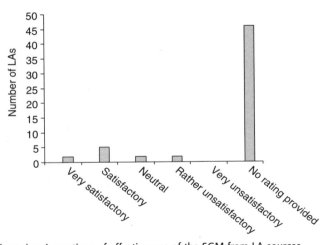

Figure 3　Bar chart showing ratings of effectiveness of the SGM from LA sources

There is a range of responses here, from:

'The impact on some children has been little short of amazing – children telling us for the first time in school they feel safe and it happens so quickly' [LA20]

and

'Excellent, helpful, empowering, solution focused – can be managed effectively by non-teaching staff' [LA27]

through to

'The response from some young people who are victims is that they see the abuser getting away without a punishment. In our LA we are very pro-active regarding anti-bullying strategies but the No-Blame approach is not one I would use' [LA4]

There are clearly a majority of broadly positive responses, often qualified by saying that this is one of a number of approaches used:

'We tend to present the approach as one of a range of approaches that schools might wish to adopt, and are always clear that there is no 'single solution' or approach that fits all circumstances' [LA8]
'We present the method as one of a range of responses that could be used according to case and according to skills and school climate' [LA7]
'I think it is an effective approach as part of a continuum of approaches to take with bullying' [LA42]

A theme mentioned in one of the more negative responses is that the approach may not be used correctly:

'Anecdotal evidence that I have picked up from children and young people is that the No Blame approach is being implemented in schools extremely badly with quite serious consequences for young people ….. which doesn't necessarily mean the approach is wrong just the way it is being undertaken in schools' [LA19]

and one of the very positive responses echoed this:

'In my experience, when the 7 steps approach is used properly (i.e. those who use it have been trained) it is very successful', going on to add that 'When parents of targets say the bullying situation is not getting better, this often means that the school has not kept them informed of what has been happening' [LA9]

There was also support for using an alternative to the No Blame label:

'Does NOT endorse No Blame name' [LA27]
'However the title is unfortunate and masks the strong developmental core of the approach' [LA48]

## School Questionnaire Analysis

Of the 59 completed school questionnaires, 32 were submitted by Primary schools; 1 by a Middle school and 26 by Secondary schools. No Special schools returned any questionnaires. School rolls ranged from 108 to 660 pupils (Primary); and 340 to 2000 pupils (Secondary). The Middle school roll was 150 pupils; for purposes of analysis we added the Middle school to the Primary schools (N=33).

*Question 1: For how long approximately (in years) have you used such an approach?*

The time span that the SGM had been used by schools ranged from 1 year (13 schools) to 20 years (2 schools); see Figure 4. The majority of schools started using the SGM in the last 5 years (69%). One school did not reply.

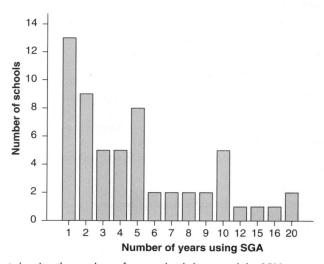

Figure 4  Bar chart showing the numbers of years schools have used the SGM

*Question 2: Are you still using it?*

57 schools (97%) continued to use the SGM; 2 schools (3%) had stopped using it.

In response to an open-ended question as to why a school had stopped using it, one primary school replied that it was still used when appropriate; one secondary school replied that it was 'Not felt appropriate or successful by Students, Staff and Parents. Many negative outcomes' (7/LA9).

*Question 3: Is (or was) the approach used across the school, or only with certain groups or years?*

44 schools (75%) used the SGM across the whole school. 15 schools (25%) used the SGM selectively. Further information about selective (or not) use of the SGM was given by 9 primary schools and 11 secondary schools. Responses were quite varied, but many of the secondary schools used it with younger pupils only (e.g. years 7–9).

*Question 4: Who generally uses (or used) the approach in your school with pupils?*

Data from all schools were considered first, and then split into data from Primary and Secondary schools. Results are shown in Table 3.

Table 3   Who uses the SGM in schools (Primary/Secondary)

| Who uses SGM | All schools | Primary schools | Secondary schools |
| --- | --- | --- | --- |
| Headteacher | 17 | 17 | – |
| Deputy head | 3 | – | 3 |
| Heads of year | 14 | – | 14 |
| Form tutor | 1 | 1 | – |
| Teaching staff | 6 | 6 | – |
| Other | 18 | 9 | 9 |
| Total | 59 | 33 | 26 |

In Primary schools (52%), the Head Teacher was the main practitioner of the SGM. In secondary schools, it was most frequently a Head of Year. 'Other' practitioners of the included: Educational psychologists; LA Anti-bullying officers; Teaching Assistants trained in the SGM; SENCOs; Home-school liaison officers; KS1, 2 & 3 leaders; Behaviour Support workers; Pupils/Peer mentors; Inclusion managers/workers; House heads; Pastoral co-coordinators/ assistants and School counsellors.

*Question 5: How did this person/these persons acquire their knowledge of the method?*

Training was provided in 18 schools (31%) by Barbara Maines and George Robinson at a training day; in 20 schools (34%) training was provided by 'someone else experienced in the method at a training day'; in 11 schools (19%), there was 'no direct training, but used the training pack, *Michael's Story – the No Blame approach video pack* or the book *Crying for Help* both published by Lucky Duck Publishing'; and 9 schools (15%) indicated that an 'other' form of training was used; and 1 school did not answer (see Figure 5).

'Train(ing) by someone else' and 'other' forms of training were identified as Educational Welfare Officers; Anti-bullying Officers trained by Maines & Robinson; Educational Psychologists; Behaviour Modification specialists; other teaching staff experienced in the SGM; and Behaviour Support service/team.

Figure 5    Bar chart showing methods of training in SGM by schools

*Question 6: Please describe how you use the method*

This was an open-ended question, which attracted responses from 27 primary schools and 22 secondary schools. We classified these into responses which were broadly in line with the Maines and Robinson approach, and those which were non-specific or which appeared to deviate in some way.

In primary schools, 12/26 responses suggested they basically followed The Support Group Method, although in some cases one takes on trust statements such as:

'As outlined in the training' [12/LA58]

Two responses were non-specific, and 5 did not answer the question, for example:

'To deal with issues which have arisen on the playground' [24/LA20].

Another 8 responses suggested some significant variation in procedure, such as:

'Sometimes the 'victim' has been involved in the meeting with the rest of the group' [3/LA7]

or seemed more similar to other approaches such as Restorative Justice approach:

'Both bully and victim are given a couple of minutes to say what it is that is causing the issue. We try to encourage the 'when you do this, it makes me feel … approach. Others are asked for their opinions on what they think might be the causes and how it might make others feel. We then move on to identify what behaviours we want to change …' [47/LA21]

or circle of friends:

'If a child is unhappy at school, whatever the reason, and needs support then a group of their friends is asked to support them. The group meets at regular intervals (usually once a week) until the child reports that they are no longer unhappy' [49/LA27]

In secondary schools, only 4/22 responses suggested they basically followed The Support Group Method. Another 7 were non-specific, and 3 did not answer the question:

'Working alongside the Local Authority anti-bullying officer' [10/LA11]

while 8 suggested a significant variation from The Support Group Method, for example:

'Parts of it – mainly the group situation' [26/LA20]

or seemed more similar to some other approach such as Pikas method:

'See pupils individually then as a group and finally with the person being bullied' [53/LA34].

*Question 7: Has your use of the method changed over time?*

30 schools (51%) responded that they had changed their use of the method over time; another 28 schools (49%) had not changed their use of the SGM; 1 school did not answer.

Those schools that had changed the method were asked to describe the alterations; [there were] responses from 16 primary schools and 13 secondary schools. Replies were very varied, though a number suggesting it was adapted to circumstances:

'How it is used depends upon the circumstances of the situation' [primary 39/LA20]

or not always used:

'It is used selectively and not at all times' [secondary 12/LA58]

Three schools mentioned greater parental involvement [35/LA20; 44/LA21; 56/LA48].

In one case it is clear the philosophy had been departed from!

'We always punish the bully for what they have done' [secondary 19/LA19]

*Question 8: From your experience of the use of the method in your school, do you have any evidence for the overall effectiveness of the approach in dealing with bullying?*

This was analysed in 3 stages. First, schools indicated if they had evidence of the anti-bullying efficacy of the SGM. 3 schools (5%) indicated there was not enough evidence; 25 schools (42%) did not have enough to give an evidence based opinion; and 31 schools (53%) indicated they did have enough evidence to give an informed opinion.

Second, if the schools had evidence of the effectiveness of the SGM, they were asked to identify who had given this feedback. This analysis was made for all schools; then Primary and Secondary schools separately. The sources of evidence of the anti-bullying effectiveness of the SGM were reported in all schools collectively as in 24 schools (41%) as person using the method; 11 schools (20%) as class teachers; in 28 schools (48%) as pupil victims; in 24 schools (42%) as other pupils; in 18 schools (32%) as parents; in 3 schools as sources other than those mentioned. No schools had any evidence from the governors (see Table 4). The distribution is fairly similar in Primary and Secondary schools, but with more information from class teachers in the Primary sector.

Table 4   Sources of evidence of anti-bullying effectiveness in using the SGM as reported by Primary and Secondary schools

| Source of evidence of effectiveness of SGM | Number of schools | Primary | Secondary |
| --- | --- | --- | --- |
| Person using the Method | 24 | 13 | 11 |
| Class teacher | 11 | 9 | 2 |
| Pupil victim | 28 | 17 | 11 |
| Other pupils | 24 | 15 | 9 |
| Parents | 18 | 11 | 7 |
| Governors | 0 | 0 | 0 |
| Other | 3 | 0 | 3 |

Third, if they had evidence, schools were asked to give a rating of the overall effectiveness of the SGM. 19 schools (32%) did not give a rating; 21 schools (36%) gave a very satisfactory rating, 12 schools (20%) gave a satisfactory rating, 7 schools (12%) were neutral, and 0 schools gave either a rather unsatisfactory or very unsatisfactory rating (see Figure 6).

A breakdown by school type is shown in Table 5. There is a trend for primary schools to give more very satisfactory ratings.

Ratings of effectiveness tend to be higher in schools where there was direct training (see Table 6).

In response to an invitation to add further comments, 20 primary schools and 20 secondary schools did so. We consider the two sectors separately.

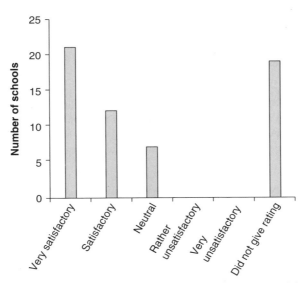

Figure 6    Ratings from all schools of overall effectiveness of the SGM in dealing with bullying

Table 5    Ratings of effectiveness of SGM from all schools, and by Primary and Secondary sector

| Rating of effectiveness of SGM | Number of schools | Primary | Secondary |
|---|---|---|---|
| Very satisfactory | 21 | 13 | 8 |
| Rather satisfactory | 12 | 5 | 7 |
| Neutral | 7 | 3 | 4 |
| Rather unsatisfactory | 0 | 0 | 0 |
| Very unsatisfactory | 0 | 0 | 0 |
| No rating | 19 | 12 | 7 |

Table 6    Ratings of effectiveness of SGM from all schools, by method of training

| Rating of effectiveness of SGM | Trained by Maines and Robinson | Trained by someone else experienced | No direct training | Other |
|---|---|---|---|---|
| Very satisfactory | 8 | 9 | 2 | 2 |
| Rather satisfactory | 4 | 5 | 2 | 1 |
| Neutral | 2 | 2 | 1 | 2 |
| Rather unsatisfactory | 0 | 0 | 0 | 0 |
| Very unsatisfactory | 0 | 0 | 0 | 0 |
| No rating | 3 | 4 | 6 | 4 |

Of the primary school comments, 13 could be classified as positive, 2 were positive but qualified in some significant way; 1 was neutral; and 4 could be classed as ambivalent.

There are many positive comments, for example:

'...the benefits are tremendous' [38/LA20]
'The 7 steps have had a positive impact on the whole school community' [40/LA20]
'We find it very effective, and use it not just for incidences of bullying but for all children who are unhappy in school' [49/LA27]
'The whole approach has been very successful in dealing with any cases of bullying' [58/LA54]

Several of the positive responses do mention the importance of parent liaison:

'Parents however do need to be made aware of how it works in the initial stages' [40/LA20]
'We found it was vital to work with parents and therefore ran an evening for parents also to inform and consult them on the approach' [58/LA54]

Of the more qualified or ambivalent comments, one theme is that the approach may not work with particularly recalcitrant children:

'Although has modified behaviour of the "one-off" bullies, it has not been so effective with two of our hardened children, whose own home life would appear to be full of bullying behaviours' [47/LA21]
'There are children in our school where trying to get the child to understand someone else's feelings can be difficult if they find it hard to understand their own. Also, there are children who are bullies and at times are labelled as such because they are manipulative and know exactly what they're doing, this approach doesn't work for them either' [52/LA51]

Of the secondary school comments, 5 could be classified as positive, 5 were positive but qualified in some significant way; 4 were neutral; 2 were ambivalent, and 1 could be classed as negative. Again there are many positive comments, for example:

'The approach is very empowering for students, victims and supportive students' [32/LA20]
'After working for over 8 years as a pastoral leader, I found it to be a much more positive approach to use than any other. It left relationships intact rather than fractured, in some cases, relationships were improved' [10/LA11]

Again the importance of exlaining to parents is stressed several times:

'The approach is something that can work well when it is appropriate to the circumstances and its use is explained to parents and students so they understand why it is being used and what the expected outcomes are' [39/LA 20]
'I frequently explain the approach to parents in workshops about Anti-Bullying matters so that they understand the No Blame approach and what lies behind it and why it works ... Parents have to feel confident with what you are doing, though, or else they undermine the process' [57/LA41]

One school doubted it would work with recalcitrant children:

'I'm not sure how it would work with certain 'hard-core' bullies' [44/LA21] but another was more optimistic:

> 'My experience of 12 years at a senior level in secondary schools is that the No Blame Approach is one of a range of approaches that works and one which is particularly effective with deeply entrenched behaviours and attitudes' [57/LA41]

Finally, from both primary and secondary schools there are several statements that this is one of a range of approaches:

> 'It is appropriate to use in the right circumstances but not always' [primary 12/LA58]
> 'I feel personally it is one of the strategies that can be employed but should not be the sole one' [secondary 35/LA20]
> 'No Blame approach is on a continuum of strategies the college use. Treat each case individually and assess what intervention is required' [secondary 4/LA9]

and that ultimately some more direct sanction may be necessary:

> 'The system does have sanctions written into it but most problems are resolved before we get to that stage' [primary 38/LA20]
> 'I would always use it first before looking at other methods if we were not moving forward in a positive manner' [secondary 55/LA58]
> 'We do use punishments in extreme cases but this is a last resort' [secondary 1/LA5]
> 'It certainly does not always work and we feel it very important that students know towards the end of the process that if behaviour is not modified now that all the issues have been explored there is a punitive process' [secondary 8/LA9]

## Discussion

One aim of the survey was to gather information on the extent of use of SGM. This was not very successful, as most LAs (51/57) did not know! Of those that did, the average (omitting special schools) was 45%. This is probably an overestimate of the national figure, as LAs that (a) replied at all and (b) knew the numbers, might be more supportive of SGM. Also of schools that replied, 58/97 used SGM, or 60%; this is almost certainly an overestimate given that (a) we targeted LAs known to have used SGM, and (b) schools that used SGM were probably more likely to reply.

The earlier estimates from the Pack surveys of 34% and 28% of schools also suggest that the 45% and 60% figures are high. A reasonable conclusion would be that some form of SGM is used in between a quarter and a half of schools in England. The qualifier 'some form of SGM' is important, as is made clear later.

So far as LAs were concerned, there was a range of attitudes to supporting SGM, although a majority of 36/57 (63%) supported it strongly or in general terms. Of those that were supportive, 16 (28%) also indicated that they supported training of SGM financially – usually the Maines and Robinson version. From the schools' point of view, training has come from a variety of sources: more often by others experienced in the method (34%) than by Maines and Robinson directly (31%) or using their training materials (19%).

For how long have schools been using SGM? Schools that replied had mostly been using it for 1 to 5 years (40/59), but some for 6 to 10 years (13/59) or even longer – although the 3 schools claiming to use it for 16–20 years have been doing so for longer than the approach has been in existence, as it started in 1991–92! A majority of schools using SGM (75%) do so across the whole school; but a number of secondary schools restrict it to lower years. In primary schools the Head Teacher often uses it, and in secondary schools it is often Heads of Year.

How satisfied are LAs and schools with the SGM? On a 5 point scale (1 = very unsatisfactory to 5 = very satisfactory), the mean rating from 11 LAs that gave a response was 3.64. The mean response from 40 schools was 4.35. The sources of evidence were mainly described by LAs as schools, parents and pupils; and by schools as pupil victims, other pupils, parents, and class teachers.

These ratings are both above the neutral point of 3, so clearly most LAs and schools find the approach useful; and indeed a majority of schools responding (21/40) rated it very satisfactory. There is possibly some bias here in that we primarily approached schools within LAs that were known to be supportive of the approach; but this is the independent response of the users, i.e. the schools. The earlier Pack survey satisfaction ratings (on an equivalent 5 point scale) were 3.5. A reasonable conclusion would be that most LAs and schools feel that the method is useful, and that a significant number of schools are actually very enthusiastic about it.

One of the more interesting findings to emerge from the survey is the range of variants of SGM that are used, and indeed there is some confusion in many schools about what it refers to. The questionnaires included the information:

USE OF THE NO BLAME OR SUPPORT GROUP METHOD IN YOUR SCHOOLS:

[This includes variants, and is sometimes called the 'seven steps' approach. The principle is that any child suspected of being involved in bullying others is not directly accused of this or sanctioned, but is introduced to a process of understanding the feelings of the victim(s) and finding ways to improve the situation. It is a group-based process which brings together non-involved children with those suspected of being involved in bullying. It is different in this and other ways from the Pikas method; we are *not* asking about use of the Pikas method here].

Despite this, three schools filled in the questionnaire fully, but it was clear from the description that two were using Restorative Justice, and one was using a Lee Canter approach which Maines and Robinson see as incompatible with their approach. In addition, the further comments from some schools suggest that they were using methods more similar to Restorative Justice, circle of friends, or Pikas; or else something that deviated substantially from SGM, for example:

'Gather groups of perpetrators victims and some neutrals and give them a project to do together, Usually in caring for other pupils' [primary 17/LA19]

or were making some significant variations to SGM, such as the way in which the victim is involved, or how parents are consulted or involved.

These misunderstandings or deviations from SGM may be more common in secondary schools. At least based on our content analysis of the descriptions provided by schools, when these were sufficiently clear, it would appear that in primary schools 12 used the method as described compared to 8 who deviated significantly; whereas in secondary schools 4 used it as described, whereas 8 deviated significantly.

These deviations may be very important. First, the more minor variants may affect the efficacy of the approach in unknown ways:

'It is very important to have everyone on board so that there is consistency of practice' [primary 38/LA20]
'It could be mishandled very easily' [secondary 44/LA21]
'The degree of criticism that NB attracts may be attached to the name of the method, to a misunderstanding of the nature of the process, or to bad practice when using or adapting the method as it is described' [LA7]

Second, quite substantial variations, not recognisable as SGM, might be used with possibly adverse consequences, and SGM gets the blame. It is possible that this may partly explain the negative outcomes reported by some parents, for example to Kidscape.

Equally, some parents may simply disagree with the non-punitive philosophy:

'Parents too frequently want to see justice and a certain degree of punishment for those who engage in bullying behaviour and for many parents the no blame approach doesn't appear to deliver either' [LA19]
'When comments are unfavourable it is usually from parents who prefer the 'death penalty' still ... When parents of targets say the bullying situation is not getting better, this often means that the school has not kept them informed of what has been happening' [LA9].

We conclude with some recommendations for Maines and Robinson to consider; and point out the need for further research beyond the limitations of this first survey.

## Recommendations

These recommendations are in the light of a generally (but not universally) positive response from LAs and schools in this survey, and intended to help further improve the effectiveness of the method in practice.

- There is support for changing the name from No Blame to Support Group:
  'We stopped calling it the 'No Blame' approach because that did not go down well with parents who wanted the bully "dealing with", and in many cases there was not a bullying focus anyway. We all just use the term Support Group' [49/LA27]
- There is considerable confusion about what is SGM and what is not. It is not infrequently confused with other methods such as Restorative Justice, Pikas, circle of friends. There are also often deviations from the standard method, perhaps more commonly in secondary schools. It may be helpful to clearly state core principles of what is SGM and what is not; or consider which variations might be useful and worth trying, and which would not be recommended.
- There is concern about the attitudes of some parents, and many schools have moved to involve parents more. It may help to consider further ways of involving parents, and of working with parents who are more 'punitive' in their outlook and expectations.

- Many schools feel that it is one of many methods to use. It may help to consider the issue of whether SGM is compatible with, or can be combined with, certain other approaches; or not.
- Some schools, even those favourable to SGM, feel that some tougher sanction may be necessary for hard core or persistent cases. Is sufficient acknowledgement given to this, and ways schools might cope within or possibly beyond the SGM approach?

## Further research

This survey is a useful step forward, with a broader and more detailed evidence base from LAs and schools than has previously been available. The findings are clearly limited by the sample; in particular the response rate for schools was very low. In addition, data has only come from LA and school representatives: we have not heard the direct voices of pupils or parents (even though schools often cited them as evidence).

The need for more research was pointed out by some LAs and schools:

'I do feel there is insufficient evidence generally' [secondary 37/LA20]
'The lack of a firm evidence base to establish what the effectiveness of punitive and non-punitive interventions actually is, has obscured and hampered the discussion about resolving bullying for too long and this, of course, does not serve well the young people who are involved in bullying. This kind of research is long overdue and may present us finally with some greater degree of certainty in our direction on interventions' [LA7]

Further research should not only examine the views of pupils and parents in SGM, but also look closely at the variant ways in which SGM is used and how they affect outcomes. We believe this range of variation in practice to be the most significant new finding arising from this survey.

## References

Department for Education and Skills (2000). *Bullying: Don't suffer in silence. An anti-bullying pack for schools* (2nd edn). London: DfES.

McGrath, H. & Stanley, M. (2006). A comparison of two non-punitive approaches to bullying. In H. McGrath & T. Noble (eds), *Bullying solutions: Evidence-based approaches to bullying in Australian schools*, pp.189–201. Pearson: Frenchs Forest, NSW.

Rigby, K. (1997). *Bullying in schools and what to do about it*. London: Jessica Kingsley.

Smith, P.K. & Madsen, K. (1997). *A follow-up of the DFE Anti-Bullying Pack for Schools: Its use, and the development of anti-bullying work in schools*. London: HMSO.

Smith, P.K. & Samara, M. (2003). *Evaluation of the DfES Anti-Bullying Pack*. Research Brief No. RBX06–03. London: DfES.

Sullivan, K., Cleary, M. & Sullivan, G. (2004). *Bullying in secondary schools*. London: Paul Chapman.

Young, S. (1998). The Support Group approach to bullying in schools. *Educational Psychology in Practice*, 14, 32–39.

Young, S. & Holdorf, G. (2003). Using solution focused brief therapy in individual referrals for bullying. *Educational Psychology in Practice*, 19, 271–282.

# Appendix 2

# Written Evidence for the House of Commons Education and Skills Select Committee Bullying in Schools and The Support Group Method

By:  *Barbara Maines*
*George Robinson*
*Lucky Duck Publishing*
*Paul Chapman Publishing*
*and SAGE Publications*
*September 2006*

## 1. Executive Summary and Recommendations

1.1   This written evidence focuses on a particular strategy to tackle the problem of bullying in schools and calls into question the Government's present policy on this matter. It does not seek to define the extent and nature of bullying as a problem, nor to consider the short and long-term effects. It is felt that many other individuals and organisations will be providing the Committee with this information.

1.2   This report does present the Committee with the **experience and research evidence for a non-punitive response to bullying amongst young people** and, in particular, highlights the significance of one particular strategy – The Support Group Method (SGM), previously known as the 'No Blame Approach'.

1.3   Barbara Maines and George Robinson started to work together in 1984 when George was the head of a special school in Bristol and Barbara was the educational psychologist to the school. Their shared belief in the importance of self-esteem and their rejection of traditional methods of behaviour management inspired them to develop new and challenging initiatives – one of them has been the SGM.

1.4   The report explains:

- the significant elements of the SGM process;
- how the Government has viewed SGM over the past decade;
- the evidence base for the Method's success;
- the importance of new research conducted in the summer of 2006;
- and provides some participant statements on DVD.

1.5   There has been opposition to SGM, primarily led by Michelle Elliot of the anti-bullying charity, Kidscape. It is noted that in her oral evidence given to the Committee in July, she chooses to refer to SGM as a 'discredited' approach. The very recent research (August 2006) outlined in this document certainly does not support this statement. In fact, the research positively endorses SGM as a successful method to be used among the full range of possible strategies to tackling bullying in schools.

1.6   This submission also outlines the change in DfES policy which has led to attempts to discredit the method since November 2005. It was previously featured positively in publications and on the website.

## 1.7   Recommendations

Bullying remains a very serious problem in most schools yet many practitioners are not sufficiently aware or have not had the training needed to use many of the strategies available to combat the problem.

There is currently very little research in the field which would endorse the use of any particular strategy or range of strategies, yet debate and criticism has been forthcoming about SGM. In reality, what research there is, *is very supportive of the SGM, when it is used appropriately and correctly*. Despite this positive research, the UK Government refuses to take an evidence-based approach to informing its policy in this area.

**Recommendation One**   Detailed and comprehensive research is needed into *all* anti-bullying strategies to ascertain how and when they are used in schools and which strategy is most effective in a range of situations.

In independent research conducted over the summer, one Local Authority commented:

> 'The lack of a firm evidence base to establish what the effectiveness of punitive and non-punitive interventions actually is, has obscured and hampered the discussion about resolving bullying for too long and this, of course, does not serve well the young people who are involved in bullying. This kind of research is long overdue and may present us finally with some greater degree of certainty in our direction on interventions.'

**Recommendation Two**   The results of this research need to inform DfES policy on bullying in schools with the outcome that appropriate *guidance* and *training* are given to all who deal with these situations across the UK.

**Recommendation Three**   A simple and user-friendly system should be devised to help teachers record the frequency of bullying incidents and to evaluate the effectiveness of how they are or are not resolved.

**Barbara Maines**
**George Robinson**

Lucky Duck Publishing
Sage Publications and Paul Chapman Publishing

# 2. Overview: The Support Group Method in Practice

2.1   All schools are likely to have some problem with bullying at one time or another and are of course required by law to have an anti-bullying policy, and to use it to reduce and prevent bullying.

The Support Group Method (SGM) originally known as 'The No Blame Approach' was devised and first used by Barbara Maines and George Robinson in 1991. By the end of the year it was available as a published training video and featured in the media on programmes including 'That's Life – BBC1 February 1993' and the BBC2 Anti-bullying series of documentaries 1997.

## 2.2   What is the SGM and how does it work?

The method is a highly structured 7-step process in which:

1. The target is given an opportunity to talk privately to an adult who will act as an advocate;
2. A group of peers is convened to include bullies, colluders, observers, friends (potential rescuers);
3. The advocate explains to the group members her worries about the target and describes his distress;
4. She makes it clear that the group members have been invited to help. No accusations are made and there is no threat of punishment;
5. The members are invited to empathise and plan actions to 'make things better';
6. The members are praised and thanked for their cooperation and a follow-up meeting is arranged;
7. At the follow-up meeting, the group members are seen individually and given an opportunity to report back but also to discuss any other concerns or worries.

2.3   From the very beginning the work was publicly criticised, particularly by Kidscape, a children's anti-bullying charity. This criticism is largely attributable to:

- A poor choice of name. 'The No Blame Approach' does imply that the bully will suffer no consequences to his actions. This is correct only in so far as no punishment is given directly to the bully by the advocate, but does not highlight the 'self-inflicted punishment' which the bully often endures. For example, if SGM is used properly, the shame and horror that bullies often experience is intense when they fully appreciate the pain they have inflicted on the target.

  With hindsight, it is easy to see that a title that explained what the approach does achieve would have been far better. During 2006, the name of the approach has been changed to The Support Group Method;

- Non-punitive methodology is counter-intuitive in UK culture where restorative practice is not well known or embraced, particularly by the media;

- A misunderstanding of the method, often seen as *any* non-punitive response and particularly as a confrontation between 'bully' and 'victim'.

2.4   The spread of the usage was significantly established through Inset training courses provided, mainly in response to invitation. During the one-day course participants experience a carefully planned and thorough description of, and rationale, for the procedure.

2.5   As the method was adopted increasingly by individual schools, by whole local authorities and in several overseas countries (Switzerland, Canada, Australia, New Zealand and Ireland), enthusiasm and confidence grew. This was further endorsed by a significant piece of research carried out in Hull, which is discussed further in section four: 'the evidence base'.

## 3. UK Policy: The Government View 1999–2006

3.1   The UK Government view until very recently has been moderately supportive of The Support Group Method.

In May 1999, the then Parliamentary Under Secretary of State for Education and Employment, Charles Clarke, said:

'Our (the DfEE's) role is to offer schools advice on tackling bullying. As their circumstances differ, we have no plans to recommend one single strategy for all schools; they need to decide which ones best meet their own pupils' needs and circumstances.

I am aware of the benefits of The Support Group Method in cases where bullying has occurred. In some circumstances, this strategy may be the answer to combating bullying, but in others a different approach may well be necessary and more effective. As you know, it is described in the Department's anti-bullying pack and we have no plans to change this at present.'

DfES publications

2nd Edition of the Department for Education and Skills (DfES) – 'Don't suffer in Silence' – Anti-Bullying Pack

3.2   This DfES support pack for schools in England was published in 1999 and evaluated in April 2003.

The Approach was nearly not included in this second edition but at the insistence of Professor Peter Smith, Goldsmiths College, University of London, it was incorporated as the 'Support Group' Approach NOT as it had been known – the No Blame Approach. The then Minister for Education, David Blunkett had vetoed any mention of 'No Blame'.

3.3   An evaluation of the Pack by Professor Smith found that:

- Schools were using a range of strategies to tackle bullying and to encourage pro-social behaviour. The most highly rated strategies were: circle time; active listening/ counselling approaches; working with parents; improving the school grounds and cooperative group work (a good example of The Support Group Method).
- Schools generally felt that the problem of bullying had slightly decreased since getting the pack.
- The Support Group Method gained a relatively high rating (5-point scale and a rating of 3.5). It was used more in Secondary Schools than in Infant and Primary Schools.

3.4   Until 2005 The Support Group Method was represented in Government publications, on the DfES website and referred to in the SEAL materials. Barbara Maines and George Robinson were founder members of the Anti-Bullying Alliance and employed as regional coordinators in the South West. A sudden change in Government policy led to the removal of previous support for our work and termination of our contracts with the Anti-Bullying Alliance. A press release was issued in February 2006 expressing significant concern. [See Appendix Two: Blair Bullies Anti-Bullying Alliance, 6 February 2006.]

## 3.5   More Recent Political Debate

Acceptance of The Support Group Method appears to have started to change during the summer of 2005. The Education Secretary at the time, Ruth Kelly, said in an interview with *The Independent* newspaper on 19 June 2005:

'We want a zero-tolerance approach to disruptive behaviour, from the low-level back chat and mobile phone texting in the classroom, to bullying or violence. Schools must have clear and consistent boundaries for what is acceptable behaviour. Pupils need to know where the limits are and what the consequences will be.'

This continued with a parliamentary question in the House of Commons on 23 November 2005:

Dan Norris (Wansdyke) | *Hansard* source:

'This Friday, as part of anti-bullying week, Lib-Dem controlled Bristol city council will call on its teachers not to punish or blame pupils who bully other pupils. What message does the Prime Minister have for those who adopt a no-blame approach, which, in my view, is dangerous and reckless, does nothing for the victims and does nothing to make bullies change their behaviour?'

Tony Blair (Prime Minister) | *Hansard* source:

'If what my hon. Friend says is correct about the Liberal Democrats, then it is an extraordinary thing for even them to do and I am shocked by it. [Interruption.] To describe oneself as shocked by the Liberal Democrats is perhaps an oxymoron.'

I profoundly disagree with the position taken by the council. Bullying should be punished. Children who bully must be made to understand the harm that they have been doing. New sanctions are available. I am pleased that in the schools White Paper we are giving teachers an unambiguous right to discipline. It is absolutely necessary, and I pay tribute to my hon. Friend's work on that serious problem.

A written question was tabled on 29 November:

Dan Norris (Wansdyke) | *Hansard* source:

To ask the Secretary of State for Education and Skills

1.    what assessment she has made of the effectiveness of different approaches to tackling bullying in schools; and if she will make a statement;

2.    what assessment her Department has made of the effectiveness of the no blame approach to tackling school bullying; and if she will make a statement.

Jacqui Smith (Minister of State (Schools and 14–19 Learners), Department for Education and Skills) | *Hansard* source:

Our guidance to schools on tackling bullying 'Don't Suffer in Silence' has been externally evaluated by researchers at Goldsmiths College, University of London. The results, though based on a fairly low response rate from schools, show that the schools found that the pack met their expectations and helped in drawing up their anti-bullying policies.

This evaluation included research into the perceived success of the anti-bullying strategies and interventions recommended in the guidance. Schools generally reported a high level of satisfaction with the interventions they had used. I have placed a copy of the research brief for this project in the Library.

The key feature of the 'No Blame' approach is that it adopts an explicit stance of discouraging punishment as a response to bullying. The Department does not support this stance and neither does the Anti-Bullying Alliance. Our guidance is clear that support and mediation strategies to change behaviour can, and should, be used in tandem with sanctions where appropriate. We are reviewing the guidance to make this even more explicit.

**As we do not promote the 'No Blame' approach for use in schools, we have not undertaken any assessment of its effectiveness.**

# 4. The Evidence Base for the Method's Success

4.1   In 1998, Sue Young published her work on an independent evaluation about the SGM.

**S. Young (1998) The (No Blame) Support Group Method to bullying in schools,** *Educational Psychology in Practice,* **14, 32–39.**

This was an independent evaluation carried out in the Kingston upon Hull Special Educational Needs Support Service (SENSS). Over a two-year period, in 80% of primary school cases treated through the modified No Blame Approach there was an immediate success.

In 14% of cases there was a delay, but after 3 to 5 weekly reviews, the bullying stopped or the victims reported that they no longer needed The Support Group.

In only 6% of cases did the victim report that the bullying continued, or that he/she was bullied by different pupils. There was a similar outcome in secondary school referrals.

4.2   Sue Young's evidence is strongly supportive of the approach but there is surprisingly little more formal evidence. During the many years which SGM has operated there are however **some powerful, personal endorsements of its success**.

There have been far too many to list but some are highlighted at **Appendix Three: Personal Endorsements of the SGM's Success**.

## 4.3   New research conducted in July/August 2006

In an attempt to understand better the use and success (or otherwise) of SGM, independent research was conducted over the summer of 2006. This was carried out by a highly respected professional, Professor Peter Smith, who heads the Unit for School and Family Studies at Goldsmiths College, University of London. Professor Smith has worked for many years in the bullying field, is a member of the Anti-Bullying Alliance and has worked in the past for DfEE on evaluating the DfES anti-bullying packs sent to schools.

This new research has not yet been published but it is clearly both recent, timely and informs greatly the current status.

Key points of the research include:

- Researchers had considerable difficulty in conducting the research due to the *political sensitivity* surrounding SGM over the last year. When attempting to build the research sample, Professor Smith planned to contact the Anti-Bullying Alliance regional coordinators to get feedback on questionnaires and to collect contact details.

  'There was fortuitously, an ABA meeting in June 2006 in London. However, the DfES representative there objected to any ABA involvement in this research…

'All 150 Local Authorities in England were approached … The speed and progress of collecting data from Local Authorities (LAs) was varied. Some refused to do the questionnaire at all, citing workload. The political sensitivity of this anti-bullying strategy at this time was a considerable hindrance in collecting data.'

- Only 11% of LAs had an awareness of how many primary and secondary schools used SGM – 89% indicated that they did not know. Yet over 60% of LAs supported the use of this approach (29% were neutral and 7% did not encourage the SGM). NO LAs discouraged its use.
- The time span that the SGM has been used by schools ranged from 1 year to its innovation in 1991. The majority of schools started using SGM in the last 5 years (69%). 97% of the schools who replied also indicated that they continue to use it, with 75% using it across the whole school.
- When schools were asked to provide evidence for the overall effectiveness of the approach in dealing with bullying, 53% indicated that they did have enough evidence to give an informed opinion.
- 56% gave a very satisfactory or satisfactory rating; 32% did not give a rating; 12% were neutral and *no* schools gave either a rather or very unsatisfactory rating.

Professor Smith's final comments summarise the state of play in 2006:

'This survey is a useful step forward, with a broader and more detailed evidence base from LAs and schools than has previously been available. The findings are clearly limited by the sample; in particular the response rate for schools was very low. In addition, data has only come from LA and school representatives: we have not heard the direct voices of pupils or parents (even though schools often cited them as evidence).

## Appendix One: Short Biographies of Barbara Maines and George Robinson

George Robinson and Barbara Maines set up Lucky Duck Publishing in 1988 to provide written materials that supported the In Service Training they provided around the UK.

**Barbara Maines** has been an educational psychologist since 1968 when the job was 'IQ testing'. In 1982 she threw away the tests so she could focus on working with teachers, in the classroom, helping to clarify difficulties and to plan interventions.

In 1997 Barbara made a career change and was appointed as a part-time support teacher for young people with emotional and behavioural difficulties in Bristol.

**George Robinson** started teaching in 1967, working in primary schools in England before teaching overseas. On his return he worked in a school for children with severe learning difficulties and then in a disruptive unit. In 1982 he took up a post as head teacher of an EBD (Emotional and Behavioural Difficulties) school.

In 1988 George moved into the field of teacher training at The University of the West of England. In 1996 he became coordinator of the Community Action Centre where he was responsible for widening access to higher education.

Barbara and George joined forces in 1988 to produce and publish their then radical approach to positive behaviour management.

**Since 2000 George and Barbara have worked together in the role of joint directors of Lucky Duck Publishing**, expanding the training and publications side of the business. They have an international reputation as lively, innovative and challenging presenters of INSET days. The publishing side of the company has expanded and can now boast the most extensive list of books and materials on humanistic education in the UK.

## Publications

When Lucky Duck started, George and Barbara wrote all the publications. As the company became successful and more widely known, other authors were added to the list. The focus of all our publications is books for practitioners by practitioners.

Since 1988 we have published more than 100 books, videos and resources to support teachers and other adults working with young people. The list ranges from such topics as Behaviour Management, Self-esteem, Special Needs and Asperger's Syndrome. We have also published several articles in refereed journals and we are presently working on new material related to Bullying and Restorative Approaches.

## Appendix Two: Blair Bullies Anti-Bullying Alliance, 06/02/06

**Embargo to 13.00 GMT, 06.02.06**

**BLAIR BULLIES ANTI-BULLYING ALLIANCE**

George Robinson and Barbara Maines, successful practitioners in helping schools to combat bullying, resigned their membership and walked out of a meeting of the Anti-Bullying Alliance in London today (Monday 6 February). It had been made clear that their contracts as regional co-ordinators for the Alliance in the south-west of England would not be renewed. This was as a result of direct intervention by the Prime Minister's office because of their advocacy of the (No Blame) Support Group Method to bullying.

This approach favours non-punitive methods to stop bullying in schools. Individuals take responsibility for their actions in a group structure and although controversial, it has proved successful across the world.

The ABA's action was taken despite positive, independent evaluation of Barbara and George's work and indications to them throughout last year that their contracts would therefore be renewed. They were told that implicit threats had been made by the Prime Minister's office to

Paul Ennals, chief executive of the National Children's Bureau, the agent of the Anti-Bullying Alliance (ABA).

He reported to the ABA that he had received repeated telephone calls, both at work and at home, implying that if he renewed the contracts, the current funding from the Department for Education and Skills (DfES) of over £0.5m would not continue.

George Robinson and Barbara Maines have been successful regional co-ordinators for 18 months and members of the Alliance since it began in 2002. 'Our membership of the ABA is no longer possible,' said Barbara. 'We have witnessed an indefensible level of bullying, manipulation and intervention, from the highest level in Government directed towards an independent organisation. How can we accept a situation where public policy is being determined to suit the current Prime Minister's obsession with punishment for any situation, whatever the circumstances?'

Barbara added: 'Not only is a democratic right at stake, but even more crucially, such actions are wholly irresponsible as they might undermine the confidence that professionals have established in using a wide range of effective measures to change behaviour and protect young people.'

Despite their complete support for Barbara and George's position and all their previous work, the ABA was forced to accept Paul Ennals' decision as members felt that this was the only practical way of protecting both future funding and the the work of the ABA itself.

George Robinson had also been a member of the ABA Advisory Group, its governing body, and was told that the Prime Minister was directly involved in the decision and that once he had made his position clear, everyone had to support it.

'But at what cost?' said George. 'And on what evidence is the Prime Minister making his judgements? Right up until last month, the DfES guidelines to schools in England fully endorsed a range of strategies, including The Support Group Method. No one has seen any evidence to suggest that this should change.'

In 2002, the DfES issued an anti-bullying pack for schools – Bullying, Don't Suffer in Silence – which was based on current legislation, recent research and relevant experience. Independent evaluation of the pack with schools showed that it was commended for maintaining awareness of the issue, and for providing a range of strategies for tackling bullying.

'The available evidence suggests that The Support Group Method has had some success,' said Professor Peter Smith, Goldsmiths College, University of London and author of the independent evaluation.

'My real concern, however, is that there does not appear to be enough substantial research which can either support or condemn any of the main anti-bullying strategies. This is a major barrier to moving on all the arguments about the benefits of one strategy to another.

Barbara Maines and George Robinson agree that more research is needed. 'We are pleased to be meeting Professor Al Aynsley Green, the Children's Commissioner for England soon,' said Barbara.

'He is treating bullying as one of his key priorities. He knows of our work and in a recent publication comments on the possible dangers of using punishment to intervene effectively when bullying happens. For example, in the case of a student called Jo, her school took firm action, but this only displaced the bullying. In Jo's view it is empathy that changed the behaviour of the young person bullying her.'

'We will be discussing with the Commissioner the need for a full evaluation of the current strategies used in schools,' said Barbara Maines. 'We hope that independent research to establish what works and what doesn't work, will prove conclusively that The Support Group Method is successful and should be used with confidence to combat bullying in our schools.'

## Notes to Editors

1. For further information about Bullying as an issue, the ABA and The Support Group approach, please go to www.luckyduck.co.uk/supportgroup.
2. The Anti-Bullying Alliance (ABA) was founded by NSPCC and National Children's Bureau in 2002. It brings together 65 organisations from the voluntary, public and private sector to work together to reduce bullying and create safer environments for children and young people. ABA is based at the National Children's Bureau. For more information, visit www.anti-bullyingalliance.org.
3. The Children's Commissioner published a short report in November 2005 – *Journeys – Children and Young People Talking about Bullying*. This is available at: http://www.anti-bullyingalliance.org/journeys.htm

## Appendix Three: Personal Endorsements of the SGM's Success 2005/6

**Val McFarlane**
**Regional Coordinator**
**Anti-Bullying Alliance, UK**

'The No Blame approach, which has been the subject of criticism from certain people, is one of many different strategies I use successfully when dealing with bullying cases, along with other methods.'

**Adrienne Katz**
**Young Voice – The national charity that makes young people's views count,**
**Member of the Anti-Bullying Alliance and Regional Coordinator for the West Midlands**

'We admire the work of George Robinson and Barbara Maines in developing new ways of thinking about resolving bullying and conflict. They have led the way to a re-think of how we teach values and behaviour. Their contribution to anti bullying work is enormous.'

**Members of the Anti-Bullying Alliance**

**Anita Compton – London Regional Coordinator**
**Val McFarlane – North East Regional Coordinator**
**Melanie Goddard and Andy Ritchie – North West Regional Coordinator**
**Peter Smith – Member of the ABA Advisory Group**

'As members of the Anti-Bullying Alliance we regret the decision by the chief executive of the NCB not to renew the contracts for George Robinson and Barbara Maines in the South West. The quality of the work they have done since their appointment in 2004 has not been in question. As originators of the No Blame, Support Group Approach they have made a valuable contribution to the range of approaches in this field and should not suffer discrimination for this reason.'

**Belinda Hopkins**
**Director, Transforming Conflict**
**National Centre for Restorative Justice in Education, UK**

'I am concerned about the proposed new, more punitive, anti-bullying policy in schools in England. Punishment may have its place but it can also be ineffective and dangerous.'

'A restorative response is not a "no-blame" response. It is a "full accountability/damage repair" response – unlike punishment. We must remember that punishment can be dangerous and ineffective. Let it be a very last resort if all else fails – but let us be aware of the potential damaging consequences to everyone involved.'

**Christopher Szaday**
**Fachstelle fuer schwierige Schulsituationen**
**Schulhaus Moosmatt, Urdorf, Switzerland**

'We've run countless training sessions for teachers on "No Blame" in the German-speaking Swiss cantons since 1998. For a few years now, the method has been spreading in Germany.

'On the basis of documented case studies and my own professional practice, I can attest to the success of the approach as one element of systematic anti-bullying provisions in schools.

'The Swiss approach is to find solutions through dialogue. The No Blame Support Group Approach fits our culture.

'We find that the victims are much more interested in having the bullying stopped than the bullies punished. The victims aren't so interested in the bullies; they just want to feel better and be able to concentrate on their school work and not be isolated during the school breaks or threatened on the way home.

'The key to the method, as I see it, is to give those pupils involved in the bullying a chance to change their behaviour. The method is about assuming responsibility for one's actions.

'I have never yet experienced or heard of a No Blame intervention which has resulted in the situation getting worse for the victim. With a week or two, we can see whether we are having an effect, and, if not, then we move to another form of intervention.

'I tell the victims that I work with that the intervention has a 90% chance of success. I tell them that if we are unlucky and the pupil is one of the 10%, then we will continue to find new solutions that will lead to a cessation of the bullying. We won't stop until the bullying stops. We always find a solution.'

**Mark Cleary**
**Principal, William Colenso College (Te Kreti o Wiremu Koroneho), New Zealand**
**(www.colenso.school.nz)**

'For the last ten years we have been using the Maines/Robinson (No Blame) Support Group Method to address bullying issues in our school. Our adoption of the method came after extensive research and experience in attempting to deal with bullying behaviour in our college.

'The approach is not only the most effective intervention method we have come across (i.e. it works), but it provides the participants with invaluable life-skills in solving relationship conflicts and provides real life opportunities for young people to intervene to challenge anti-social behaviour and support victims.

'I am horrified that this programme is under attack.'

**Thomas Brown**
**The Broken Toy Project**
**LionHeart Multimedia Productions**
**National Anti-Bullying Awareness Speaker**
**School Violence and Bullying Film Creator**
**The United States of America**

'Regarding the "no-blame" approach to dealing with school bullying … it's not always easy for people to understand how effective it can actually be. I have shared the no blame concept at every parent and teacher group I've ever been at, and the results are mixed. But thank goodness, there is always one wonderful teacher who stands up and shares a personal story that completely legitimizes the "no blame" concept.

'And the only way to even "have a chance" of getting a bully to turn their attitude around, is by helping them understand how much it hurts to be bullied in the first place, by using non-threatening tools and awareness, and certainly not by punishing them with suspension or expulsion … or punishing their parents.

'Punishment is too easy … too convenient … and it NEVER does any good. For fifteen years, I've been incorporating the no blame concept in my films and in my school programs, and I will continue to do so … simply because IT WORKS.'

**Judith Moore**
**CHIPS Coordinator SW**
**Childline in Partnership with Schools (CHIPS), UK**

'I have met George and Barbara on several occasions now and I have always found them most genuine, helpful and clearly committed to promoting the health and wellbeing of children and young people.

'During my work with pupils and staff on tackling bullying we discuss a variety of strategies including the "No blame support group approach" as well as peer support schemes etc.

'I receive feedback from young people in my workshops and they are very clear that punitive approaches do not always work and may make a situation worse – clearly schools need to have a variety of strategies to use.'

**Keith Sullivan PhD**
**Professor of Education and Head of Department**
**The National University of Ireland, Galway, Ireland**

'I am a great supporter of the No Blame Approach to bullying. I have been aware of it as a method for dealing sensitively and effectively with bullying when it occurs and also for teaching observers and perpetrators of bullying that they can contribute constructively to solving it. Bullying can be an ongoing process of intended nastiness and violence and can also be the result of ignorance and a lack of thought about its effects.

'The No Blame Approach not only provides an excellent well-structured process to empower children to stop bullying (including the perpetrators of bullying and their supporters), it also provides students with conflict resolution skills and a sense of being able to deal constructively and positively with negative situations. In the short term, it is a powerful tool for dealing with bullying, in the longer term an investment in our children's future.

'In 1995–96, I was elected to the Charter Fellowship in Human Rights at Wolfson College, University of Oxford. My time at Oxford was spent visiting and getting to know the various initiatives that had been developed in the UK. .... Two practically based and very effective initiatives were my most memorable experiences. One of these was the Dundee-based Tayside initiative ... the other was the No Blame Approach of Bristol-based psychologist Barbara Maines and lecturer George Robinson.

'In terms of my own publishing in the anti-bullying area, I have written about and provided instructions for how to use the No Blame Approach in two highly successful books. 'The Anti-Bullying Handbook' was published by Oxford University Press in 2000.

'The second book ('Bullying in Secondary Schools: what it means and how to manage it') was published by Sage Publications in 2004 and also contains a chapter on the No Blame Approach.

'A few years ago, I was approached to be the New Zealand representative at a historically significant OECD conference in Stavanger, Norway (held in September,

2004). On this occasion, my paper focused on the efforts of one New Zealand High School's very innovative approach to bullying. Those that ran the anti-bullying program stated that although the school had chosen a variety of both proven and new strategies to meet a diversity of needs and situations, the unifying theme to their approach was an underlying philosophy of No Blame.

'In my experience, the No Blame Approach has been used extensively to very good effect. I know of one case in a New Zealand primary school where after the No Blame Approach had been adopted to solve a bullying situation that the perpetrators not only ceased their bullying (and bullies are often powerful individuals who misuse their power), they became the school's main defenders against bullying in general.

'The No Blame philosophy and approach has proven to be very successful in providing positive and empowering solutions not only for victims of bullying but also for those who bully and for those who are forced to observe it.

'If you punish perpetrators of bullying what often happens is that, although the problem may appear to have been solved, it can often just be driven underground. In such cases, victims of bullying are held responsible for any consequences or punishment meted out to the perpetrators and are punished for this (in effect being bullied again).

'The perpetrators will also make certain that no one is aware of this reoccurrence of bullying. The No Blame approach is a much better response to such situations as it intentionally brings bullying out into the open and makes transparent what is hidden.

'In a non-confrontational way, it also encourages those who are responsible for the bullying-problem to contribute to the finding of solutions (and therefore to take responsibility for their actions). It also assists the hidden and quiet (and uncomfortable) majority (the observers and secondary participants) to claim their power and act in a unified way to solve the situation. They also see that when they act together they are more powerful than those who bully.

'For the victim of the bullying, it firstly stops the bullying from occurring and also provides a process of positive support that both affirms their right not to be bullied and supports the normalising of their life.'

**Tony Kerr**

'I am writing as a retired Principal Educational Psychologist and Assistant Director of Education to say how sad I am that an anti-bullying method of proven effectiveness appears to have become a political football, and will, as a result, become less available to many of the children whose lives could be improved by its use.

'During my period of responsibility for educational psychology services, I was much impressed by the powerful testimonials from headteachers and support staff in schools which had used the method. It was abundantly clear that, in appropriate cases, the effect of using The Support Group approach was to harness and redirect the normal group processes of childhood and the teenage years into productive channels, both solving the initial problem and helping the bullying children to mend their ways.

'I can quite understand that the "no-blame" label gives the wrong message to some parents, but that suggests to me a need for better presentation rather than abandoning a tried and tested approach. There is no single answer to all the different types of bullying, so the last thing we need to do is to deprive teachers of this powerful tool in their repertoire.'

DIANA WINTERBOTHAM, Lancashire Local Studies Librarian, 1971–93
(photo courtesy of the *Bury Journal*)

# Acknowledgments

I T IS A PLEASURE to thank the contributors to this volume for their enthusiasm and for choosing subjects which so well reflect Diana's own interests. I am very grateful to Diana's sister, Joan French, for her help with the biographical note (although she is not responsible for its content!) and to Frank Sunderland for his assistance. Frank Booth, editor-in-chief of the *Bury Journal*, generously allowed the photograph of Diana to be reproduced. The sources of other illustrations are acknowledged as appropriate, but thanks go to all those who helped in this respect, including Cath Rees who did much of the photographic work. Thank you, too, to the various members of the Lancashire Local History Federation who knew of this project and offered support and encouragement.

The following abbreviations are used in the notes and references:

| | |
|---|---|
| B.A.L.H. | British Association for Local History |
| C.N.W.R.S. | Centre for North-West Regional Studies |
| L.R.O. | Lancashire Record Office |
| P.R.O. | Public Record Office |
| R.S.L.C. | Record Society of Lancashire and Cheshire |
| T.H.S.L.C. | Transactions of the Historic Society of Lancashire and Cheshire |
| T.L.C.A.S. | Transactions of the Lancashire and Cheshire Antiquarian Society |

# Contents

# About the contributors

P. H. W. BOOTH, a former chairman of the Lancashire Local History Federation, is senior lecturer in the Department of History, University of Liverpool, and for over twenty years has been lecturer and organiser for the university's continuing education history programme. In 1992 he became the eleventh president of the Chetham Society.

ALAN CROSBY is a freelance local historian living in Preston. He is chairman of the Lancashire Local History Federation, an honorary research fellow of the University of Liverpool, and general editor for the British Association for Local History. He is currently writing a history of food in Lancashire.

MARY HIGHAM is an about-to-retire schoolteacher and a well-known lecturer who has done extensive research on the landscape history of medieval Lancashire. She has recently been awarded a doctorate from Lancaster University for her work on the impact of the Norman Conquest in north Lancashire.

ZOË LAWSON is an assistant librarian in the Local Studies Department of Lancashire County Library Headquarters in Preston. She has a degree in history and a diploma in local history from the universities of Liverpool and Lancaster.

JUDITH SWARBRICK is a librarian in the Local Studies Department of Lancashire County Libraries. She is the secretary of the Garstang Historical and Archaeological Society.

GEOFF TIMMINS is senior lecturer in history and university INSET co-ordinator at the University of Central Lancashire in Preston. His important work on the history of early industrial housing in Lancashire is widely known, and he has recently published a major study of the handloom weaving industry.

ANGUS WINCHESTER is lecturer in history at Lancaster University. Between 1981 and 1991 he was organising lecturer in extra-mural studies in mid-Lancashire for the University of Liverpool. His particular local history interests are in the medieval landscape and the development of rural society.

# Diana Winterbotham

*Lancashire Local Studies Librarian, 1971–1993*

THIS FESTSCHRIFT VOLUME, *Lancashire Local Studies*, has been written and published to mark the retirement, in March 1993, of Diana Winterbotham, who was for twenty-two years the Lancashire Local Studies Librarian. The book is intended as an expression of thanks for Diana's special contribution to the development of local history in the county and beyond, and it marks our appreciation of her great warmth, friendship, humour and good sense.

Some of us have worked alongside Diana as colleagues in the library service, and have found it a rich, rewarding and immensely enjoyable experience – she will be sorely missed within her profession. Other contributors have been associated with her through a shared involvement in local societies, the Lancashire Local History Federation, and a vast range of events and activities over the years. We have all been full of admiration for her energy and enthusiasm, while the breadth of her knowledge, the eminently practical nature of her organisational skills, and her warm personality have been instrumental in making possible so much of what we have tried to achieve. Her good-humoured presence makes even long committee meetings a pleasure!

In choosing subjects for our contributions to this volume we have tried to reflect Diana's own historical interests. Angus Winchester writes about the medieval Lancashire landscape, using, as he points out, Diana's own approach of combining documentary and cartographic evidence with what is to be seen in the landscape itself. Diana has for many years been collecting material on roads, bridges and the experience of travellers, and has lectured extensively on Lancashire maps, so Mary Higham's paper on the medieval Gough Map seems particularly appropriate. Paul Booth investigates seventeenth-century Toxteth Park, a township with an unusual and unexpected history. His example of the detailed social history

1

of a community is both intrinsically interesting and highly relevant to wider historical issues – not least, that existing published sources are not necessarily reliable. I hope that my own, somewhat eccentric, contribution on geese in Lancashire will appeal to Diana's interest in the lesser-known aspects of agriculture.

In his paper on two-up, two-down housing Geoff Timmins reassesses one of the commonplaces of the history and landscape of Lancashire, and especially of south-east Lancashire which is Diana's home territory, and suggests that there is a great deal more than we might at first suspect behind the plain brick façades in the long terraced streets. In another contribution which looks at a detail of Lancashire agriculture, Judith Swarbrick has plumbed much murkier depths – probing (metaphorically) the recesses of cesspits and urine tanks to find out about the manuring practices of early nineteenth-century Lancashire farmers, and to make interesting comparisons with the experience of their Flemish contemporaries.

Diana is a very keen cyclist, and has awed all of us with casual descriptions of popping down to Hereford or cycling round the Lake District in the torrential rains of December. Who else would have a favourite route into Cheshire which involves a bumpy track across Chat Moss and the toll bridge at Warburton? Zoë Lawson investigates the early history of cycling in Lancashire, looking at the growth of the different types of cycling clubs in the late nineteenth century, and Diana's pioneering predecessors among the lady bicyclists.

## A biographical note

DIANA WINTERBOTHAM was born at Swinton in 1933, but was brought up in Worsley and educated at Eccles Grammar School. She had hoped to train as a teacher, but family circumstances prevented this, and instead she reluctantly became the most junior library assistant at the Weaste branch of the Salford libraries, for a wage of £3 10s. a week. The switch from teaching to librarianship was undertaken without enthusiasm – she once told me that 'after the first ten years it got better' – but working in the severely deprived districts of Salford was an important formative influence. She may not have loved the job, but she loved the people, who brought her apples and sweets. It was here that she was first able to make use of her great gifts of communication and sympathetic understanding.

During her time with the Salford Corporation libraries Diana moved from branch to branch – Regent Road, back to Weaste, Peel Park, then to Hope – but at the same time she was, between 1953 and 1962, undertaking a lengthy part-time course at the Manchester College of Science and Technology to obtain her Library Association qualifications. In 1960 she had been appointed as readers' adviser and senior assistant librarian at Eccles Public Library, dealing with the immensely varied requests from the general library users. It was while she was working there, in 1962, that she completed her final examinations.

While she was with Salford, and especially after the move to Eccles, Diana was developing a particular interest in local history. Although she had enjoyed history at school she had not hitherto seen it as significant in career terms, but this began to change in her late twenties. In 1961 she joined the Eccles and District Local History Society, which had been founded in 1956 and of which she eventually became president. With this growing interest came the opportunity for specialisation within the library world, and in 1964 she moved to the Swinton and Pendlebury libraries as reference and local history librarian. Being in charge of the local history material at Swinton confirmed her love of the subject, and she has always emphasised the importance of the seven years she spent there. On her departure in 1971 she said, with characteristic modesty, that 'I know quite a lot now about the history and books associated with South East Lancashire' – a typical understatement.

In 1971 Diana was appointed County Local Studies Librarian with Lancashire County Library in Preston. This was a new post, in a newly created section of the library service. The intention was to develop a major collection of printed material relating to Lancashire, basing it partly on the existing stocks of local history material scattered across the many branch libraries, and partly on new acquisitions and purchases. The collection was to be based at the headquarters building of the library service in Corporation Street, Preston, and it would complement the specifically local collections in particular towns.

Diana began work at Preston with nothing: there was no core collection, and the shape and character of the county local studies library was to be entirely the result of her policy and philosophy. She knew that it was a considerable task, and anticipated that creating even the basic collection would take five years, but in a newspaper interview she pointed to the rare opportunity which was hers: 'I am able to start from scratch and to use many of my own ideas. It will be fascinating building up the collection [and] it is something I am really looking forward to'. Any local historian who has used the County Local Studies Library will be able to testify that the result is a triumph. Diana built up, by perseverance, patience and persuasion, a superb collection of Lancashire material – books, journals and transactions, photographs, and maps. Her own knowledge was another crucial resource, put to good use by searchers and visitors for over two decades, and always willingly given.

There was another aspect to the job. In the early 1970s, when Diana was settling into her new role, local history and family history were at the beginning of the great expansion which has been such a feature of the development of history in the past two decades. New local societies were being formed, national bodies were becoming concerned with, or created for, local history, and thousands of individuals – whether 'professional' or 'amateur' – were undertaking local history research. As well as dealing with the library work which the job required, the Lancashire local studies librarian was inevitably destined to be a significant figure in the development of local studies within the county.

There could not have been a better incumbent for the new post. From the beginning Diana has given immense amounts of time, labour and enthusiasm to this task. Within the county, and nationally, her part in the shaping of local history as we know it today has been outstanding. In 1981 the Librarians' Association recognised this when it bestowed on her the first Dorothy McCulla Award for her contribution to local history librarianship. The award, named after the founder of the L.A.'s local history group, was in special recognition of her work in promoting the educational use of local studies material, and of her dynamic and vigorous forwarding of the cause of local studies within her profession. She has been a leading member of the L.A. Local Studies Group for many years. Her great contribution to librarianship and local history was recognised by the award of the MBE in the 1993 New Year's Honours, an award richly deserved and widely welcomed.

Diana was active in the erstwhile Standing Conference for Local History, and in 1982 was a founder of the British Association for Local History. She was a member of the original B.A.L.H. Steering Committee, and subsequently served as a committee member and chairman of the

Publications Committee, and ultimately as vice-chairman of B.A.L.H. itself.

She was also one of the founders of the lengthily titled Federation of Local History Societies in the County Palatine of Lancaster. This was established in 1973 and ever since then Diana has been instrumental in ensuring that its work (and that of its more succinctly named successor, the Lancashire Local History Federation) has been effective. The L.L.H.F., co-publisher of this festschrift volume, has drawn heavily upon her reserves of energy and enthusiasm, and has relied on her common sense, practical understanding and organisational skills, and her love of history: she has been, in large measure, responsible for its present-day strength.

Diana has also been closely associated with the Lancashire and Cheshire Antiquarian Society, is a council member of both the Historic Society of Lancashire and Cheshire and the Friends of Lancashire Archives, and is chairman of the Ranulf Higden Society. There can be few local history societies in the county which she has not addressed, and thousands of local historians benefited from her patient, good-humoured, and informed assistance – whether they were experienced academics or those completely new to local history. Her own historical interests are wide. She has written in fascinating detail of the social and economic history of the area around her home in the Irwell Valley. Her retirement will not, of course, be idle: she is currently engaged on a history of Lancashire agriculture, a subject which she has always found of particular interest, and is also researching domestic life in Lancashire and the experiences of travellers on Lancashire's roads.

We give these essays to Diana with our warm affection and gratitude, and with our best wishes for a long, healthy and happy retirement.

*Alan Crosby*
*March 1993*

5

# Field, Wood and Forest – landscapes of medieval Lancashire

*Angus Winchester*

I F ASKED to select the one book which has been most influential in engendering interest in local studies in England, my answer would have to be *The Making of the English Landscape* by W. G. Hoskins. Since its publication in 1955 (and particularly after it appeared in paperback in 1970) Hoskins' classic study has fired the enthusiasm of numerous local historians, encouraging them to pursue a topographical approach to the study of history – literally a 'down to earth' approach, which aims to bring alive the history behind the fields, woods, hedgerows, farmsteads, roads and other man-made features of the countryside. The 'Hoskins' school of local history is one which appeals greatly to Diana Winterbotham and she has been keen to encourage local historians to apply a topographical approach to the study of Lancashire's history. This essay is offered as a small contribution towards such an approach, in the hope that it will encourage others to undertake further research into the making of the Lancashire landscape.

Since Hoskins published *The Making of the English Landscape* there has been an explosion in topographical study of the English countryside. As a result, the past thirty years have seen the revision of many older views (including some of those put forward by Hoskins) and the development of new understandings of the ways in which settlement and landscape have evolved across the centuries. One theme which has come to the fore in recent years is the image of rural England as a patchwork of regional landscapes, areas which shared not only distinctive patterns of settlement and land use, but also particular types of local economy and society. To English men and women in the sixteenth and seventeenth centuries, these distinctive regions were 'countries', in the sense that the word is still used

in phrases such as 'the fell country'. A Furness man visiting Amounderness, for example, would feel himself to be visiting a 'country' which
differed from his own, not only in its landscape but also in a host of cultural
features: dialect, building styles, customs and religion. The 'countries' of
pre-industrial England were often remarkably durable, their roots extending back into the medieval centuries and elements of their distinctive
character persisting into modern times.

Mapping the English 'countries' tends to be difficult, as one distinctive
area of countryside shades off into the next, but the complexities of pattern
can be reduced by seeing most 'countries' as variants of two contrasting
types of regional landscape. On the one hand are those anciently settled
areas where extensive cultivation was occurring by early medieval times
and, on the other, areas which contained considerable tracts of late
surviving woodland or untamed moorland or marsh until well into the
Middle Ages.[1] It has been convincingly argued that the two types of
countryside were complementary and inter-dependent in the pre-Conquest period, the areas of woodland and waste providing important
reserves of natural resources (particularly pasture) for communities in the
anciently settled areas. In lowland England, where most of the recent
research and analysis has taken place, several features are repeated
sufficiently often for a model of early medieval landscape evolution to be
built.

In such a model the anciently settled areas lie along river valleys,
where early place-names, known Anglo-Saxon estate centres, and early
parish churches tend to be concentrated. They are set against a backdrop
of uncleared woodland, a frontier zone, often on poorer or heavier soils
along the watersheds. Here the place-name record indicates the late
survival of woodland, and charter evidence and the pattern of parish
boundaries suggest links of lordship between outlying settlements in the
woodland areas and estate centres in the river valleys. The untamed areas
were particularly important in the period of population growth between
the eleventh and thirteenth centuries, as they provided reserves of 'empty'
land from which new settlements could be carved.

Such a pattern has been described in Kent and Surrey, where ancient
settlements around the coast and up the Thames valley were linked with

---

[1] For a good brief introduction to the mosaic of regional landscape types, see J. Thirsk, *England's
Agricultural Regions and Agrarian History, 1550–1750* (1987).

pasture and woodland on the Weald and Downs; and in Warwickshire, where the anciently settled 'felden' landscape of open-field villages in the valleys of the Avon and its tributaries contrasted with the woodland frontier zone of the Arden district in the north west of the county.[1] The thesis to be presented below is that it is possible to identify a similar contrast between areas of ancient settlement and reserves of colonisable woodland and waste in medieval Lancashire, and that the contrasting landscapes which developed have left an enduring legacy in the countryside of Lancashire today.

A useful starting point for a survey of this kind is to reconstruct the distribution of woodland in the early medieval period. Elsewhere in the country the local historian is able to turn to the evidence of the Domesday Book, which records woodland as a source of income to lords of the manor in 1086. The late H. C. Darby's painstaking mapping of Domesday woodland has painted a vivid picture of those areas where substantial tracts of woodland remained in the eleventh century.[2] In Lancashire we are less fortunate, as the bald list of geld assessments, which is all that Domesday records for the county north of the Ribble, provides no reference to woodland, while the idiosyncratic descriptions of the great hundredal estates of south Lancashire provide only a very incomplete picture. In Leyland hundred, for example, it records woodland two leagues long and one wide at Leyland itself, an unspecified quantity of woodland at Penwortham, and further substantial quantities of woodland in unnamed locations elsewhere in the hundred.[3] We are therefore thrown back on another source, the evidence of place-names.

Three place-name elements may be used to gain an impression of the distribution of woodland in the centuries before 1300. They are *wudu* (as in Fulwood, Harwood, Heywood) and *skógr* (as in Myerscough and

---

[1]  Among the most important papers on this theme are: A. Everitt, 'River and Wold: reflections on the historical origin of regions and pays', *Journal of Historical Geography*, iii (1977), pp. 1–10; H. S. A. Fox, 'The People of the Wolds in English Settlement History', pp. 77–101, in M. Aston, D. Austin and C. Dyer (eds.), *The Rural Settlements of Medieval England* (1989); W. J. Ford, 'Some Settlement Patterns in the Central Region of the Warwickshire Avon', pp. 274–94, in P. Sawyer (ed.), *Medieval Settlement* (1976); T. Williamson, 'Explaining Regional Differences: woodland and champion in southern and eastern England', *Landscape History*, x (1988), pp. 5–13; D. Hooke, 'Regional Variations in Southern and Central England in the Anglo-Saxon period', pp. 123–51, in D. Hooke (ed.), *Anglo-Saxon Settlement* (1988); J. Blair, 'Frithuwold's kingdom and the origins of Surrey', pp. 97–107, in S. Bassett (ed.), *The Origins of Anglo-Saxon Kingdoms* (1989).
[2]  See H. C. Darby, *Domesday England* (CUP, 1977), pp. 171–207.
[3]  *Domesday Book*, f. 270a.

Burscough), respectively the Old English and Old Norse terms for 'wood'; and *leah* (as in Chorley, Burnley, Cadley, Lea, Leigh and many other names), an Old English word which has a spectrum of meanings associated with woodland and which appears to have meant 'glade' or 'woodland clearing' when used in the name of a settlement.[1] The distribution of names containing these elements in mid-Lancashire is mapped in Figure 1. The pattern it portrays cannot be located at one particular point in time: only *skógr* can be pinpointed fairly precisely, as names containing this element were probably coined during the tenth century when Norse-speaking immigrants settled in the North West. Both *wudu* and *leah* were used in name formation for several hundred years, through the Anglo-Saxon period and into the twelfth century.

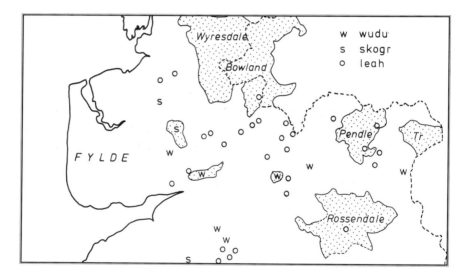

FIGURE 1.   Woodland elements in Lancashire place-names before 1300

Nevertheless, the distribution enables us to recapture something of the extent of woodland in early medieval Lancashire. It is striking how the woodland names avoid both the high land of the Bowland Fells and the

---

[1]   M. Gelling, *Place-Names in the Landscape* (1984), pp. 198–207, 209–10, 227–9.

Rossendale Moors, and the coastal plains of the Fylde and south-west Lancashire. Woodland appears to have been concentrated along the skirts of the hills and in the Ribble valley. It is also striking that the names are far from evenly distributed within the area in which they do occur: their clustering suggests discontinuous areas of woodland rather than any major wooded belt. The evidence suggests, therefore, that we can postulate a zone of patchy remaining woodland between the coastal lowlands and the hills.

The significance of the woodland names is highlighted when they are contrasted with the name of the largest lowland area in Lancashire, the Fylde. The term 'Fylde' is derived from the old English *filde*, 'a plain', a word closely related to *feld*, meaning 'open country' as opposed to wooded country.[1] The contrast, in the minds of our medieval ancestors, between the treeless Fylde and the more wooded zone to the east is highlighted in the names used to distinguish between the two settlements in Amounderness hundred called Plumpton. That near Lytham in the heart of the Fylde, now called Great and Little Plumpton, was called Field- or Fylde-plumpton in the fourteenth century;[2] the name of the other, on the edge of the woodland zone to the east, was and still is Woodplumpton. This terminology, and the restricted distribution of woodland in mid-Lancashire, suggest that the contrast between the two landscapes was a real feature of the medieval countryside, akin to that found in counties further south.

In the north of England, however, a third landscape zone needs to be identified, namely that of the upland moors. In the medieval period most of the Bowland and Rossendale fells were, like much of the rest of the Pennine chain and the Lake District fells, described as 'forest' or 'free chase' – that is, land reserved (in theory at least) for the exercise of hunting rights by the king or one of the great feudal overlords. Thus, Pendle and the moorlands of the Rossendale block together constituted the forests of Pendle, Trawden, Rossendale and Accrington, which were the private forests of the honour of Clitheroe. The Bowland fells comprised the forest of Bowland to the east; the forest of the earldom of Lancaster (covering Quernmore, Wyresdale and Bleasdale) to the west; and the

---

[1]  Ibid., pp. 235–45.
[2]  Their names occur as 'Little Fildeplumpton' and 'le Graunte Fildeplumpton' in 1323: W. Farrer (ed.), *Lancashire Inquests, Extents and Feudal Aids, part II*, R.S.L.C., liv (1907), p. 158.

11

chase belonging to Hornby castle (the valleys of the Roeburn and the Hindburn) to the north.[1] These forest areas were not necessarily wooded (the term 'forest' signifying that they were *foris* (that is, outside the normal land laws) but, like the wooded areas of the woodland zone, they contained important reserves of pasture and they constituted 'empty' land, awaiting exploitation and settlement.

The threefold division outlined above – the open and treeless Fylde or 'field' land; the woodland zone; and the upland forests – provides a framework within which to examine some of the detailed documentary evidence which enables us to reconstruct the medieval landscape of Lancashire.

## 1. *The 'field' lands of the coastal lowlands*

The lowlands of the Fylde and south-west Lancashire are areas of gently undulating plain, consisting of 'islands' of glacial drift material interspersed with wet, often peat-filled hollows. The balance between the drier ridges, on which settlement and agriculture were possible, and the wetlands, which could not be cultivated but yielded peat for fuel and rough pasture for cattle in the summer months, varied across the lowlands. Much of the Over Wyre district of the northern Fylde consisted of the extensive peat wetlands of Pilling, Rawcliffe and Winmarleigh mosses, while a vast tract of peatmoss stretched across south-west Lancashire, from Tarleton to Altcar. However, in the southern Fylde and in what is now South Ribble District, the proportion of wetland was less: and in these areas a landscape of nucleated villages surrounded by open fields developed.

The chronology of these village settlements is difficult to pin down. As land suitable for cultivation was comparatively scarce, we may assume that the drier ridges and 'islands' would have been settled early. Many of the village names are of Anglo-Saxon origin, pre-dating the Scandinavian settlement of the tenth century, but the evidence of the names must be

---

[1] For the upland northern forests in general, see A. J. L. Winchester, *Landscape and Society in Medieval Cumbria* (John Donald, 1987). For the Lancashire forests, see R. Cunliffe Shaw, *The Royal Forest of Lancaster* (Preston, 1956); G. H. Tupling, *The Economic History of Rossendale*, Chetham Society, new series, lxxxvi (1927). The 'chase' or 'forest' pertaining to Hornby is recorded from 1199: W. Farrer (ed.) *Lancashire Inquests, Extents and Feudal Aids*, R.S.L.C., xlviii (1903), pp. 92, 261.

viewed in the light of archaeological and documentary work from elsewhere in the country which has revolutionised our view of the antiquity of village settlement in England. An early Anglo-Saxon name for a village need not imply that the nucleated village and its open fields date from that early period: landscape historians are becoming increasingly aware of a 'rural revolution' in the period AD 850–1150. The engine of change was growth in the power of the lord of the manor: the expressions of lordly control included a tendency to concentrate population in nucleated settlements, and the laying-out of open field systems.[1]

The extent to which such a process occurred in Lancashire is difficult to assess, but there are villages in the Fylde (such as Elswick, Hardhorn, Clifton and Newton) with regular, planned layouts very similar to those in Yorkshire and Durham, which it has been suggested were laid out afresh in the aftermath of the Norman Conquest.[2] Domesday Book's comment on the settlements in the Fylde, that of the sixty vills listed as members of the huge estate centred on Preston only sixteen possessed 'a few inhabitants', suggests a major disruption in the eleventh century, possibly the result of Malcolm III's invasion from Scotland in 1061. Such destruction would be compatible with a post-Conquest re-planning of settlement in the area. The landscape of these western lowlands described in detail in charters from the thirteenth century and later was one which possessed a great time-depth but which may have undergone a wholesale transformation in the aftermath of the Conquest.

A case study will give an impression of the look of the 'field' landscape in the medieval period. It is Longton, 'the long village', set in the midst of a landscape of long, strip-like fields which were the result of piecemeal enclosure of open fields and common meadows, probably in the seventeenth century.[3] Several title deeds of the thirteenth and fourteenth centuries survive, giving details of holdings in the township. Longton was one of a string of townships from Penwortham to Hoole, settled along the drier ridge between Preston and the river Douglas and hemmed in by the Ribble marshes on one side and the great mosslands which stretched towards Leyland on the other. The township boundaries were drawn in

---

[1]  See C. Taylor, *Village and Farmstead: a history of rural settlement in England* (1983).

[2]  See B. K. Roberts, 'Village Plans in County Durham', *Medieval Archaeology*, xvi (1972), pp. 33–56; J. A. Sheppard, 'Medieval village planning in northern England: some evidence from Yorkshire', *Journal of Historical Geography*, ii (1976), pp. 3–20.

[3]  Enclosure of an open field at Longton *c.* 1655 is recorded in L.R.O., DDHe 115/2.

such a way that each settlement had a share of each category of land – the marshes as pasture and meadowland, the ridge for cultivation, the mossland for fuel. A series of title deeds from the early fourteenth century enables us to recapture a landscape of open-field agriculture, in which the land of each farm consisted of strips scattered across the open field furlongs around the village. For example, the land granted by Henry Ploket to his brother Adam in 1318 was described as:

> all my land which I had by gift of my father Hugh in the township of Longton, except a house with four selions [open field strips] on le Ston . . . namely: a croft with houses built upon it, lying between the land of Robert de Shireburn on one side and the land of the said Robert on the other side; all my land in Turmeracreflat; all my land in Scortebuttes and in le Rodedoles; all my land in Houwcomkar; all my land in le Beremersse and all my land in le Reodheved and a selion with a tongland [tongueland = a tapering strip] in le Tunstedes.[1]

Enough of the medieval field names survived into the nineteenth century at Longton to enable us to locate most of the areas in which Henry Ploket's land lay. Turner Acre, Reed Dow, Short Butts and Reed Head were furlongs in the open fields to the north of the village; Stone and Tunsteads were similar blocks to the south; and Bare Marsh lay on the edge of the wetland to the south-west (see Figure 2).

Several of these field names occur in charters describing other hold-ings in the village, confirming that land was intermixed in these fields. Sometimes the fields are described as 'furlongs' (for example, 'le Ston' is 'Stanfurlong' in a thirteenth-century charter).[2] Sometimes the term *campus* ('field') is used, particularly for larger sections of the open fields. Turner Acre, described as a *campus* in the early thirteenth century, appears to have been subdivided into at least three furlongs, as a 'Middilfurlong in Turmirakyr' is recorded in the mid-thirteenth century.[3] While it is clear that much of the villagers' land at Longton, as in other villages in the coastal lowlands, was held as strips in open fields, we know little about how these field systems operated during the Middle Ages. There is little evidence for the regular division into two, three or four cropping units (the 'Midland' system); rather, the north-western open fields appear to

---

[1]  L.R.O., DDHe 25/25.

[2]  A. N. Webb (ed.), *An Edition of the Chartulary of Burscough Priory*, Chetham Society, third series, xviii (1970), p. 137.

[3]  Ibid. and L.R.O., DDHe 25/4.

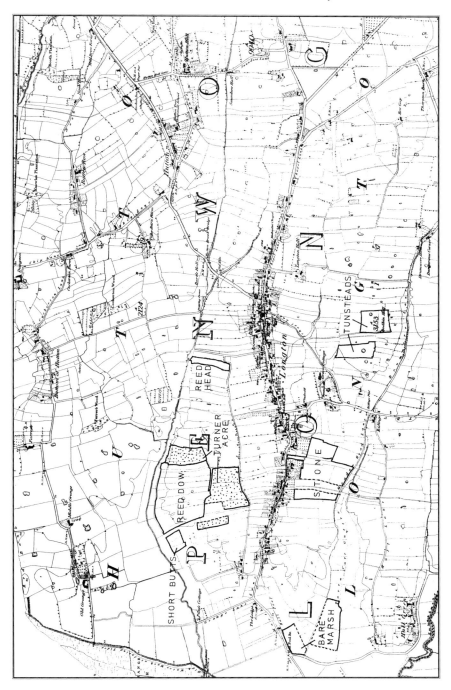

FIGURE 2.   Medieval field names in Longton township (on 1st edition 6" map base)

have taken the form of something more akin to the Scottish 'infield', a nucleus of intensively cropped ploughland.

By the end of the Middle Ages the term 'townfield' came to be used to describe this vital core of open-field land which yielded harvests of oats and barley year-in, year-out. Also within the limits of land held by members of the village community were meadows, often held as common meadows within which each farmer held a share, and enclosed pasture. By the seventeenth and eighteenth centuries there is evidence of land around Lancashire villages being cultivated on a long rotation, whereby two or three years' cropping was followed by six years' fallow as pasture. This was closely paralleled by the 'outfield' cultivation found further north, in Cumberland and Scotland, but it is not clear how far back into the Middle Ages such long rotations stretched.[1]

Beyond the settlements and their fields were areas of scrubby waste termed 'moor', 'carr' or 'moss' depending on their wetness. As we have seen, little woodland remained in these areas by the early medieval period: it is striking that the only woodland place-names in the Fylde proper are Preesall and Preece, both of which contain the Old Welsh element *pres*, 'brushwood', implying both that we have to go back before the Anglo-Saxon period to find significant woodland in the Fylde and that, even in the British period, this woodland was scrubby brushwood rather than a substantial tree cover. Most of the scrubby waste land between settlements was wetter than the precious free-draining plough-land of the village fields, but the three terms by which the unenclosed waste was known described distinct types of land. 'Moor' was the driest, tolerably good rough grassland which provided valuable grazing for livestock in the summer months. 'Carr' (from the old Norse *kjarr*, 'marsh overgrown with brushwood') was probably the wettest, a tangle of alder and willow scrubland with pools and morasses. The 'mosses' were the peatmoss proper, a spongy waste, the character of which can be seen in the surviving untamed mossland at Winmarleigh Moss. These unenclosed wastes are not described in the land charters, as common rights on the waste of the township (particularly rights of pasture and turbary – the right to cut peat and turf for fuel) were appendant to holdings of land in the open fields.

---

[1] G. Youd, 'The Common Fields of Lancashire', *T.H.S.L.C.*, cxiii (1961), pp. 1–41, is still the most comprehensive discussion of open-field systems in the county.

So far, the lowlands have been portrayed as a static landscape in the Middle Ages, but in fact major changes took place, particularly during the period of sustained population growth in the twelfth and thirteenth centuries. To feed more mouths more land had to be put under the plough and greater numbers of livestock had to be raised. The Middle Ages saw a determined assault on the remaining areas of lowland moor and the edges of the wetlands. By 1300 new hamlets had been founded along the margins of the waste, some bearing names which reflect their location: for example, Mosshouses, a hamlet on the edge of the mossland north-east of Much Hoole village, is recorded from 1296.[1]

Boundaries were drawn across the moorland and through the wetlands to assign exclusive rights to settlements adjacent to them. In the Fylde, for example, a ditch had been excavated by *c.* 1250 through the wet valley separating the manor of Staining from the manors of Little Carleton and Great and Little Layton.[2] Such an attempt to tame the waste would have improved drainage and enabled the limit of cultivation to be extended further towards the wetter land. On the other side of Staining manor the carr land between Todderstaffe, Singleton and Preece continued to be used for grazing and digging fuel in the early sixteenth century, when attempts to enclose it led to a series of disputes over ownership.[3] A sustained attack on the lowland wastes took place in the sixteenth century. In some places this was restricted to piecemeal nibbling at the edges, as the numerous references to small acreages 'lately enclosed from the moor' testify. But wholesale enclosure of lowland moors also took place, as at Kirkham *c.* 1555.[4]

The medieval landscape of the Fylde and south-west Lancashire was essentially one of open land: a landscape with few trees and few hedgerows, of villages set in open fields and common meadows, beyond which stretched unenclosed moorland and peatmoss.

---

[1] *V.C.H., Lancashire*, vol. VI, p. 151n.

[2] W. A. Hulton (ed.), *The Coucher Book of Whalley Abbey*, Chetham Society, old series, xi (1846), pp. 421–2, 443.

[3] P.R.O., DL 3/10, f. 100; DL 3/16, ff. 61–9.

[4] For examples of piecemeal intaking see rentals of Hambleton and Carleton, 1567 (L.R.O., DDSt, rentals and surveys, box 1); for Kirkham Moor, see R. Cunliffe Shaw, *Kirkham in Amounderness* (1949), pp. 113–15.

## 2. *The woodland zone*

In marked contrast to the coastal plain, the woodland zone was a land-scape of broken terrain, numerous trees, and dispersed hamlets and farmsteads set in a patchwork of small, enclosed fields. Although wood-land names are found on the lowlands, notably along the eastern edge of the Fylde from Lea and Fulwood north to the Garstang area, the majority are found as the land rises to the eastern moors. We have already noted that the place-name evidence suggests that survival of extensive areas of woodland in Lancashire was more patchy than in some other counties. Noteworthy clusterings include those around Leigh (including Hindley, Astley, Tyldesley, Worsley and Kearsley) and Chorley (recorded not only in a cluster of *leah* names but also in the suffixes of Clayton-le-Woods and Whittle-le-Woods).

There are some hints that parts of the woodland zone along the skirts of the hills might at an early date have been linked to older settlements in the lowlands, perhaps to provide reserves of grazing. The evidence is tentative and is based on the patterns created by ancient territorial boundaries, where places in the woodland zone were, for administrative purposes, detached portions of territorial units centred further west. There are three instances of this: the chapelry of Goosnargh, north of Preston, which was a detached part of the parish of Kirkham throughout the medieval period; the township of Chorley, a detached portion of Croston parish until 1793; and Astley, near Leigh, which was an outlying member of the post-Conquest fee centred on Widnes. These are tantalis-ing suggestions that the ancient settlements along the coastal plain were set against a backdrop of woodland and pasture along the skirts of the hills, which provided them with a valuable resource, used as distant grazing grounds.

By the time of the Norman Conquest parts of the woodland zone had long been settled, but this belt also contained areas which were to become the frontier of active colonisation in the twelfth and thirteenth centuries. Charters from these areas paint a picture of a landscape in the making, as colonists carved new farms and enclosures from the wood and waste. Let us start with a thirteenth-century charter from Tottleworth, a hamlet of the edge of Great Harwood (a name probably meaning 'the great grey wood'). Tottleworth itself presumably originated in the Anglo-Saxon period, as *worth* is a common Old English term for an enclosed settlement. The charter grants a compact block of land within the territory of Tottleworth and spells out its boundary thus:

> beginning at the water of Hyndburn and following the stream on the south side of the tree called 'Hyere', ascending straight to the ash tree near the assart of Henry of Tottleworth, and following Henry's assart as far as the oak tree near the little way, and so descending as far as the apple tree standing near the great way, and following the way, descending to John's assart, following the wood on the south side of the said assart down to the Hyndburn, and ascending by the Hyndburn as far as the afore-named stream.[1]

Notice, firstly, that this is a single block of land rather than a number of small strips in the open fields. The land is not named and was granted by Richard of Tottleworth to his daughter as her marriage settlement. It could be that this was land literally on the frontier. It is striking that several of the boundary points are trees and that the land being granted adjoined two 'assarts' – that is, clearings in woodland made for cultivation. The nineteenth-century field pattern at Tottleworth, as in other parts of the woodland zone, was one of small, irregularly shaped enclosures, many of which, it seems reasonable to suggest, came into existence during the winning of new lands by assarting during the twelfth and thirteenth centuries.

A few miles north of Tottleworth lies Dinckley and, across the Ribble, the township of Aighton, Bailey and Chaigley along the southern slopes of Longridge Fell. These *leah* names imply the existence of late-surviving woodland and even Aighton, the exception, means 'oak tree settlement'. The field pattern and field names in the area tell again of medieval assarting as farms and fields were carved out of the woods. The settlement pattern is one of scattered farms, several of which bear names recording woodland: *hurst*, meaning 'wooded hill' (as in Stonyhurst); *ridding*, meaning 'land cleared for cultivation, an assart' (as in Riddings). Field names recorded on the 1733 plan of the Stonyhurst estate (see Figure 3) tell the same story, the name Stubbings ('a clearing') being particularly evocative as it refers to land in which the stumps ('stubs') of cleared trees remained. Surviving charters confirm this picture of a landscape of assarting, but they also make it clear that some small patches of open field arable agriculture had come into existence by the later thirteenth century.

---

[1] L.R.O., DDHe 36/1.

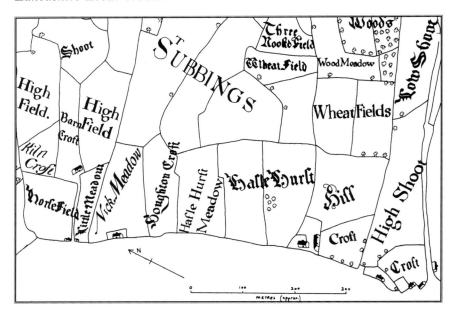

FIGURE 3.    Extract from estate plan of 1733
(copy of photograph of original at Stonyhurst College)

For example, a charter of *c.* 1280 concerning land in Dinckley grants a mixture of meadowland and ploughland bearing field names which evoke a landscape of woodland clearings and wet meadows:

> all my part of le Paddakelache ['the toad ditch'] and of le Eyeskar ['the island carr'] and of le Milngreves ['the mill groves'] and of Abraham's meadow; and that half-acre which Henry Spot formerly held; and all my part of Tulleriding and of Appeltreriding and of Utrethecroft and one acre in le Cocshute [a woodland glade where nets were stretched to catch woodcock] on the west side of Alexander's land; and one butt [a short open-field strip] on le Eyes ['the islands'] abutting on Appeltreriding, and another butt at le Thisteliflat with meadow adjacent abutting on le Staniriding.[1]

The references to individual 'butts' imply that some, at least, of the arable land was divided into open field strips. But these patches of shared ploughland appear to have been small: both the 'Eyes' and the 'Thisteli-

---

[1]  L.R.O., DDHe 12/1.

flat' ('flat' is synonymous with 'furlong') abutted on fields bearing the name 'ridding' (a clearing). The landscape of late thirteenth-century Dinckley was probably one of small patches of shared ploughland surrounded by assarts from the woodland.

The extensive collection of medieval title deeds preserved in the Stonyhurst collection in the Lancashire Record Office appears to chart the evolution of a similar landscape in the township of Aighton, Bailey and Chaigley. Early thirteenth-century charters grant blocks of land specifically described as 'assarts'. Their boundaries follow cloughs, minor streams, other assarts and, in some cases, named or marked trees. The boundaries of an assart near Aighton mill, for example, ran from a stream to 'Thirledake' (probably 'the hollow oak') to four marked oaks (*quatuor quercus mercatas*) to 'Burrilake' (presumably another oak tree). Similarly, land in 'le Bouhurstes' was bounded by a series of cross-marked oaks and other trees.[1] By the fourteenth century settlement and cultivation had resulted in a landscape which contained some open field land. A charter of 1318 granted three 'selions' (strips) in 'the field [*campus*] of Acghton-felde'. Each lay between land belonging to other landowners, confirming that the deed is describing dispersed strips in an open field but, like the land described in the charter from Dinckley, one of the selions abutted head and foot on assarts.[2] Similarly, in 1335 three selions in 'Aghtonfelde' were granted 'with meadow and wood lying at the head of the said selions', again painting a picture of a small open field set in a landscape of woodland and meadow.[3] By the mid-fourteenth century, however, the open field of Aighton was sufficiently large to contain named subdivisions, charters of the 1330s referring to 'le Westfeld' (implying that there were other 'fields') and to a furlong (*cultura*) called 'Kirkwro'.[4]

The picture painted by these charters from the woodland zone is of a landscape akin to that found in areas of late-surviving woodland elsewhere in England. The scale of the landscape was small, intimate and 'hand-made'. Small nuclei of open-field arable land were set in a patchwork of

---

[1]  L.R.O., DDSt, unlisted deeds in box labelled 'Aighton Medieval Deeds'. Those cited here are: Osbert *molend'* to Alan *carpentarius*, undated; and Ralph of Mitton, kt, to Ralph his son, undated.

[2]  Ibid. Ralph, s. of William, s. of Ely of Aighton, to John, s. of Walter of Bailey, 6 Jan. 1318.

[3]  Ibid. Henry, s. of Robert of Halle, to John, s. of Walter of Bailey, 22 Dec. 1335.

[4]  Ibid. William, s. of Robert of Halle, to John, s. of Walter of Bailey, 7 Nov. 1334; Henry of Halle to Richard, s. of Gilbert of Aighton, 8 Feb. 1336; Ralph, s. of Robert of Halle, to John, his son, 17 Mar. 1336.

small enclosures which had been created by grubbing up woodland in the twelfth and thirteenth centuries. Such features were common to much of the western Midlands and the Welsh Marches, as well as to the broken terrain of the upland margins of other parts of northern England.

## 3. The forests

The third distinctive landscape of medieval Lancashire, the 'forest' landscape of the upland east, was defined in part by the physical topography of the peat-capped, gritstone moors with their limited acreages of potential ploughland. Extensive, as opposed to intensive, grazing of livestock was bound to be the natural means of exploiting the particular resources of these areas. We may assume that the upland district of eastern Lancashire contained more woodland in the medieval period than it has done subsequently, but the tops of the Bowland fells and the Rossendale moors had long since been denuded and had supported peat moss and moorland vegetation since the prehistoric period. Woodland would have remained along the slopes of the hills and in the valleys penetrating the uplands.

We have already seen that large sections of the eastern uplands shared with much of the fell country of northern England the designation 'forest' or 'chase'. In theory, therefore, the uplands were hunting preserves, retained in demesne by the great feudal landowners. Being demesne land, they were exploited directly by the overlords and comparatively good records survive to shed light on the ways in which their resources were used. The bulk of the Lancashire forests fell into two groups, those belonging to the earldom of Lancaster (the forests of Quernmore, Wyresdale and Bleasdale and, from 1311, the forest of Bowland) and those forming part of the great honour of Clitheroe (the forests of Pendle, Trawden, Rossendale and Accrington).

When the uplands were first designated as forest is not known, but the origins of the forest areas of upland northern England are probably bound up with the distinctive pattern of large, composite estates which was found across the north in the early medieval period. The honour of Clitheroe, for example, appears to have been the Norman successor to such a multiple estate or 'shire', known as Blackburnshire. Like other large pre-Conquest estates in the north, Blackburnshire may have been an ancient and stable unit of landholding, its origins perhaps stretching back to the Celtic society which pre-dated the Anglo-Saxon settlement.[1] Many of these multiple estates or 'shires' of the north bore similar relationships to the landscape and included within their bounds both lowland areas, in which the lord's court lay and where early settlements were concentrated, and a share of the uplands which, arguably, constituted a major resource of grazing land for the lowland communities. In Lancashire the place-name record contains one hint of such a linkage between upland and lowland. This is the name Ortner in Over Wyresdale, which is a contraction of 'Overton-erg', that is, the *erg* or summer grazing ground belonging to Overton, the lowland township on the Lune estuary.

By the later thirteenth century, when documentary evidence enables us to gain some detail of the land use and topography of the upland forests, the forests of both the earldom of Lancaster and the honour of Clitheroe were being managed in similar ways. No longer was the whole of the forest preserved for hunting, since special deer parks had been enclosed for that purpose. Instead, the bulk of the land within the forests was being exploited as pasture, much of it through a system of large dairy farms or 'vaccaries'. In the honour of Clitheroe the vaccaries formed a system of demesne cattle husbandry on a large scale. In 1295 the lord's chief stockman (or 'instaurator') for Blackburnshire had under his control no fewer than twenty-eight vaccaries, five in Trawden forest, eleven each in the forests of Pendle and Rossendale, and one in Accrington forest. With the exception of the single large vaccary in Accrington, which ran over 100 cows, 125 younger cattle and three bulls, each of the vaccaries supported herds of around fifty milch cows, as many younger cattle, and a bull. In all, the demesne vaccary herd amounted to 2,500 head of cattle.[2]

The forests of the earldom of Lancaster also contained vaccaries, though many of these appear to have been leased rather than farmed directly for the earl. There were said to be twenty vaccaries in Wyresdale (which probably included Quernmore and Bleasdale) in 1297 but eight had already been leased by 1248, when vaccaries are first recorded in the forest.[3] The vaccaries were named in 1322, by which date they were all leased. Then there were twelve vaccaries in Over Wyresdale. Their

---

[1] R. B. Smith, *Blackburnshire* (Leicester, 1961).

[2] P. A. Lyons (ed.), *Two 'compoti' of the Lancashire and Cheshire manors of Henry de Lacy, Earl of Lincoln, 24 and 33 Edward I*, Chetham Society, old series, cxii (1884), pp. 129–40.

[3] W. Farrer (ed.), op. cit., pp. 169–70, 290–1.

23

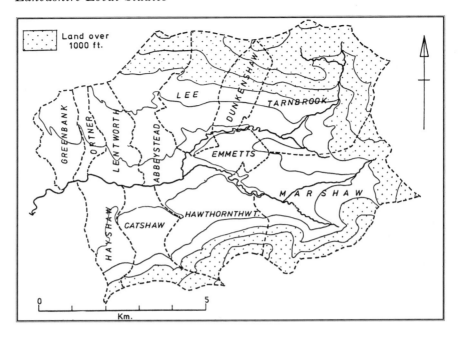

FIGURE 4.    Over Wyresdale vaccaries, 1833

boundaries, stretching up to the moorland watershed on each side of the valley, continued to be recognised in the nineteenth century (see Figure 4). Bleasdale had four vaccaries (Blindhurst, Fairsnape, Hazelhurst and 'between the Brokes') in its great amphitheatre scooped out of the fells, but the northern part of the township formed the separate pasture of 'Calder and Grysdale'. This was physically divided from the vaccary lands by the earthwork named on modern maps as Calder Dyke and apparently marked as 'the fence' on a sketch map of Bleasdale drawn in the sixteenth century.[1]

Out of the cattle-ranching economy of the forests in the thirteenth and early fourteenth centuries there developed a landscape of small pastoral hamlets during the later Middle Ages. The vaccaries formed the framework within which the new settlement pattern evolved, each vaccary coming to be divided and leased in smaller units, particularly after the forest law was relaxed in 1507. By the middle of the sixteenth century

---

[1]    R. Cunliffe Shaw, *Royal Forest of Lancaster*, p. 375; P.R.O., MPC 77, f. 10d.

most had become hamlets of small farms and cottages, and the vaccary lands, which had previously been the domain of the lord's livestock, now supported a considerable human population.

A contrasting element in the upland forest landscape was provided by the parks enclosed to provide a safe haven for the lord's deer. These were probably comparatively heavily wooded areas which had been enclosed with a wooden stockade or pale in the thirteenth or early fourteenth century. Four major parks were associated with the Lancashire forests: Ightenhill Park, on the edge of the forest of Pendle (recorded from 1296); Musbury Park, enclosed in 1304–5 on land outside the forest of Rossendale;[1] and, within the bounds of Bowland forest, Radholme Park (recorded 1322) and Leagram Park (recorded 1348).[2] How long the parks continued to be actively managed for hunting is difficult to ascertain.

In the case of Leagram Park, in the saddle between the Bowland and Longridge fells, just to the east of Chipping, we can chart the decline and eventual conversion of the deer park during the fifteenth and sixteenth centuries. By 1422 the hunting lodge had fallen into disrepair and the 'agistment' of the park (the right to receive payment from the owners of livestock grazing there) had been leased for ten years. The park had presumably ceased to be treated as a game reserve and was seen simply as another tract of land from which income from grazing could be received. By 1556, when it was disparked and converted into farmland, Leagram Park presented a picture of wilderness and neglect. At its lower end it contained

> a great carr and marsh ground . . . a very deep and wet carr, overgrown with thick ollerwood [alderwood] and a few hollies, hazels and thorns; also two great and barren mosses called Hoddes Mosse and the Parke Mosse . . . The pale of the said park . . . is in great decay and quite unable to keep any deer in the park, if there were any there.[3]

In this case lordly indifference appears to have preserved a piece of landscape in something approaching its 'natural' state. But this was the exception. In the forest landscapes the principal theme is that direct lordly influence, in the form of active exploitation of the resources of the upland pastures through the system of vaccaries, retarded the development of the

---

[1]  G. H. Tupling, op. cit., p. 15.

[2]  R. Cunliffe Shaw, *Royal Forest of Lancaster*, p. 426 (Radholme Park 1322 reference).

[3]  Quoted in T. C. Smith, *History of Chipping* (1894), pp. 192–3.

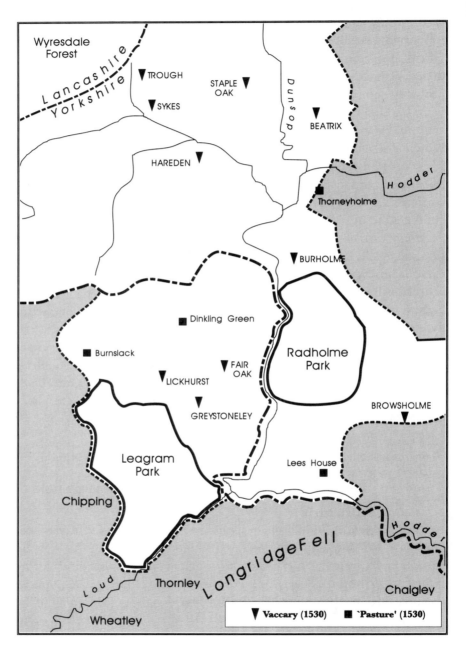

FIGURE 5. Parks and vaccaries in part of the Ribble Valley, 1530

peasant farming communities which were the main agents of landscape change in the lowlands and the woodland zone. Lordly influence delayed, but ultimately did not prevent, the settlement of the uplands. If the woodland zone was the frontier of active colonisation during the thirteenth century, the former forests were able to absorb considerable numbers of new settlers during the population expansion of the sixteenth century.

The agricultural and industrial revolutions wrought profound changes on the Lancashire landscape. Field drainage and mossland reclamation in the nineteenth century have rewritten much of the rural landscape of the coastal lowlands, while urbanisation and industrialisation have dominated the former woodland zone and the fringes of the upland forests. Nevertheless, legacies from the medieval landscapes described above abound, not only in churches and manor houses which contain medieval fabric, but in the positioning and alignment of landscape elements of later dates. The modern garden fences in the core of an old village may be determined by property boundaries originally laid out in the twelfth century; the sudden curve in the route taken by a country lane may follow the edge of an assart enclosed by a medieval frontiersman in the thirteenth century. Only detailed local historical research will make possible the elucidation of such minutiae. The tradition of local topographical study springs ultimately from a quest for enjoyment of the environment in which we live. As W. G. Hoskins put it in the introduction to *The Making of the English Landscape*, 'one cannot understand the English landscape and enjoy it to the full, apprehend all its wonderful variety from region to region (often within the space of a few miles), without going back to the history that lies behind it'.

## Acknowledgment

We would like to thank the rector of Stonyhurst College for permission to reproduce the drawing in Figure 3, which is taken from the college's 1733 estate map.

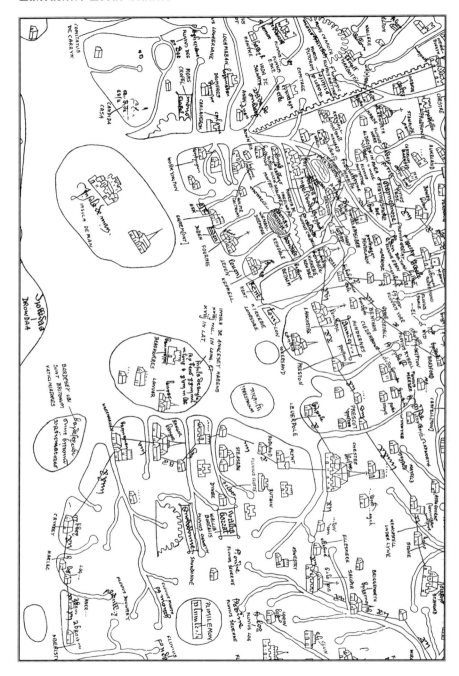

FIGURE 1. The Gough Map

# Through a glass darkly – the Gough Map and Lancashire

*Mary Higham*

THROUGHOUT the time I have known Diana and her work, I have always been impressed by her knowledge and enthusiasm for local history in general and Lancashire history in particular. One of her many areas of expertise concerns maps, with an obvious emphasis on maps of Lancashire. There are many people, myself included, who have enjoyed and learned a great deal from her lectures on 'the traveller and his maps', and my choice of the Gough Map as the basis of this article must not be taken as suggesting that Diana's knowledge is in any way deficient. In addition, as will become obvious from the sources quoted later, there is an already existing *corpus* of published material on this important document, so I feel I must emulate A. G. Hodgkiss,[1] in trusting that this article will 'add to the enjoyment of the converted' rather than 'persuading an unbeliever of the attractions of early maps'.

The Gough Map takes its name from Richard Gough, who purchased it for half-a-crown at an auction in 1774.[2] It is currently in the Bodleian Library, with two facsimiles having been published, in 1870 by the Ordnance Survey and in 1958 in a joint venture by the Bodleian Library and the Royal Geographical Society. The original map, made up of two joined skins of vellum, some 49 inches from north to south, gives the names of certain places in England, Scotland and Wales, and also sketches in certain roads linking some of these places. The road network recorded is much denser in the south of England than for areas further north, and inaccuracies of location occur in direct correlation with the distance from

---

[1] A. G. Hodgkiss, *Discovering Antique Maps* (4th edn, Shire Publications, 1983), p. 3.
[2] E. J. S. Parsons, *The Map of Great Britain c. 1360 known as the Gough Map* (Oxford, 1958), p. 1.

London. It is probable, therefore, that the map was compiled in the south, possibly for use by 'official' travellers, rather in the same way that the Roman itineraries were used.

It is, however, unlikely that the map itself was ever used 'in the field', for expert examination has suggested that it had been fixed either on a board or a wall. Even fixed to a board its portability would have been suspect, for the actual map of Britain is some 45 inches in length (the north–south axis) and some 22 inches wide. The map itself is usually dated to the middle of the fourteenth century, from the palaeographical evidence and from the inclusion (or omission) of certain place-names the use of which can be dated fairly precisely from other sources. For example, the royal borough of Queenborough in Sheppey was founded in 1366 and named in honour of Queen Philippa, but is not shown and only the name 'Sheppey' appears on the map. That Whalley Abbey, unlike the other major monastic houses in the area, is not named would also support the dating, for the monks only moved from Stanlow in 1296,[1] and it took some little time for them to construct adequate conventual buildings because of problems with the supply of good building stone and timber. Even the church was not begun until 1330,[2] so the Cistercian house of Whalley would scarcely have warranted inclusion, being unfinished and probably most uncomfortable for the high-status visitors who would have had access to the Gough Map.

It has been suggested that this was an official map for government use,[3] probably intended for use by royal couriers, royal officials and the judiciary, the people most likely to travel around the country as a whole rather than just in one small area.[4] If this was indeed the case, this particular group of people may well have determined what was included on the map.

Following medieval convention, the 'top' of the map is east, which poses some initial problems of orientation for the modern reader, this not

---

[1] Not *c.* 1175, as quoted by Michael Morris, *The Archaeology of Greater Manchester*, vol. I (G.M.A.U., 1983). This date is probably the date of the foundation of the monastic centre at Stanlow on the Mersey, by John Halton, Constable of Chester. The monks left this site at the end of the thirteenth century and relocated at Whalley, although they still retained the estates which had been attached to Stanlow.

[2] L. Butler and C. Given-Wilson, *Monasteries of Great Britain* (1979), p. 387.

[3] B. P. Hindle, *Medieval Roads* (2nd edn, Shire Publications, 1989), p. 17.

[4] That the distances on the map were apparently computed in a unit very close to the old French mile of 1.25 statute miles possibly supports this theory: see B. P. Hindle, 'The Towns and Roads of the Gough Map *c.* 1360' *The Manchester Geographer*, new series, vol. 1, no. 1 (Autumn 1980), p. 41.

being helped by the omission of Morecambe Bay and the Wyre, which results in the distortion of the coastline and an increase in the extent of the Fylde. Even so, the standard of cartography is surprisingly high considering the suggested date of compilation, there being no maps of even comparable accuracy until Saxton drew his county maps in the late sixteenth century. As can be seen from Figure 1, which shows that section of the Gough Map covering Lancashire, Westmorland and some of Yorkshire, there had obviously been some rationale behind the selection of the information to be included. Two 'district' names shown – *Kendale* and *Aundernes* [Amounderness] – are placed in gold cartouches on the original map. Not including the rivers, which are all shown in the conventional medieval fashion as issuing from lakes (including Windermere, which is specifically named), there are only fourteen separate places shown for Lancashire, with a further eight for Westmorland, implying a *raison d'être* for the choice of those particular places. What is particularly striking, given that the Gough Map was intended for travellers, is the paucity of information regarding roads within the area – only two are shown in Lancashire, and one fringing the county to the east.

Even in the medieval period it would have been essential that important messages got through quickly, and it is unlikely to be a coincidence that the few roads shown in the North West are apparently on the line of important Roman routeways. The northern stretches of the road identified as 'M4'[1] by Parsons (London–Newcastle-under-Lyme, Warrington, Wigan, Preston, Lancaster, Kendal, Shap, Penrith, Carlisle) correlate well with a general northern route identified by Margary.[2] The Skipton–Settle–Kirkby Lonsdale group of places also lies on what Margary suggests is a putative Roman road, through Ingleton and linking with his route 7c east of the Lune at Kirkby Lonsdale.

Hindle, although agreeing that 'some of the lines follow Roman roads',[3] has certain reservations regarding the use of such roads in the medieval period, commenting that 'it does not follow that those roads were in use or even passable'. He implies that there had been little or no maintenance of the road network of Britain for some seven centuries.

---

[1] E. S. J. Parsons, op. cit., p. 36.
[2] I. D. Margary, *Roman Roads in Britain* (3rd edn, 1973): road refs. 70a, 70b, 70c, 70d, 705, 7c (from Overburrow), 806, 707, 7d, 7e.
[3] B. P. Hindle, 'Towns and Roads of the Gough Map', p. 44.

If one then takes into account his further comment that 'no major roads were constructed after the Romans left until the Turnpike Era', the implication seems to be that traffic on the move consisted of pedestrians, men on horseback and pack-horses. If this was indeed the case, one has to wonder at the temerity of the Prince of Wales who, at the end of the thirteenth century, was apparently unable to campaign in Scotland without his lion, 'which travelled in a special cart and enjoyed its own commisariat arrangements'.[1] Other records relating to the Edwardian wars against the Scots suggest that decent well-made roads (apparently following the line of earlier Roman roads) were in existence on both sides of the border, enabling large and heavy equipment to be used and allowing the rapid transit of lighter goods. For example, 'wages money was conveyed from York to Stirling in the summer of 1304 in two carts each pulled by five horses, taking only seven days, a rate of over 30 miles a day'.[2]

It could be argued that the easier routes afforded by the Roman roads on the eastern side of the country meant that they were more likely to be kept in repair, but evidence exists to suggest that in the North West, too, Roman roads remained and continued in use. This is not really surprising, for they usually took the best available routes through very difficult terrain, and there were no sensible alternatives. For example, the record of the *Quo Warranto* proceedings of 1293 includes a reference to the *via regia* through the middle of the forest of Ingleborough,[3] which is the Roman road (Margary 73) from Bainbridge to Ingleton. This road, although very direct, takes a far from easy route over the fells, reaching a height of 614 metres [2014 feet], but – as the petitioners noted – the alternative was a detour of some '50 leagues'. Even allowing for a degree of poetic licence in the distances stated, the detour must have been quite unacceptable. That the line of this Roman road, over Cam Fell, was indeed the best available route is illustrated by its continuing in use through to modern times, even being improved by Fothergill as part of the Richmond to Lancaster turnpike in the mid-eighteenth century. Despite the importance of this east–west route, that it was omitted from

---

[1]  G. W. S. Barrow, 'Land routes – the medieval evidence', in A. Fenton and G. Stell (eds.) *Loads and Roads in Scotland and Beyond* (Edinburgh, 1984), p. 53.

[2]  Quoted by G. W. S. Barrow, op. cit., p. 52.

[3]  M. Hartley, J. Ingilby, D. S. Hall and L. P. Wenham (eds.), *Alexander Fothergill and the Richmond to Lancaster Turnpike* (North Yorkshire County Record Office Publications, no. 37, 1985).

the Gough Map would seem to suggest that the map provided only very basic information regarding major routes in the North West for the medieval traveller who was unfamiliar with the area.

Additional and more detailed local information, as well as suitable overnight accommodation and other necessities, could, however, be obtained at the various places shown on the map. It cannot be coincidence that, with the exception of Whalley, the major religious houses are shown, including the Premonstratensian houses of Shap and Cockersand [*cokersand*], the Cistercian abbey of Furness [*fournes*], and the Augustinian priory of Cartmel [*kartmell*]. In the medieval period these were the equivalent of the modern 'motel', providing food and shelter for any *bona fide* traveller. The quality of such provision depended on the status of the traveller. Ohler notes that 'accommodation, service and care should be suited to the visitor's rank' and goes on to quote from a commentary on St Benedict's rule regarding hospitality: 'for it is not right that bishops and counts should be placed with poor people, abbots and strangers'.[1] If means allowed, a separate bedroom was to be offered. Like the accommodation, the quantity and quality of the food offered varied, but even the poorest traveller might count on soup, possibly bread and cheese, and weak beer. The rich traveller would expect to fare better, for there were other considerations to be taken into account besides that of the Christian duty of the monks to provide appropriately. It was the well-to-do and important person who was most likely to repay the kindness with 'treasure on earth' – provision of protection, assignment of property or privileges and, at least, expensive votive offerings.

The provision of overnight hospitality would not have been the only advantage for the traveller. Because the monastic houses held lands over such wide areas they were ideally placed to provide essential information regarding local routes which linked up with the major road networks shown on the Gough Map. Cockersand Abbey, for example, held large areas of land in Amounderness, some forty separate places being named in its Chartulary[2] together with over eighty places south of the Ribble in

---

[1]  N. Ohler, *The Medieval Traveller* (1989), pp. 82–3.
[2]  W. Farrer (ed.) *The Chartulary of Cockersand Abbey*, vol. 1, parts 1 and 2, Chetham Society, new series, xxxviii and xxxix (1898).

Leyland, West Derby, Makerfield and Salford hundreds.[1] As might be expected, it had large holdings in Lonsdale as well.

Many of the parcels of land defined in the charters have roads as part of their boundaries, these roads obviously being in existence and in use when the documents were first drawn up. The following three examples illustrate the type of reference found within the Cockersand material:

> Grant in frankalmoign from Roger, son of Henry [to the monks of Cockersand], of three strips of land in Stainall; one in the Longfurlong in the southern part of the town, extending from the *highway* called Alsergate to the *way* running between Stainall and Combelaw [SD 1246–1268].[2]

> Quitclaim by Ralph, son of William de Garstang [to the canons of Cockersand] of all his right in three acres of land in Hutton . . . extending in length from the ditch of Swain, son of Robert de Hutton, unto the *wain-gate* [ road suitable for carts and wagons] on the west [SD 1236–1246].[3]

> Grant in frankalmoign from Margery de Pennington [to the canons of Cockersand], of a portion of her land in Pennington, within these bounds, from Oldmiln-ford going up the *road which comes from Bedford*, following that road towards the church to a certain ditched place [SD 1220c–1246].[4]

Furness Abbey had lands both local to Beckansgill and also extending deep into the Lake District, and would have been well placed to aid travellers in those areas. What is rather more surprising is that the Lancashire abbeys had lands in Yorkshire, particularly within the Mowbray honour of Burton-in-Lonsdale (Figure 2). For these areas, too, the monks would have been able to provide information about the best routes to take, For example, there appears to have been a route from the Furness grange at Newby through the forest of Mewith, crossing the Hindburn at 'Furnessford' (SD 663669) and the Lune by Castle Stede [Hornby], then possibly using closes called 'Furness' in Arkholme as 'overnight stock stances' for cattle or sheep. continuing to the abbey grange at Beaumont (SD 485652), close to Hest Bank on the shores of Morecambe Bay, which is still a recognised starting point for the hazardous journey to their grange

---

[1] W. Farrer (ed.) *The Chartulary of Cockersand Abbey*, vol. 2, part 1, Chetham Society, new series, xl (1898); vol. 2, part 2, xliii (1900); and vol. 3, part 1, lvi (1905). Hereafter all references to the Chartulary of Cockersand Abbey will be *Cockersand*.

[2] *Cockersand*, vol. 1, part 1 (1898), p. 120.

[3] *Cockersand*, vol. 2, part 1 (1898), p. 421.

[4] *Cockersand*, vol. 2, part 2 (1900), p. 713.

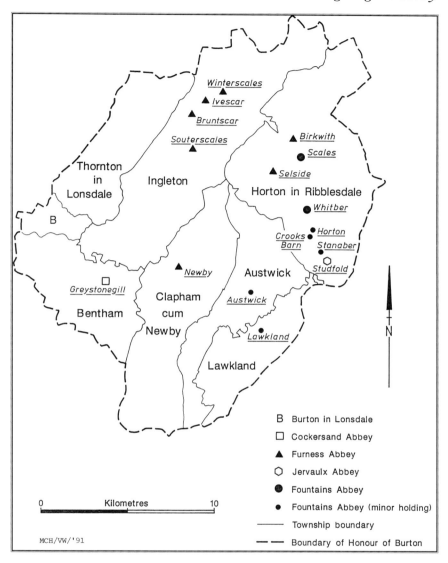

FIGURE 2.   Monastic holdings in the honour of Burton

'over sands'. Access to the specialist knowledge of the 'over sands' routes, essential today, would have been equally invaluable to the medieval traveller, particularly if he were a stranger to the area. Some idea of the possible consequences of an 'over sands' crossing were noted by the abbot

35

of Furness, who in 1325 recorded that even 'at the ebb tide, up to sixteen people could be drowned at any one time'.[1]

One of the attractions of early maps noted by Richard Muir is that 'the old map is a safer conveyance than a real time machine because it does not put us in risk of . . . hazards' which would have been an integral part of the traveller's lot at the time the map was compiled.[2] One such hazard would have been that posed by the 'over sands' crossings. Another was that of rivers. It is often forgotten that today's rivers are emasculated versions of the ones which flowed in the medieval period. They are now much better controlled, both by regulation of run-off and by extraction of water for greatly increased human consumption. Documentary evidence for a period a century or so before the Gough Map illustrates the potential problems of crossing even at recognised places. The assize rolls for Lancashire 1246/7 give several examples:

*Leyland Hundred*
Thomas son of Siward le Oterhunte fell from a horse in Yarewe water and was drowned . . . verdict, misadventure

*Wapentak of Salfordshyre*
Richard son of Eugenia de Ratcliue drowned from a horse in Irwel water . . . verdict, misadventure

*Blackburneschyre*
Robert de Grimsharke was drowned in Rybel water . . . verdict, misadventure

*Wap. of Lonnesdal*
Henry son of Alice of Melling was drowned in Lone water . . . verdict, misadventure

Gilbert Grosman was drowned in Candovere water [Conder]. No judgment as Adam de Kellet, who should have attached Mabel de Caldecotes, first finder, to attend the assize had not done so

One Ivo, a lay brother [*conversus*] of Foprnell [Furness] was drowned from a horse in Levene water . . . verdict, misadventure[3]

---

[1]  This 1325 extract is taken from the display at Furness Abbey (English Heritage), which quotes the Society of Antiquaries, London, as its source.
[2]  R. Muir, *Portraits of the Past* (1989), p. 153.
[3]  J. Parker (ed.), *Lancashire Assize Rolls, 30–31 Henry III*, R.S.L.C., first series, xlvii (1904), pp. 65, 69, 87, 104, 105, 102.

As even local people, who presumably knew the problems posed by local rivers better than travellers from the south of the country, could be drowned, the emphasis placed by the compiler of the Gough Map on the location of the rivers is not surprising.

As has been demonstrated, the inclusion of the monastic houses can be easily explained. There would have been certain problems, however, as the monasteries themselves were in the north of the county and, in all cases, in somewhat remote locations. There would have been a need for more convenient stopping places south of the Ribble. On the map west of Wigan [. . . *ig* . . .] there is a place with a completely indecipherable name, which Parsons suggests could be Burscough. Certainly there was an Augustinian priory there, and in view of the role played by monastic houses with regard to travellers this possibility should be borne in mind. An alternative suggestion is Ormskirk, a pre-Conquest ecclesiastical centre and a medieval borough.[1] The prior and canons of Burscough had been granted a market at Ormskirk by Edward I in 1286 and, Philpott notes, the town was probably granted a borough charter in the same year. A settlement with borough status would have provided a good service to travellers. There would have been inns where accommodation could be obtained, and tradespeople would have provided essential services. The boroughs were administrative and judicial centres (the gallows often associated with the latter being a useful impetus to trade, hangings being a favoured medieval spectator sport, with people coming to town to watch and take the opportunity to buy and sell goods). Local gentry, too, often had their town houses in the boroughs, and these also provided quality accommodation and information for travellers of high status.

Possibly for the reasons outlined above, there does seem to be a strong bias towards boroughs in the 'lay' places named on the Gough Map. Indeed, there seems to be a certain emphasis on those places with firm royal connections. Liverpool [*leverpole*], Wigan [. . . *ig* . . .], Preston [*preston*] and Lancaster [*lancastre*] were all royal boroughs, with Lancaster the *caput* of a large honor. Clitheroe [*clederhowe*], which was the *caput* of the honour of Clitheroe, encompassing the hundred of Blackburnshire together with Bowland, also had its borough charter (probably obtained by the de Lacy family) and by the early fourteenth century was, like

---

[1]  R. A. Philpott, *Historic Towns of the Merseyside area: a survey of urban settlement to c. 1800* (Liverpool Museum Occasional Papers, no. 3, 1988), p. 43.

Lancaster, firmly in royal hands. The honour of Clitheroe had passed to Thomas of Lancaster, nephew of Edward I, on his marriage with Alicia, daughter and sole heiress of Henry de Lacy, earl of Lincoln, in 1294. Following Thomas' revolt in 1322, and his subsequent beheading at Pontefract, his lands were forfeit to the Crown and henceforth were effectively under royal control.

Warrington [*w . . . ington*], created by William le Boteler before 1233[1] and Prescot [*prescot*] were apparently both seigneurial boroughs, but it is not possible to date the creation of that at Prescot because the charter has not survived.[2] There are, however, numerous references to burgages, which Beresford considers to be sufficient evidence for borough status, commenting that 'in the absence of borough charters we must rely on the accidental mention of the place as a borough in some other documentary source, or on the presence of burgages'.[3] Manchester, too, was a borough, and a rental of 1282 includes an item of £7 3s. 2d. for burgage rents, 'which would imply that there were approximately 143 burgage properties' at that date.[4]

This leaves just two places to be discussed. The identification of *Wynwyke* with Winwick is obvious. This place, although not a borough, was an important pre-Conquest ecclesiastical centre for a very large area, and it continued to have this function until well into modern times. It is very close to Newton-le-Willows, the administrative and judicial centre for the same territory. Winwick also lies on the Roman road. These factors might well explain its inclusion on the Gough Map. The Ordnance Survey facsimile identifies the final place, apparently close to Winwick, as *stowe*, for which there is apparently no record in the place-nomenclature of the county, while Parsons interprets the name as '*k . . . ow . . .*', which he suggests is Knowsley. This would seem to be unlikely, particularly in view of its position on the Gough Map relative to the places identified as Wigan and Prescot. Where and what *stowe* or *k . . . ow . . .* was cannot be easily ascertained, unless detailed research in the vicinity of Winwick reveals some clues.

---

[1]  Ibid., p. 49.

[2]  Ibid., pp. 22–4.

[3]  M. W. Beresford, *National Register of Archives: Annual Report and Bulletin of the West Riding Northern Section No. 8* (1965), p. 3.

[4]  M. Morris, op. cit., p. 38.

Detailed local research has certainly helped to provide what I see as a rather more satisfactory explanation for the inclusion of Bentham on the Gough Map. Hindle[1] suggests that this township, lying just outside Lancashire, was included because it lay on a route between Settle and Lancaster. It is true that, latterly, until the building of the M62, coaches from Leeds and Bradford regularly used the route through Skipton to Settle and then through Bentham to get to Morecambe and its Illuminations, and it is possible that such a route has been used for centuries. However, although Bentham was an ancient ecclesiastical centre it was not the *caput* of a major medieval estate. Its claim for inclusion may lie instead in its position relative to the forest of Bowland, for it does appear to have lain on a well-known routeway linking Bowland with Lonsdale in the medieval period. This routeway was apparently known and used by the Scots, who made periodic incursions into the area. There was a series of invasions, both 'formal' and 'informal', in the twelfth and thirteenth centuries, and these seem to have created havoc in the North West, but it is the record of the early fourteenth-century activities of the Scots which might be thought to provide reasons for Bentham's inclusion on the Gough Map.

The early fourteenth-century series of raids seems to have been in part a response to bad harvests and the incidence of cattle *murrain*, as a result of the climatic deterioration which began in about 1315,[2] and also as a result of the weakness of Edward II, which allowed the Scots, apparently with the connivance of Thomas of Lancaster,[3] to 'make deep forays as far south as the West Riding and Lancashire'.[4] The Scots seem to have come south to settle old scores and, if possible, to get grain and cattle – a practice which continued for centuries – and this certainly caused problems in parts of Lancashire and the adjoining areas of the West Riding. As a result of Scottish raids many of the settlements were either excused contributions to subsidies, or were assessed at a much lower rate, with the large monastic houses also suffering great losses. The smaller landowners felt the effects of the raids. The *Inquisition Post Mortem* taken in May 1325, on the death of Mathew de Burgh, stated that he held a 'ruinous messuage,

[1]   B. P. Hindle, *Medieval Roads*, p. 20.

[2]   J. M. Stratton and J. H. Brown (ed. R. Whitlock), *Agricultural Records, AD 220–1977* (2nd edn, 1978).

[3]   J. Edwards, 'The cult of Thomas of Lancaster and its iconography', *Yorkshire Archaeological Journal*, lxiv (1992), pp. 105–6.

[4]   J. Kershaw, 'The Scots in the West Riding, 1318–19', *Northern History*, xvii (1981), pp. 231–9.

10 bovates of land laying waste from the devastations of the Scots and 20 acres of pasture called *Groskolm* [Gruskham] destroyed by the Scots', this some three years after the major incursion of 1322.[1]

Gruskham (SD 683669) is one of the three large farms lying to the south of Mewith Lane, mentioned earlier as part of a probable route between Newby and Furness Abbey. Even today, Mewith Lane (SD 708670 – SD 640678) exhibits all the characteristics of a major stock route, formerly with wide verges which are still recognisable in places, either by lines of 'ancient' hedges parallel with the modern road, or marked by encroachments of squatter settlements whose rear boundaries are obviously fixed by the line of the former track. The settlement at Gruskham would not have been readily visible to any band of raiders moving along this track and this would suggest one of two things – either the *I.P.M.* is inaccurate, or the present route from the Forest of Bowland via the Cross of Greet and Burn Moor to Bentham was well known in the medieval period, not only to local travellers but also by those from much further afield. The evidence suggests that the latter is more likely.

The subsidy records show that Slaidburn, *caput* of the former de Lacy estates in Bowland, suffered quite badly from the Scots at this time. As Slaidburn is somewhat 'off the beaten track', even as far as major medieval routes northwards are concerned, this implies that the settlement, like Gruskham and Bentham, lay on a route over the fells both known and previously used by the Scots. There is certainly evidence surviving which suggests that the Slaidburn–Bentham route was used by drovers, with a close named Galloway Parrock[2] off the track which leads from Burn Moor down to the Wenning and on to Bentham. The field name itself is significant, particularly when applied to a close with two gated 'stock funnels' from the lane, one at the top and another at the bottom. This would suggest a stock stance (an 'overnight stopping place') or a form of 'by-pass' to avoid the mixing-up of herds or flocks moving to and from Bentham.

It is not possible to say how old such a drove route might be, but the 1325 evidence, together with that afforded by the inclusion of Bentham on the Gough Map, would suggest that it may have already been in use and well known, even in Scotland, in the medieval period. Certainly it

---

[1]  P.R.O., *Cal. Inq. Post Mortem*, vol. viii (1909), p. 53.
[2]  West Yorkshire Archives, Sheepscar, Leeds: BD 118.

was one of two medieval routes (the other being via Bowland Knotts and Keasden) linking the forest of Burton with the forest of Bowland. Bentham's position, at the junction of two routeways, one linking Settle with Lancaster, and another linking the *caput* of Bowland at Slaidburn (itself a 'failed' new town and the medieval judicial centre of West Staincliffe wapentake[1]) with Lonsdale and routes further north, would explain its inclusion on a map which concentrated on recording the high-status boroughs and major monastic houses.

From six centuries on, it is only possible to speculate about the motives behind the compilation of the Gough Map, the reasons for the inclusion of certain places (and the omission of others), and the paucity of roads shown for Lancashire and the North West. What the Gough Map does provide is a fascinating 'window' into the fourteenth century. As might be expected of a medieval window, the view is limited and somewhat blurred. I hope Diana feels that the effort of peering through it has been worthwhile.

## Acknowledgment

I would like to express my thanks to Val Winchester, who drew the map used as Figure 2.

---

[1]  M. C. Higham, unpublished MA thesis, University of Hull (1978).

# Fowl play? Keeping and stealing geese in Lancashire, 1550–1850

*Alan Crosby*

I N *Lark Rise to Candleford* Flora Thompson describes an elderly woman whose father, when a young man in the late eighteenth century, kept 'a cow, geese, poultry, pigs, and a donkey cart to carry his produce to the market town. He could do this because he had commoners' rights and could turn his animals out to graze'. His daughter had tended the beasts: she had to 'mind the cow and drive the geese to the best grass patches. It was strange to picture Sally, a little girl, running with her switch after the great hissing birds on the common, especially as both common and geese had vanished as though they had never been'. Enclosure of the commons, and the abolition of commoners' rights, had put an end to goose-keeping among the cottagers of Lark Rise.[1]

In characteristically lyrical fashion this passage evokes a scene typical of much of rural England two hundred years ago. Although Flora Thompson described Oxfordshire, geese grazing on the common would have been an equally familiar sight in late eighteenth-century Lancashire. There were differences, though. In Lancashire, as in parts of East Anglia and Yorkshire, urban growth and the consequent demand for food had given early encouragement to a trade in geese which developed beyond the domestic scale. This paper considers some of the evidence for goose-keeping in Lancashire before the 1850s. The first part is a general survey, while the second looks in more detail at the quarter sessions records which relate to the stealing of geese in the period 1623–48. These records, as well as being of intrinsic interest, shed valuable light upon the keeping of

---

[1]  F. Thompson, *Lark Rise to Candleford* (O.U.P., 1954 edition), p. 74.

geese – and upon the ways and habits of those who could not resist temptation.

## *The use of a goose*

Those sentimental Victorian paintings of tranquil rural scenes and cottages garlanded in flowers often include a few geese and hens, perhaps tended by an apple-cheeked old lady or a demure maiden in a spotlessly white apron. Although their detail is often false, the images are authentic. Geese, together with ducks and hens, were part of the important, but almost unsung, domestic agriculture of smallholders and cottagers throughout the country. They provided eggs for the family and, when death came as the end, meat as well. With luck there would have been a surplus of eggs, to be sold for cash, while those with a small flock might also sell birds on a local market.

Geese were relatively low in value when compared with the larger livestock, and even with pigs, but to the smallholders and cottagers they were valuable and very economical, as they cost little or nothing to feed. It was proverbial that with a pig everything could be used apart from the squeal, and the same was true of a goose, as it still is in France.[1] An adult goose had plenty of meat, which was especially appreciated because it was rich and fatty. For those who could keep it, buy it or steal it, a goose was a welcome change in what was often a monotonous and frugal diet. Thus, goose was associated throughout Europe with feast days and festivities – notably, of course, Michaelmas and Christmas.[2] In some parts of Lancashire a 'goosefeast' was traditionally held at or near Michaelmas. Nicholas Blundell makes several references in his diaries to the Crosby Goosefeast, which was a special occasion not only for the villagers but also for the local gentry, who joined with them in communal celebration.

---

[1]  James Bentley says of goose-killing in the Dordogne that 'when they [the women] have finished, not a morsel remains on their work-benches. The feathers are saved for pillows and duvets. Even the feet of a goose eventually make glue . . . Of the rest is created all manner of delicious dishes. As usual nothing goes to waste', *Life and Food in the Dordogne* (Weidenfield & Nicholson, 1986), 59–60. I have found no record of a Lancashire equivalent of *pate de foie gras!*

[2]  For example, Lesley Chamberlain notes that 'Roast goose was long the common man's festive dish, particularly in western Russia and the Baltics', *The Food and Cooking of Russia* (Allen Lane, 1982), p. 161.

Goose meat can be preserved, by smoking, salting, or cooking and sealing in its own fat, and lends itself well to all these methods. It could therefore be stored for future use and still remain more or less palatable. The eggs, much larger than hen's eggs, were widely claimed to be the best of all in baking, as well as being a substantial meal in their own right. Goose blood was traditionally used in Scotland to make a close relative of black pudding,[1] and it is reasonable to suppose that a similar dish was made in Lancashire. Goose fat is excellent for cooking and was universally valued in medical remedies – as a liniment and 'cure all' for chest complaints, a winter safeguard against colds, and as a base for ointments and salves. The harder feathers were used for quills and small brushes and, in cooking, for basting and applying melted fat to pans and dishes, while the soft feathers and down were prized for stuffing pillows and quilts.

## *Evidence for goose-keeping: probate inventories*

Goose-keeping, like other aspects of domestic agriculture, has left few specific records despite its ubiquity and importance: in Lancashire, as elsewhere, documentary evidence is limited and unsystematic. The apparent insignificance of poultry in national and regional terms means that they have not been the object of detailed research. It is, however, possible to build up at least a partial picture of the subject from scattered sources – probate inventories, farm and household accounts, and casual references in material relating to other topics. Probate inventories, widely recognised as a key source of information on early modern agriculture, have considerable potential, but they must be treated with caution. Their recording of poultry is erratic, and can be misleading.

In some areas local custom may have dictated that geese, ducks and hens were completely omitted from inventories: for example, those from pre-industrial Trawden 'showed no evidence at all of the keeping of poultry or geese'.[2] It is highly improbable that poultry were not kept, and deliberate exclusion is a likely explanation for their absence. Where poultry *are* included in inventories they are often recorded in what appears to be an unsystematic or sporadic fashion: in Colne chapelry and Pendle

---

[1]  F. M. McNeill, *The Scots Kitchen* (Blackie, 1929), p. 222.
[2]  R. Schofield, 'Trawden before the Industrial Revolution', *Lancashire Local Historian*, iii (1985), p. 7.

forest between 1580 and 1640 only 6.7 per cent of the inventories of *infra* (poorer) testators listed poultry, a suspiciously low proportion.[1] In instances where the deceased kept only a few hens or a couple of geese these may have been ignored by the appraisers, who only paid serious attention if there were sizeable flocks. On the other hand, in an admittedly tiny sample of early seventeenth-century inventories from Childwall, most included poultry or geese.[2] Differences in local inventory-making practice are almost certainly responsible for such variations across the county.

Sometimes geese were not listed in inventories although it is known from other sources – such as farm accounts or court cases – that they were kept. It has been suggested, on the basis of evidence from Manchester township, that 'presumably the tradition that barnyard fowls belonged to the wife rather than to the husband accounts for their absence from inventories'.[3] However this argument is contradicted not only by their inclusion in many inventories (including some from Manchester itself) but also by specific statements that the fowls belonged – as indeed did all else – to the husband.[4] If such a tradition really did exist, it was by no means general.

The terminology used in describing poultry is also arbitrary: there was no standardisation of description. Sometimes poultry are grouped with other livestock: thus, the inventory of Richard Aiskrigg of Gressingham (1558) includes 'Swyne geys & pulletts' worth seventeen pence, lumping together the low-value livestock in a miscellaneous category. Sometimes geese appear in separate entries, but more often they are grouped with ducks and hens. An entry in the inventory of Roger Day of Knowsley (1592) is typical: 'Duckes, gisse, & other pullone' worth five shillings. The use of the general labels 'pullen' and 'poultry' must often conceal the presence of geese. Other inventories are more specific, and so more helpful. In 1564 Lawrence Almond of Kirkham had 'thre geese & gandre' valued at two shillings; John Dale of Clitheroe (1574) had 'v Gyse' worth 2s. 6d. and 'vij hendes & a cocke' with the same value. It is sometimes

---

[1]   J. T. Swain, *Industry before the Industrial Revolution: north-east Lancashire, c. 1500–1640*, Chetham Society, third series, xxxii (1986), p. 49.

[2]   R. G. Dottie, 'Childwall: a Lancashire township in the seventeenth century', *T.H.S.L.C.*, cxxxv (1985), p. 5.

[3]   T. Willan, *Elizabethan Manchester*, Chetham Society, third series, xxvii (1980), p. 46.

[4]   See, for example, L.R.O., QSB 1/85/42, in which it is stated that the wife tended the flock, but that they were the husband's birds.

possible to ascertain the exact composition of the flock: Hugh Appleton of Bold, miller (1592) owned 'one goose and a gander and seven yonge geese' worth 2s. 3d., while John Dowson of nearby Winwick (1579) had 'one gander one gouse & iiij goslinges' worth twenty pence.[1]

## The commercial trade in geese

A distinction may tentatively be drawn between those who kept substantial flocks of geese and other poultry, perhaps on a commercial scale, and those with one or two birds purely for domestic use. The larger flocks were often found close to towns, although this is certainly not a hard and fast rule, and the evidence is subject to the general reservations about probate inventories outlined above. There are many examples: William Johnson of West Derby, a butcher (1613); William Darbyshire of Urmston near Manchester (1595), a husbandman; and George Darlington of Roby (1561), each had geese, hens and ducks worth ten shillings.[2] These are – in relation to poultry – large sums and imply sizeable flocks. At Chipping in the early seventeenth century several farmers kept large flocks of geese: James Dewhirst had fourteen birds, worth 6s. 8d., and Ellin Richmond had sixteen, worth eight shillings.[3] Proximity to the flourishing markets of Preston and Blackburn may have been significant here.

The major urban markets drew their food supplies from a ten- to fifteen-mile radius. Usually live birds were sent: in Liverpool in 1568 the corn merchants complained of 'gese tearyng [and] breakyng theyr sackes, destroying theyre corne in the market place upon the market dayes'.[4] The limited evidence available suggests that even in the late sixteenth century some Lancashire farmers had begun to raise poultry on a commercial scale to supply the growing urban communities with eggs and meat, or for organised sale to more distant purchasers. Such a trade was noted by

---

[1] L.R.O., WRW (L) 1558, Richard Aiskrigg of Gressingham; WCW 1592, Roger Day of Knowsley; WRW (A) 1564, Lawrence Almond of Kirkham; WCW 1574, John Dale of Clitheroe; WCW 1592, Hugh Appleton of Bold; WCW 1579, John Dawson of Winwick.

[2] L.R.O., WCW 1613, William Johnson of West Derby; 1593, William Darbyshire of Urmston; 1561, George Darlington of Roby.

[3] C. Ironside, 'The parish of Chipping during the seventeenth century', *T.H.S.L.C.*, cxxvii (1977), p. 39.

[4] J. A. Twemlow (ed.), *Liverpool Town Books, vol. 1, 1550–71* (Liverpool University Press, 1918), p. 402.

agricultural writers from the middle of the eighteenth century, but it must have originated well before that time.

The accounts of the Shuttleworth family of Gawthorpe near Padiham, between 1581 and 1621, support this view, at least as far as south Lancashire is concerned. They list regular payments for geese from Hoole, in the mosslands near Douglas estuary, where the family had estates. Eighteen geese were brought from there in April 1592, for example, and six more in September. Geese were also purchased from the Leigh area, which other contemporary evidence shows had a significant goose trade: nine birds were bought from Astley Green near Leigh in April 1592. These were long-distance purchases, comparable to the buying of cattle from Garstang and other fairs, and it is clear that the areas concerned were beginning to develop a specialist trade.[1]

In some parts of Lancashire this specialism was significant well into the nineteenth century. One such area was Martin Mere, only three miles from Hoole. In 1795 it was said that on the mere were 'turned a number of flocks of geese . . . brought from different parts of the county . . . Upon this Mere they continue till about Michaelmas'.[2] Although such flocks were perhaps small compared with those grazed on the Lincolnshire and Norfolk fens, which were driven to London for the Michaelmas and Christmas markets, they had assumed considerable importance in the regional economy and food supply by the late eighteenth century. Peter Brears notes that from the early 1790s geese were farmed on a large scale in Wensleydale, where previously they had been kept only by cottagers and grazed on commons. Each August, after the harvest, Dales geese were herded together and driven down in large flocks to Lancashire and the industrial West Riding to be fattened on stubble for Michaelmas and Christmas.[3] Even this could not meet the demand, and geese were imported to Lancashire from further afield: in 1835 Sir George Head observed a vessel from Drogheda unloading Irish geese at Clarence Dock, Liverpool.[4]

---

[1] J. Harland, *The House and Farm Accounts of the Shuttleworths of Gawthorpe*, Chetham Society, old series, xlvi (1858), pp. 653–4.

[2] J. Holt, *General View of the Agriculture of the County of Lancaster* (1795), p. 176.

[3] P. Brears, *Traditional Food in Yorkshire* (Edinburgh, 1987), pp. 110–11.

[4] Sir G. Head, *A Home Tour through the Manufacturing Districts of England in the Summer of 1835* (repr. Frank Cass, 1968), p. 27.

Fattening geese on stubble was an ancient custom. In the 1580s and 1590s the Shuttleworths usually bought geese twice yearly – 'green geese' (young birds which had been grazed on grass) between April and June, and 'field geese', which had grazed on commons and on harvest stubble, during September and October ready for Christmas.[1] Nicholas Blundell noted the practice in his journal for 16 September 1709: 'I had two Flocks of Gees brought which William Ainsworth had bought to put into the Stubble'.[2] The tradition of wintering geese on watersides and marshes is recalled in another entry in his diary. He made a decoy pond in 1711, and stocked it partly with geese: in December he recorded that 'I put up some Geese to feed in the Duckcoy it being the first time it has been put to use'.[3]

The price of a goose varied according to age, quality and season. In inventories before the 1620s the value of a full-grown bird is usually about sixpence, and that of a gosling two or threepence. This accords reasonably well with what is known of the market prices. The Shuttleworth accounts record payments of eightpence for a goose in 1584, 1s. 8d. for eight goslings in May 1586, and ten shillings for no fewer than thirty geese bought in June 1586 – the price then was fourpence each, probably because they were young birds. Prices mentioned in quarter sessions papers for the mid-seventeenth century are somewhat higher. In 1627 Robert Collinge of Castleton bought five geese for five shillings. Three years later Ellen Proctor of Hornby claimed to have paid one shilling, two flagons of ale and a loaf of bread for two geese sold to her by a pair of travelling women, and in 1628 a goose stolen in Didsbury was sold for elevenpence.[4] In comparative terms, geese were worth considerably more than other poultry, and were broadly equivalent in price to swine.

## Evidence for goose-keeping: the quarter sessions records

Although stealing geese and other livestock was a time-honoured pastime – in April 1522, for example, Thomas Butterworth was fined by the

---

[1]  J. Harland, op. cit.

[2]  J. J. Bagley (ed.), *The Great Diurnal of Nicholas Blundell, vol. 1, 1702–11*, R.S.L.C., cx (1968), p. 229.

[3]  Ibid., p. 309. The decoy was probably intended to attract wild geese, which were shot in considerable numbers in the coastal and mossland areas of the Lancashire plain.

[4]  L.R.O., QSB 1/38/39; 1/16/31; 1/35/41.

Accrington manor court because he was a 'petty thief, and takes his neighbours' geese away'[1] – not until the early seventeenth century do any detailed records survive. Thirty definite cases of goose-stealing between 1623 and 1648 have been identified.[2] The incidents are widely dispersed across the county, and although there are some geographical gaps – most of the Fylde and Leyland hundred are unrepresented – these are likely to be the result of the small statistical base. In contrast, the thefts show an unquestionable, and very pronounced, seasonality. No fewer than 92 per cent of cases occurred between October and January, and 44 per cent were in the peak month – November. This pattern is clearly related to the market for geese: they were fattened ready for Christmas sales, and so reached their maximum size and availability in early winter. It is striking that, despite the dark nights, there were no thefts at all between late January and the end of March.

## *The grazing of geese*

Many of the quarter sessions records refer to the use of commons for grazing geese, and this accords well with other contemporary evidence. The practice, in which geese grazed alongside cattle, goats and swine, was a widespread feature of 'traditional' agriculture everywhere in England. Its supposedly harmful effects were noted in the sixteenth century by Thomas Tusser – 'Some pester the common with jades and with geese'[3] – and the bitterness which was felt towards the enclosure of common land was summed up in the well-known seventeenth-century verse:

> The law locks up the man or woman
> That steals the goose from off the common
> But leaves the greater villain loose
> Who steals the common from the goose.[4]

---

[1] W. Farrer (ed.), *The Court Rolls of the Honor of Clitheroe*, vol. iii (1913), p. 40.

[2] There may well be other examples which are described in the Lancashire Record Office calendars simply as cases of 'theft'. Several earlier (pre-1623) quarter sessions cases are published in E. Axon, *Notes of Proceedings before Oswald Mosley, 1616–30*, R.S.L.C., xlii (1901), which deals only with the Manchester sessions.

[3] D. Hartley (ed.), *Thomas Tusser: his good points of husbandry* (1969), p. 62.

[4] Quoted by, among others, C. Hill, *The Century of Revolution, 1603–1714* (2nd edn., Routledge, 1980), p. 129.

In Lancashire the common pastures, lowland mosses, coastal marshes and upland moors were all widely used by farmers and cottagers for grazing their geese. This made sound economic sense: keeping geese gave a useful return from marginal land, and feeding them involved no financial outlay. The use of the commons for geese was frequently confirmed in specific local regulations: at Clitheroe, for example, the right to graze geese on Low Moor and other town commons was one of the privileges of the burgesses. A comparable use of marginal land may be seen in the moorland townships of upland Lancashire. In 1631 Thomas Wilson of Roeburndale testified that 'upon Saturday morneinge last beinge the viijth day of this Instante December betweene day breakinge and sun rysinge, Three of this Informers Geese and one of Richard Betts of Roeburndall his geese were stolne and taken off A Comon called Whitmore'.[1] Whit Moor, which is still open moorland, lies on the west side of Roeburndale at 750–1,000 feet above sea level.

Coastal marshes and saltings were also widely used. In November 1636, for example, three birds from the flock belonging to William Birkett of Middleton by Heysham were stolen at night from the marsh, where they had been put to graze.[2] The exploitation of such areas could be very intensive. At Preston the court leet resolved in 1597 that 'noe person nor persons . . . shall putt anie geese to the Marshe from the 25th of March untill after Midsummer', because overgrazing by geese during that period was damaging the marsh grass. In 1653 the closure period was extended until 15 August because of the loss 'especiallie to the poorer sorte of the ffree Burgesses', and the pinders were ordered to impound any offending birds. Nevertheless, only three years later there were numerous complaints about the 'wasteinge and destroyinge of ye Arbish [herbage] of ye marsh' by grazing geese.[3]

Where there were no moors and mosses, or where larger commons were distant or inaccessible, cottagers might use any available corners and fragments of roadside waste for grazing geese. In November 1628 Richard Lynney of Didsbury confessed that he 'did steall two Geesse forth of a Lane nere unto the house of Thomas Garnett of Withington, husbandman'.[4]

---

[1] L.R.O., QSB 1/112/22.
[2] L.R.O., QSB 1/60/20.
[3] A. G. Hewitson (ed.), *Preston Court Leet Records* (1905), pp. 28, 61.
[4] L.R.O., QSB 1/35/41.

Numerous minor place-names, such as Goose Lane in Castleton, Goose Green at Coppull and Pemberton, and Gander Green, Waddington, derive from this practice. Birds grazing by the roadside were particularly at risk from casual thieves: at Orrell in December 1640 two witnesses watched Margaret, wife of William Barton, as she 'did dryve seven geese unto a hedge & tooke one of them & put it Into her coate & carred the sayd goose away wither'.[1]

Geese were also kept in enclosed fields, which might receive their name as a result: Goose Hey at Rivington is an example. In the urban areas of the county, where geese were still being kept in the mid-eighteenth century, grazing was inevitably scarce. The birds would usually be kept in sheds or yards, but were sometimes turned into the streets to scavenge with the pigs. In sixteenth-century Manchester this caused a considerable public nuisance, and cases were brought before the court leet: 'divers inhabitants of this towne doe keepe geese and ducks ordinarye in ye highestreets to ye annoyance of divers of others the inhabitants of ye said towne'.[2] In rural areas, too, geese would be housed in barns and outhouses, with the other poultry: the pens or sheds sometimes gave rise to minor place-names, such as Goosecote Hill in Turton.

A fascinating instance of geese being kept in the dwelling house comes from Astley, one of the places where the Shuttleworths bought geese. In 1623 there was a dispute over tithe rights between Astley and Bedford townships, because their boundary ran through the house of Adam and George Hindley – indeed, through the middle of a bench in one of the rooms. Thomas Gellibrand, the owner of the Astley tithes, 'did demaund a tyeth goose of George Hindley . . . in respecte the yonger ones weare hatched in the newe house at the end of Adam Hindleyes ould howse'. The owner of the Bedford tithes won the case, however, 'by reason that the Gooselinges weare as hee [Hindley] said hatched under the higher end of a benche then in the newe howse, saying that soe much under the same benche as a goose could sit on was in [Bedford]'.[3]

Although enclosed fields might have seemed more secure, thefts from them were no less frequent than from the mosses, moors and byways. In

---

[1] L.R.O., QSB 1/242/33.

[2] A. G. Earwaker (ed.) *The Court Leet Records of Manchester, vol. II, 1586–1618* (Manchester Corporation, 1885), p. 196.

[3] L.R.O., DDHm (uncatalogued) Astley manor court roll: I am indebted to Angus Winchester for this reference.

November 1634 William Smith, a weaver of Atherton, was out walking at night when he 'came away by the dwelling of old Mistress Atherton . . . and [saw] a Company of Geese, in a close near unto thafforesaid house'. He saw his chance and 'tooke upp a stone and threw the same amongst the said Geese and struck one of the same Geese on . . . which said Goose hee confesseth hee presently tooke upp'. In the same month John Tickle of Ditton confessed that 'he came into a feilde neare adioyneinge to Willm. Martins house and then and there did kill three geese with a staffe and soe tooke them away with him'. Geese could also escape into adjacent fields: in November 1628 James Hardman of Barton stole two of his neighbour's geese 'in one of his own closes upon Sunday last about 7 of the clock'. His defence, which was unsuccessful, was that he thought they were his own birds.[1]

## Planned and unplanned thefts

Vagabonds and vagrants were often suspected of stealing geese, or were accused by those who, when found with the evidence, tried to shift the blame onto someone else. In at least one instance genuine vagrants were caught red-handed: Thomas Goulden of Winwick testified in October 1638 that 'yesternight betwixt 6 and 7 of the clocke this informer and one John Ormston of Hulme being togather, sawe neare to the Stone delph of Hulme twoo wandringe rogues, haveinge eyther of them a Goose under theire armes; the bigger of them did let the goose in his armes fall w[hi]ch thother little rogue tooke up'. The culprits had made an unfortunate error in choosing those particular geese, for when they and the birds were taken before the constable of Winwick he confirmed that the geese were indeed stolen, since one was from his own flock.[2] In another case, Ellen Proctor of Hornby, was questioned in December 1626 after the remains of geese were found in her house. She claimed that two travelling women had lodged there the previous night, and that 'shee did bye the said two geese of . . . the above said woemen upon the xiij of December last past', but she did not know who these women were.[3]

---

[1] L.R.O., QSB 1/146/43; 1/146/60; 1/51/48.
[2] L.R.O., QSB 1/210/38.
[3] L.R.O., QSB 1/16/31.

In 1631 William Whitecarre stole several geese at Fox Denton near Chadderton. For reasons which are unclear, but which he must later have regretted, he decided to involve Jane, wife of Hercules Smith of Chadderton, in his plans. Jane was very ready to gossip, and later told the magistrates how, in the early hours of a November morning, she was shown the geese in Whitecarre's house, and overheard him saying to another man that 'the geese kaickled as they came over the White Mosse'. Although the alarmed cackling of geese when in danger is the stuff of legend, this is the only one of the thirty cases where it is mentioned. Whitecarre admitted taking two of the geese, which he said he had found 'on the Mosse called Theale Moor' – another example of geese being grazed on the waste – but, in good Lancashire fashion, shifted the real blame onto not just any nameless rogue, but a real villain: the others 'hee had of a Man born in Yorkeshire whose name hee knoweth not'.[1]

These were apparently unplanned thefts, but others were carefully prepared and executed. Perhaps the clearest instance of a premeditated theft is from Samlesbury, where one night in December 1631 a gander was stolen from John Haidock. He suspected that the thief was a boy called Fish, who lived nearby in Balderstone. The boy eventually confessed to stealing the gander, but said that he had delivered the bird to Ann, wife of Alexander Garner of Balderstone, 'the said An haveinge entreated the said boy (and withall tould where hee might best be lurkeinge to doe the deed and also gave him a penny for his paines) to doe the deed & all'.[2]

Sometimes, in the dead of night, a passer-by would come upon thieves who had made a special expedition to steal birds. In another case from Samlesbury, John Whalley and an unknown accomplice stole geese from Ellen Smyth in November 1639. They were seen coming from the direction of her house at midnight, Whalley carrying 'in his handes twoe staves . . . and the other man . . . carried a burthen upon his backe'.[3] When, at midnight on a Tuesday in December 1636, Richard Pilkington of Lostock was going home, he 'did meete two men, Coming frowards Lostock, who carryed burdens upon their shoulders; in black poaks like unto cole poaks wherein seemed to bee things which stood out in lumps;

---

[1] L.R.O., QSB 1/99/65.
[2] L.R.O., QSB 1/97/63.
[3] L.R.O., QSB 1/225/11.

and the one of the said men carryed a Cugell in his hands'. The following morning another witness saw two women leave 'one Cole poake wherein was a goose dressed' in a nearby field.[1]

## Organised theft

The great estates were not immune from theft: the rich pickings which they offered probably represented an additional temptation to serious thieves. In November 1627, for example, 'there was a flocke of geese to the number of sixteene, or thereabouts, stolen out of the demaine of Rawcliffe, all in one night, being the goods of Richard butler of midle Rawcliffe'. This was the largest single theft recorded during the period 1623–48, and it was undertaken by professional thieves – two brothers from Pilling, five miles away across the moss, who were later found to be prime suspects in thefts of other livestock, including several sheep.[2]

There is evidence to suggest that in south-east Lancashire professional thieves stole livestock, including geese, on a substantial scale, with the aim of supplying the urban market – primarily in Manchester but also in Rochdale, Bolton and Bury. Several cases involved stealing geese for sale on Manchester market, or for informal distribution in other towns, and these examples parallel the organised thefts of other foodstuffs, including sheep and cows, cheeses and grain, which can also be traced in quarter sessions records.

Abraham Scolefield of Castleton, the sort of nosy neighbour whose detailed reporting of goings-on makes quarter sessions records so valuable and entertaining to the historian, claimed in October 1627 that James Whiteley 'came unto the place where this ex[aminant] dwelleth and brought with him on horse backe geese but howe manie [he] knoweth not which geese the said Whiteley unloaded at his brother John Whiteley's dooer'. After lengthy examination of witnesses it emerged that James Whiteley, who lived at Colne, had stolen twelve geese, five from Ambrose Barcroft in Foulridge and seven from George Emmott of Mackrode in Colne. He had brought the carcasses down to Castleton for sale to his brother's neighbours. The lengthy and detailed examinations of witnesses

---

[1]  L.R.O., QSB 1/179/50.
[2]  L.R.O., QSB 1/193/23.

in this case suggests that the whole affair was carefully planned and organised.[1]

In December 1636 two geese were stolen at Holcombe near Bury. A witness claimed that he had been 'goeinge towards Manchester in the company of . . . John Brooke, who drove a horse and pannyers covered with a cloth'. A woman, known to them both, joined them, 'which said wyfe asked the said Brooke what hee carried who answered hee carried fustian yarne, but afterwards the said wyfe as shee said saw geese without their heads'. It was said that the geese were sold on Manchester market,[2] a fate shared by those which had cackled coming over the moss. Jane Morris of Manchester, spinster, said that on Monday 16 November 1631 'by 7 of the clocke in the Morninge one William Whitecar and Robert Tompson brought five geese to the house where [she] dwelleth in Manchester and desired [her] to helpe them to sell the said geese and they would give her 4d. which shee refused to doe and afterwards the said Whitecar sould the said geese in the open market'. The network of gossip soon carried the news back to the owner of the geese, William Ratcliffe of Fox Denton, who heard that 'William Whitecare and Robert Tompson, being men of evill fame had five geese in Manchester which they offered to sell'.[3]

## Eating the evidence

For those who stole a single goose, whether casually or in a planned expedition on a dark autumn night, commercial gain was not usually a consideration. Instead, the thief looked forward to a feast. The eating of a succulent and tasty goose was an occasion for company – but that held its dangers. Questions might be asked about the origins of the bird, and word might slip out, to circulate among neighbours all too willing to report what they heard to the authorities. In July 1630 a witness said that he had seen 'the Carkasse of a goose' at the house of Abraham Hallowes of Rochdale, while others claimed that John Briggs had boasted that 'hee should have beene att the eatinge of a goose in the house of one Abraham

---

[1] L.R.O., QSB 1/38/39.
[2] L.R.O., QSB 1/179/25.
[3] L.R.O., QSB 1/99/6.

Hallawes'.[1] To issue an invitation to such a meal was to bestow an honour, but it was advisable to prepare the guest list carefully.

The thief might take the stolen bird to someone else's house, perhaps to hold a party. The three geese stolen from Middleton Marsh in November 1636 were intended as a feast for the local tradesmen. The suspects – Thomas Nickson, miller of Middleton; Thomas Storey, miller of Overton; and Richard Thompson of Gressingham in Lonsdale – were in league with Nicholas Turner, the blacksmith of Overton, and took two of the geese to his house, 'theone wherof the said Thomas Story Thomas Nickson & the said Turners wyfe did eate'.[2] After a spate of goose-stealing in Burscough in 1638 one unconvincing witness said that he 'did eate the sayd geese in a house in Ormskerke but which howse it was [he] nowe remembereth not'. However, another recalled that it was at the house of widow Poole, who seems to have received and cooked the stolen birds.[3] In November 1628, when Richard Marler had stolen two geese from a lane in Withington, it was said that 'the said Marler was at the eatinge of one of the said two geesse' at another man's house, while in 1618 Thomas Travis of Pendleton (Salford) admitted that on All Saints Day a goose had been roasted and eaten at his house but – somewhat implausibly – that he did not know who had eaten it 'since he was sicke and then in his bedd'.[4]

Perhaps the most complicated theft involved a goose stolen by Raphe Pircroft of Failsworth from Robert Odcrofte of Reddish in October 1647. Pircroft took the goose to the house of William Booth in Reddish and there, before witnesses, handed it over to Robert Chetham. Chetham then stole a horse and delivered the bird to John Jackson's alehouse at the Lancashire end of Stockport bridge. The reason for this odd procedure was that the thief, Raphe Pircroft, was 'purposinge to meete there upon Munday night after with some other Companie viz: the said Robert Chetham Willm. Booth John Jackson & the rest of John Jacksons ffamilie & to be merrie with [the] goose'. In fact, he was unable to get to the feast and the others enjoyed his stolen goose without him.[5] The thieves were discovered because the arrival of the goose at Jackson's alehouse, late at

---

[1]  L.R.O., QSB 1/79/40.
[2]  L.R.O., QSB 1/160/22.
[3]  L.R.O., QSB 1/198/60.
[4]  L.R.O., QSB 1/35/41; E. Axon (ed.), *Notes of Proceedings before Oswald Mosley, 1616–30 . . . and other Magistrates at Manchester Sessions*, vol. 1, 1616–22/3, R.S.L.C., xlii (1901), p. 64.
[5]  L.R.O., QSB 1/297/27.

night, had been observed by the Stockport watchmen and bridgemen, who also saw that the horse had no saddle or bridle – just a string in its mouth.

Even feasting upon a single stolen bird could therefore be risky: there was a good chance of somebody giving the game away. Thieves often seem to have been unsure how to deal with their bounty. The geese could not be kept alive, for there was the ever-present danger of discovery, and gossiping neighbours might comment upon their sudden appearance. Sending the stolen birds to market or selling them locally was potentially hazardous for the same reason. The birds therefore had to be killed, but this led to another difficulty: what was to be done with the large quantity of meat, and with the waste? The meat could be cooked and in some way preserved, or it could be discreetly given away to friends and neighbours. Such gifts might, if the thief was lucky, be construed as mere good neighbourliness and not too many questions would be asked. A goose was a welcome gift even among the gentry: Nicholas Blundell noted that when he and his family went visiting in February 1705 'we took a Fat Goose with us for Betty Fazakerley'.[1] But suspicions might well be aroused by a sudden onset of lavish generosity: herein, too, was the danger of discovery.

Jane Smith of Chadderton, 'called out of her bedd' by William Whitecarre in 1631, was told that 'Tom had brought two geese thither and they had rosted the one and boyulde the other and Tom had taken the Rost goose home and if shee would Come shee should have part of that was boyld'.[2] In January of that same year Ann, wife of James Winder of Aughton, admitted that, at Christmas, she 'being at the house of Oswold Heesham of Aughton saw Anne the wife of the said Oswold take a goose puddinge out of a pott on the fyre and gave this Informer a peece thereof'. Goose pudding was similar to steak and kidney pudding – meat cut up and boiled in a cloth with suet pastry, onions and herbs. Two days later, when Ann Winder again visited her neighbour, Anne Heysham 'gave to this Informer about half a goose pye', appealing to female solidarity by asking Ann Winder 'to keep secret for that she bought the goose at highfeild without knowledge to her husband'.[3]

---

[1]  J. J. Bagley (ed.), op. cit., p. 77.
[2]  L.R.O., QSB 1/99/65.
[3]  L.R.O., QSB 1/84/10.

## *Cooking your goose*

If immediate consumption was not intended, the meat might be preserved. It could be salted; made into a pie or pudding; or sealed in its own fat in earthenware pots and stored in a cool place. It was possible to keep goose pie for a considerable period. In his autobiography Adam Martindale recalled how, in the 1640s, his sister Jane was living in poverty in London and 'she concealed her straits from us. Onelie in a gentile way she writ for a goose-pie to make merrie with her friends; and a lustie one was immediately sent her, cased in twig worke' – the journey from Lancashire to London took a week and a half, but a good thick crust and a stout travelling basket were sufficient to ensure that the pie survived the journey.[1]

Inventories, which regularly list certain foods, such as dried or salted beef, cheese and bacon, which were kept in store for long periods, do not refer to goosemeat. The term 'salt meat', which is sometimes found, could include meats such as goose, lamb and pork, all of which were preserved by this method. Alternatively, local custom in the making of inventories may have determined that 'non-standard' commodities were excluded. For example, there are very few references to the preserved foods such as salted or dried fish which were probably found in many households. The inventory of Thomas Allen, a prosperous Warrington draper who died in 1593, does include 'four mugges of goose grese' valued at 7s. 0d., but this is the only instance found in a sample of more than three hundred pre-1600 probate inventories.[2]

The preserved or cooked meat of stolen geese was often discovered by the constables and their fellow-searchers. In December 1626 a search at the house of Francis Proctor in Hornby revealed 'Two geese cut in quarters, And likewise . . . three goose wings'. At Balderstone, in January 1627, Edward Carter and others searched the house of a neighbour, William Walton, and found 'eight quarters of geese salted in an earthern pott hid with clothes in a secrit . . . place And fower wings of geese and not more.'[3]

---

[1]  R. Parkinson (ed.), *The Life of Adam Martindale*, Chetham Society, old series, iv (1845), p. 8.
[2]  L.R.O., WCW 1593, Thomas Allen of Warrington.
[3]  L.R.O., QSB 1/16/31, 1/17/27.

The theft of sixteen geese from the Butler demesne at Rawcliffe in November 1637 was followed by impressively large finds of meat at the homes of Edward and John Williamson of Pilling. Thomas Sykes of Pilling tipped off the searchers by reporting that 'it had formerlie been observed, that the dogges had sometymes found fflesh, that had been hidden in holes made in the ground, neare unto those two houses'. In Edward William-son's house the searchers found, hidden under straw 'in a lofte over a beddechamber, a tubbe or woodden vessell with in which vessell, there was founde tenne quarters of goose flesh lately salted'. In the same house the constable came across 'a pye, where in was one whole quarter of goose flesh which was baked therein . . . and also the bones of two other quarters, but whether those two other quarters were baked therein, or in some other, he doth not knowe'. Looking for other evidence, and for traces of sheep believed to have been stolen from Winmarleigh by the same men, they found 'upon a hay mough in a barne, or out house, A mugge or earthen potte, wherein were eleven other quarters of goose flesh, which seemed likewise to be latelie salted'.[1]

## Identification of stolen birds

The presence of large quantities of goosemeat in the houses of those who did not keep geese, could not have afforded to buy them, and were not known to have acquired them openly, was damning. Often there were neighbours to testify against the accused and frequently the crime was so recently committed that there was other evidence still present. Dressing and cooking a goose produces large quantities of feathers, bones and trimmings. The feet, heads and wings were not easily hidden, and the owner could readily identify those parts of the goose. The feathers would have recognisable marks of colour and pattern, and the shape of the head, beak and feet would also be characteristic. Moreover, as with sheep, it was customary to give geese identification marks. The usual methods were to clip the wing tips in a particular pattern – which also prevented the geese flying away – and to nick the feet with distinctive cuts. In 1795 Holt,

---

[1] L.R.O., QSB 1/193/23.

referring to the geese summered on Martin Mere, noted that 'these flocks are so marked, as again to be known'.[1]

George Emmott of Colne went to Castleton in October 1627 to look for his seven stolen geese, and he 'found one ould goose in the handes of one John Collinge of Castleton, husbandman which goose [he] verilie thincketh was his goose . . . for that shee not onely agreed in cullor but alsoe hadd the same marke in the foote that his hadd'. Ambrose Barcroft of Foulridge, victim of the same thieving brothers, likewise found geese 'not onely like the geese which [he] hadd taken from him, in Cullor, but alsoe have ther wyngs and feete cutt Just as his said geese were'.[2] In December 1636 William Wilkinson of Eskriggs near Hornby testified that wings found in the house of Francis Proctor were those of his own geese, while in 1631, when Hester Arter, servant to John Croskell of Aughton, went to Oswald Heesham's house to search for her master's geese, 'lookinge under a Chist in the said house she found under the same two geese which had the foote marke of the geese of the said John Croskell'.[3] Thomas Wilson, whose geese were stolen from the moor in Roeburndale, found in the house of Richard Skirrow of Roeburndale no fewer than eight goose wings, five goose feet, three goose necks, five pinions and a dressed goose carcass – he recognised them because 'the said winges and ffeete were of the three geese stolne'.[4]

Sometimes geese were identified by more subtle means. Forensic evidence was used in November 1618, when two geese were stolen from Thomas Lightbowne of Pendleton near Salford. In the house of Thomas Travis were found 'twoe geese wings a ducke winge and the panche of a goose newlie killed, in which theare was found much french wheate, and by reason the said geese taken from this informer did goe & feede in stubble of French wheate, as allsoe by the coller of the winges theare found this informer verilie thinketh it was one of the geese stollen from him'.[5] William Martin of Parr, who lost three geese at night in November 1634, went in the morning to the field 'to seeke for all his geese [and] founde a trale way in the grasse where the rest were . . . leadinge over hedge and ditch to one William Houghes house with in Windle' where a search

[1]   J. Holt, op. cit., p. 176.
[2]   L.R.O., QSB 1/38/39.
[3]   L.R.O., QSB 1/16/31, 1/84/10.
[4]   L.R.O., QSB 1/112/22.
[5]   E. Axon (ed.), op. cit., p. 64.

revealed 'in a poake on houghes hay moughe two geese dresst [in a sack on the haystack, two geese prepared for cooking]'.[1]

In contrast to these gruesome discoveries of dismembered corpses, a delightful pastoral image is found in the report of a theft in November 1630. Isabel Ingham of Hurstwood tended a flock of geese from which five birds were taken. Soon afterwards her husband's shepherd, William Ekroyd, told Isabel that he had seen two of them grazing with the geese of William Shackleton, a neighbour. Ekroyd, when questioned by the examining magistrate, said that he was in no doubt as to the identity of the geese because he had 'divers and often times seen William Ingham's flock of geese, and that hee knoweth all those geese very well'. Isabel, evidently a determined woman, confronted Shackleton and claimed the two geese back, but he and his wife denied that they were hers. However, the resourceful Isabel was able to recover her birds by making use of the well-known gregariousness of geese: she 'did fetch her owne flocke of geese to ye said Shackleton geese & presently those two geese yt shee claymed came unto her owne flocke & did goe quietly with them'.[2]

## Acknowledgments

An early version of this paper was read at a reunion dinner of the first intake of students from the Liverpool and Lancaster Universities Diploma in Local History course: I am grateful to those present for their helpful comments and suggestions. The staff of the Lancashire Record Office produced many dozens of probate inventories and quarter sessions documents, and their assistance was invaluable. The extracts from documents are published with the kind permission of the County Archivist of Lancashire. My wife Jacquie read the text and commented upon it – sometimes with approval.

[1]  L.R.O., QSB 1/146/40.
[2]  L.R.O., QSB 1/85/42.

# From medieval park to puritan republic

*P. H. W. Booth*

IN THE SUMMER of 1522 King Henry VIII ordered a stag to be sent as a gift to Henry Courtenay, Earl of Devon. Sixteen years later this recipient of royal favour was to be executed on the king's orders. He should not have been surprised, since his father had suffered the same fate in 1509. The two Courtenays had committed the crime of being too closely related by blood to the royal monster. The order to gift-wrap and dispatch the venison was conveyed by a letter, signed by the king himself, and sealed with his signet, to the keeper of Toxteth Park, in distant Lancashire. It now lies among the Molyneux of Sefton muniments in the Lancashire Record Office (see Figure 1).[1]

So it was that Toxteth continued in its way of singularity: a medieval deer-park which had once been the site proposed for a great Cistercian abbey; a community which, a century after Henry's letter, had come to be dominated by extreme Protestants who paid their rent to a Catholic landlord; a community which organised its own religious worship, which instituted public support for elementary education, which played an important role in the scientific revolution of the seventeenth century, and which had as little as possible to do with the great and dignified authorities of the early seventeenth-century state – king, bishop, or gentry in quarter sessions. Its singularity was also written in the pattern of the hedgerows that surrounded its farms and their fields. Seventeenth-century Toxteth had a landscape that was radically different from those of any of the adjacent communities in south-west Lancashire.

---

[1] L.R.O. DDM 50/1. For a brief history of Toxteth Park from the eleventh to the nineteenth centuries see the chapter by P. H. W. Booth, 'The Background: People and Place', in *Sefton Park* (1984), pp.19–43.

FIGURE 1. Signet letter of King Henry VIII,
ordering the dispatch of a deer from Toxteth Park, 1522

The story of how such an unusual community came to be has long
been regarded as interesting and important, and has been told several
times. According to the *Victoria History of Lancashire* Toxteth was 'disparked' around 1592, and in 1596 William Stanley, the sixth earl of
Derby, sold the entire park, together with the associated property of
Smithdown, to Edmund Smoolte and Edward Aspinwall for £1,100.
These two men 'subsequently made a number of grants to kinsmen and
others'.[1] In 1604, however, the earl sold the park a second time, to Sir
Richard Molyneux of Sefton. A chapel, which is now called 'The Ancient
Chapel of Toxteth', was built by the inhabitants of the park at the
beginning of the seventeenth century, but the editors of the *Victoria County
History* were doubtful whether Anglican services were ever held in it.

---

[1] *V.C.H. Lancashire*, vol. III (1907), p. 42.

Our secondary sources have also told us something about the nature of the community which came to be established on the shore of the river Mersey following the 1592 'disparking'. Robert Griffiths, who wrote in the early twentieth century, depicted a second journey of the Children of Israel to the Promised Land, in the band of Lancashire puritans who emigrated from Bolton, the 'Geneva of the North', to settle themselves in Toxteth.[1] Griffiths thought they were only a small number, since he held that there were only four farms in the entire township as late as the second half of the eighteenth century. This migration is confirmed, with only a slight hesitation, by John K. Walton in his recent book *Lancashire: a social history, 1558–1939*. Griffiths even claimed that he could see the evidence of this long-vanished community before his own eyes, in Toxteth's physical features: farms and places (Jericho, David's Throne, Adam's Buttery), streams (the river Jordan) and whole districts (the Holy Land – the unlikely name for the area round the Pineapple Coffee House).[2]

The story, as we have received it, presents considerable problems. First, how could Toxteth have been sold twice by the earl of Derby within the space of eight years? Secondly, if the community did consist of only four farms in the eighteenth century, how did it manage to build and pay for both a chapel and a school in the seventeenth? Is the migration of an entire community from Bolton credible without direct supporting evidence? After all, Edward Aspinwall, the acknowledged social and religious leader of Toxteth in the early seventeenth century, is described in 1596 as belonging to Scarisbrick – hardly an obvious temporary resting-place on a journey from Bolton to Toxteth.[3] Can the late nineteenth-century names of Toxteth landscape features be regarded as evidence of the religious views and practices of those who lived there a quarter-millennium before, when there is no evidence of the use of those names before the nineteenth century? If the ancient chapel was not used for Anglican services in the 1620s and 1630s, why was Richard Mather, its most famous minister, ordained to priest's orders by the bishop of Chester in 1618, or not long afterwards? (What sort of services could have been held

---

[1]  R. Griffiths, *The History of the Royal and Ancient Park of Toxteth* (1907), pp. 27, 50.

[2]  J. K. Walton, *Lancashire: a social history, 1558–1939* (1987), p. 49; Griffiths, op. cit., p. 27.

[3]  L.R.O. DDM 50/3. For a detailed examination of this document see pp. 68–9. According to Aspinwall's *inquisition post mortem*, dated January 1634, he owned land in Scarisbrick, Ormskirk, Rosacre, Wesham and Liverpool: S. B. Gaythorpe, 'Jeremiah Horrocks', *T.H.S.L.C.*, cvi (1954), p. 27.

in a chapel in north-west England in the 1620s anyway, if not Catholic or Anglican?).[1]

History is the study of the past through the critical use of documentary sources. Some of the problems outlined above can at least be addressed through the examination, and reinterpretation, of sources which have long since been published, with the addition of some unpublished material. Two previously unpublished documents are given in appendices 1 and 2 at the end of this article.

Part of what made Toxteth a particular place was its inheritance from its medieval past. It had been both a deer-park and one of the three areas of the great forest of West Derby in which the forest law continued to be applied in full rigour after the early thirteenth century.[2] This meant that both settlement and development of the land for farming were virtually impossible from the thirteenth to the sixteenth centuries. Furthermore, it meant that Toxteth and Smithdown entered the early modern period as an 'extra-parochial' township, one which was not included within an ecclesiastical parish. Despite strenuous efforts to prove otherwise, the township retained this status until the nineteenth century.[3] Consequently, a late sixteenth-century estate agent, had such existed, could have described the park as 'ripe for development' once the planning-controls had been lifted, and could also have hinted at its attractiveness for religious dissidents in that it was not a full part of the disciplinary structure of the Church of England.

It was the Stanley family who were to take advantage of these investment opportunities. They had a connection with Toxteth which went back to 1447, when King Henry VI had granted the park to the controller of his household, Sir Thomas Stanley.[4] Unfortunately, the Lancashire

---

[1] *The Life and Death of Mr Richard Mather* (published in 1670, with an introductory letter by Increase Mather, the supposed author).

[2] Because of the formlessness of R. Cunliffe Shaw's massive *History of the Royal Forest of Lancaster* (1956) it is difficult to follow what happened as a result of Count John's forest charter of 1189–94. It appears that the inhabitants of West Derby forest, except for the three areas of Toxteth, Croxteth and Simonswood, were exempted from forest law in relation to assarts and purprestures (that is, cutting down trees, taking land into cultivation, erecting buildings and so forth). The law concerning the preservation of deer remained in force, however, throughout the whole of the old forest area. In the three places mentioned, the forest law remained in force in its entirety. See the record of the 1359 forest eyre in Cunliffe Shaw, *Royal Forest*, pp. 173–5.

[3] It was the Tithe Redemption Commissioners who in 1847 finally decided that Toxteth was part of Walton on the Hill parish: L.R.O., DRL 1/80.

[4] L.R.O., DDK 3/14.

*V.C.H.* embarks on the first of two major blunders by calling this a grant of the *custody* (that is, the office of keeper) of the park, and going on to state that it was a grant 'in fee', and that the office of keeper thereby descended from Sir Thomas to the sixth earl of Derby.[1] Henry VI's grant makes it clear beyond doubt that it was the *land* of Toxteth Park and Smithdown Moss that was granted, and that it was granted not in 'fee' but in 'fee farm' at an annual rent of 11s. 7½d. Moreover, the grant was made to Sir Thomas and the heirs male of his body (that is, to his own male legitimate children, and their heirs). Although the grant gave Stanley the actual land of the park (and not just the office of keeper), it did not give him the full freehold or 'fee simple', and it was this that appears to have caused some difficulty when the park came to be sold at the end of the sixteenth century. For example, if Stanley should leave no male heirs of his body, then the ownership of the park might revert to the duchy of Lancaster.

A second grant of the park was made by the Crown in 1593, which R. Cunliffe Shaw calls, mistakenly, 'a life grant of Toxteth'.[2] The original letters patent show that this was a straightforward confirmation of the 1447 grant to Sir Thomas's descendant, Henry, fourth earl of Derby. It spelled out that the property was to be held by Henry and his heirs male, in default of which it was to descend to the remaining heirs male of Sir Thomas. Earl Henry was to continue to hold the park and moss in fee farm, and to pay the original rent of 11s. 7½d.[3]

Earl Henry died not long after the issue of the 1593 confirmation, and was succeeded by his elder son Ferdinando, who died in 1594. The earldom then passed to Henry's second son, William (the sixth earl). With his title he inherited massive debts, some of which his father had incurred, and some because of the compensation that he himself had to pay to Ferdinando's widow, the dowager countess Alice, and to her three daughters.[4] At first he had to borrow very large sums of money, and when that did not prove sufficient he had to sell landed property, even some from the heartland of Stanley power in Lancashire, a compelling indication of financial straits. So it was that Toxteth and Smithdown came on the market, a short time after the sixth earl's succession.

---

[1]   *V.C.H. Lancashire*, vol. III, p. 42.
[2]   R. Cunliffe Shaw, op. cit., p. 466.
[3]   L.R.O., DDK 6/19.
[4]   B. Coward, *The Stanleys, Lords Stanley and Earls of Derby, 1385–1672*, Chetham Society, third series, xxx (1983), p. 49.

Gaps in the documentary record make it difficult to disentangle the complications of what turned out to be two sales, in 1596 and 1604, both of which were of the whole property, so the first one must therefore have been abortive for some reason. The gaps are largely because the actual title deeds have been lost in both cases, and all we are left with are subsidiary papers. Conveyances of substantial pieces of real estate generated whole files of documents by this time, as a result of the elaboration of conveyancing procedures that had taken place in the fourteenth and fifteenth centuries. One single transaction might leave a written agreement between the parties to the sale, the actual conveyance or title deed itself, a letter of attorney to deliver seisin (that is, the actual physical possession of the property), a note that seisin had in fact been delivered, a recognizance by which the seller agreed to perform the sale itself, and another in which the purchaser agreed to perform the covenants connected with the sale, a bill of legal expenses, a final concord (by which the transfer was registered and confirmed in a court of law, and which could itself consist of several documents), and a history of the title to the land.

So it was that on 11 November 1596 the earl of Derby conveyed Toxteth and Smithdown to Edward Smoolte 'of Lathom' and Edward Aspinwall 'of Scarisbrick'.[1] The deed has not survived, as we have seen, and so the evidence consists of two related documents. The first is the appointment on 16 November, by Smoolte and Aspinwall, of William Foxe as their attorney to receive seisin of the property from the earl's attorneys, James Pemberton and Thomas Ballard. The second, which is physically attached to the first, is the memorandum of the livery of seisin itself – that is, of the public ceremony (which took place on 24 November) through which possession was legally transferred by the earl.

Because of the loss of the title deed, we do not know what estate Smoolte and Aspinwall received in the land, or what the 'consideration' was – the price that they had to pay. The deed might well have told us that they were acting, as was most likely the case, for a third party, to whom they would convey the land in their turn. The memorandum does tell us, however, that when Foxe received seisin of Toxteth and Smithdown, he also received twenty separate holdings of land, held by named tenants. This is the origin of the *V.C.H.*'s second blunder, which arises

---

[1] L.R.O., DDM 50/3.

from a misinterpretation of this transfer of tenanted holdings from the earl to Smoolte and Aspinwall as grants made by those two to their 'kinsmen and others'.[1] The august editors should surely have noticed that their interpretation could not be tenable, partly because two of the 'kinsmen' to whom Smoolte and Aspinwall supposedly 'granted' this newly acquired land were the two men themselves! No, the memorandum records that by November 1596 there were already twenty tenant farmers with holdings in the newly developed Toxteth park.

We have to go back seven years, to 1589, to find when the process had begun. In that year Earl Henry had proposed to the government that he be allowed to develop both Toxteth Park and Macclesfield Forest, in order to help to deal with his serious financial problems. The following year the queen gave permission with regard to Toxteth, and on 8 March 1591 the mayor of Liverpool had an exciting announcement to make to the borough assembly. He had been told that Toxteth was to be 'disparked', and that the earl of Derby was planning to develop the park for agriculture. A hundred acres were to be reserved for the inhabitants of Liverpool, should they want to take it up.[2] Obviously the earl felt that the original grant of 1447 allowed him, as the virtual owner of the park, to do this, since the letters patent of 1593 only confirmed the original grant, and were probably intended, unsuccessfully as it turned out, to remove any uncertainties about the earl's title. It is possible that the initial surveying and letting of the park had begun even before 1591, since Thomas Seddon, who made his will on 26 February 1591, says that he was 'of Toxteth parke'.[3] He may, of course, have lived as a sub-tenant in one of the two medieval park lodges, and not in a newly built farmhouse. Seddon's will goes on to say that the park was 'within the parish of Lancaster', the conventional description of the remaining places which were in the forest, and might be taken to imply that the disparking had not then taken place.

It is strange that there is no mention of the permission to dispark in Elizabeth's 1593 letters patent, and that legal proceedings had to be taken in 1604 to confirm the 'disparked' state of Toxteth and Smithdown. This was done by a form of legal inquiry called a 'special commission and

---

[1]  *V.C.H. Lancashire*, vol. III, p. 42.
[2]  B. Coward, op. cit., pp. 34–5; J. A. Twemlow (ed.) *Liverpool Town Books*, vol. II (1935), p. 586.
[3]  L.R.O., WCW 1591, Thomas Seddon.

certificate' in the supreme court of the duchy of Lancaster – the court of duchy chamber at Westminster.[1] The record, which is published as appendix 1 of this article, shows that Toxteth had been 'disparked' and divided into farms 'for the space of this twellve yeres last past and above' (i.e. from before 1592). The document as a whole will be discussed later (pp. 71–2) but we should note here that it is consonant with other evidence that the initial impetus to survey, enclose, and let out holdings in the park came not long after the 1590 permission to dispark – that is, towards the end of the life of Henry, the fourth earl of Derby, whose activities in improving the financial yield of his estates at a time of rising population and increasing demand for land are well attested.[2] A considerable part of the task must have been achieved with some speed for there to have been twenty holdings with tenants by 1596. How many of those tenants were actually resident by 1596 cannot be determined.

The necessity for the 1604 commission seems to imply that the permission from the Crown to 'dispark' Toxteth in 1590 was not wholly secure in law. Worries on this score may not have been ill-founded. Compare the disparking of Toxteth with the enclosure of part of the duchy of Lancaster's forest of Bowland in the latter part of the sixteenth century.[3] Although the same procedure of commission and certificate was employed, there was a difference, of course, in that the duchy was the actual landowner in Bowland forest, whereas in Toxteth the virtual ownership had passed to the Stanleys in 1447. The apparent clarity of the legal situation in Bowland did not prevent James I's government from reopening questions of legal title, and compelling those who regarded themselves as undoubted owners to pay large fines to have their titles confirmed.[4] The prospective purchaser of Toxteth, Sir Richard Molyneux, may have been quite right to have had reservations about buying the park when its legal status might remain open to challenge.

As neither the deed by which Derby conveyed the property to Smoolte and Aspinwall in 1596, nor that by which Derby conveyed it to Molyneux in 1604, has survived, we can only surmise the reason it took eight years for the transaction to be completed. It is most likely that the difficulties

---

[1]  P.R.O., Duchy of Lancaster, Special Commissions, DL 44/671.
[2]  B. Coward, op. cit., p. 49.
[3]  J. Porter, 'Waste Land Reclamation in the Sixteenth and Seventeenth Centuries: the case of south-eastern Bowland, 1550–1630', *T.H.S.L.C.*, cxxvii (1978), pp. 1–23.
[4]  Ibid., p. 23.

which arose out of the 1447 grant in fee-farm were the main reason for the delay, compounded by uncertainty with regard to the 1590 'disparking'. It is significant, perhaps, that Earl William had run into similar difficulties with other sales he had been compelled to make. In 1595/6 he had agreed to sell the two manors of Cheetham and Cheetwood near Manchester to Sir Nicholas Mosley. Mosley, however, refused to pay the full purchase price until the reversion of the two manors had been obtained from the Crown.[1] As part of the final agreement to sell Toxteth and Smithdown in 1604, the question of acquiring the 'reversion' from the Crown was also mentioned.[2]

Attached to the 1604 sale's 'articles of agreement' is a rough draft of a final concord, by which the conveyance was to be given additional legal force.[3] In the notoriously vague way employed by such records, the property is described as sixteen messuages, six cottages, two mills, twenty gardens, 600 acres of (arable) land, sixty acres of meadow, 300 acres of heath and 600 acres of moss. This implies the existence of twenty-two dwellings, and a recorded acreage of 1,560. If we assume, as we surely have to, that the acre in this document was measured by the 24-foot perch (that it was the 'big acre', therefore), then that figure can be taken to equal 3,276 statute acres. This is not far off the township's area as it was measured by the Ordnance Survey in the nineteenth century, namely 3,598 acres.[4] In fact, Molyneux did not manage to take possession of the whole of Toxteth Park, at least immediately. As part of the settlement which the earl had to make with his sister-in-law, the dowager countess Alice (who was born a Spencer of Althorp, and thus was initiating a notable family tradition) part at least of Toxteth had to be handed over to her, for life.[5] This meant, for example, that at Michaelmas 1618 she was able to lease the old lodge in the park to Richard and Alexander Molyneux.[6]

The report of the 1604 commission tells us that there were twenty-three named tenants with holdings in the park, but that only thirteen of the farms had houses built on them. The table compares the data given in the 1596 and 1604 documents.

[1]  B. Coward, op. cit., p. 49.
[2]  L.R.O., DDM 50/8; Coward, op. cit., p. 199; *V.C.H. Lancashire*, vol. III, p. 42.
[3]  L.R.O., DDM 50/8.
[4]  *V.C.H. Lancashire*, vol. III, p. 40.
[5]  B. Coward, op. cit., p. 206.
[6]  L.R.O., DDCl 268.

## Tenancies in Toxteth in 1596 and 1604

|  | *(20 tenants)* |  | 1604 *(23 tenants)* |
|---|---|---|---|
| *1596* |  |  |  |
| 1 | Richard Harrington |  | – |
| 2 | Edwarde and Anne Aspinwall | 1 | Edward Aspinwall |
| 3 | Edmunde Smoolte | 2 | Edmond Smoote |
| 4 | Raphe Whitfielde |  | – |
| 5 | George Laurenson |  | |
| 6 | Edwarde Hutchin | 3 | Edwarde Hytchyne* |
| 7 | Roberte Roos | 4 | Roberte Rosse* |
| 8 | James Fraunce | 5 | Henry Fraunce |
| 9 | William Foxe | 6 | Wylliam Foxe |
| 10 | Thomas Terbocke |  | (Thomas Seddon, in his 1591 will, referred to his house bought from 'Mr Tarbucke') |
| 11 | John Blundell |  | – |
| 12 | Thomas Bickerstaffe | 7 | Robert Bixteth* |
| 13 | Johne Byrde | 8 | Wife of John Bird |
| 14 | Myles Mather | 9 | Mylles Mather |
| 15 | Thomas Foxe | 10 | Thomas Foxe |
| 16 | Richard Hodgsonn | 11 | Wife of Richard Hodgesone |
| 17 | Gyles Broockes | 12 | Gylles Brockes |
| 18 | Edward Terbocke (or Thomas, his son) |  | – |
| 19 | Robert Berrie | 13 | Robert Barrye |
| 20 | William Coocke | 14 | Coocke's wife |
|  |  | 15 | Thomas Bowlton* |
|  |  | 16 | Raphe Gryffid* |
|  |  | 17 | John Bannester* |
|  |  | 18 | Evann Thomassone* |
|  |  | 19 | William Banaster* |
|  |  | 20 | Thomas Blymston* |
|  |  | 21 | Henry Mossock* |
|  |  | 22 | Thomas Lacke* |
|  |  | 23 | Alexander Molyneux |

The names are given, first, in the order of the 1596 list, and then those names in the 1604 list which appear to correspond with them are placed opposite. Names asterisked are those with tenements described as not having houses erected on them in the 1604 list. Alexander Molyneux, gentleman, appears at the head of the 1604 list. He was, presumably, the same as 'Alexander Molyneux Esq.' who paid an entry-fine of £40 for 'the oulde lodge' in 1610/11 (L.R.O., DDM 1/36) and 'Alexander Molyneux, rector of Walton', who leased the same from the countess of Derby in 1618 (L.R.O., DDCl 268).

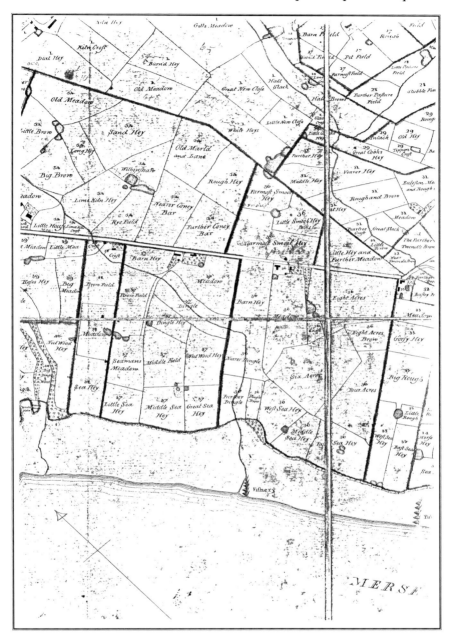

FIGURE 2. A section from the plan of Toxteth Park, undated but likely to have accompanied the survey of 1769 (L.R.O. DDM 14/57). The lighter boundary lines show the field boundaries, the darker ones farm boundaries (the latter being coloured in the original).

Using the data given above, we can begin to say something about the nature of the community that was planted in the former deer-park from the late sixteenth century. As far as its size goes, we first have to rule out Robert Griffith's strange estimate of there having been only four farms in the eighteenth century, a mistake based on the fact that only four farms are actually named on Yates and Perry's inadequate *Map of the Environs of Liverpool* of 1768.[1] Twenty farms had been surveyed and rented out by 1596. Although we do not know the name of the surveyor, the later plans of the park make it clear that the new techniques of surveying were employed in laying out new farms and fields in an 'undeveloped' land-scape (figure 2). The rectangular shapes of the farms and the highly regular boundaries of individual fields were similar to the lay-out of the new settlements that the colonists were founding in America. By 1604 the number of holdings in the park had risen to twenty-three (not far from the figure which is recorded in the 1604 final concord, of sixteen mes-suages and six cottages). Of the twenty-three holdings, ten had no house built on them in 1604; seven of those ten were held by tenants who did not appear in the 1596 list. Four of the tenancies in the earlier list cannot be traced in the later one, suggesting that some of the pioneers did not necessarily see their land as a permanent acquisition.

Because of the lack of parish registers, understandable in a township which was extra-parochial, and whose inhabitants seem to have chosen for themselves the local churchyard in which they preferred to be buried,[2] it is difficult to trace Toxteth families through the seventeenth century. A Hearth Tax return for 1673 records the names of thirty-two taxpaying households in the township. Of those, twenty-one were houses with one hearth only, four with two, two with four, one each with three and five, and six with six. Unfortunately this return does not give the names of those who were too poor to pay the tax, and so it is not possible to do more than suggest a total population of between forty and forty-five households.

What is surprising is to find that only six of the family names in the 1596 and 1604 lists were represented in the Hearth Tax return. Yet another list of tenants was made in 1717, as part of the process of valuing

---

[1]  R. Griffiths, op. cit., p. 57.

[2]  For example, five christenings, one marriage, and fourteen burials of Toxteth people are recorded in the Liverpool chapelry/parish registers and bishop's transcripts between 1620 and 1701: H. Peet, (ed.), *Registers of Our Lady and St Nicholas, Liverpool*, Lancashire Parish Register Society, xxxv (1909).

Lord Molyneux's estate as a 'papist' following the 'Fifteen rebellion.[1] This includes forty-three holdings which had either a farm-house or a cottage on them, plus twelve described simply as 'parcels' of land. Five of the holdings were held by tenants whose surnames appeared in the 1596 or 1604 lists. Even allowing for women's changes of name at marriage, and for the possibility of some of the original families surviving as under-tenants of those listed, the evidence does witness both to a substantial growth in the population of the community, by over three times, from the thirteen families resident in 1604 to the forty-three in 1717, as well as to a high level of turnover of tenants during that period.

The involvement of the Molyneux family in the history of Toxteth Park went back even further than that of the Stanleys. In 1394 Richard Molyneux had been granted a lease of the office of keeper of the park,[2] while in 1446 Sir Richard Molyneux was granted the hereditary office of master-forester of West Derby, of steward of the hundreds of West Derby and Salford, and of constable of Liverpool castle.[3] A similar grant was confirmed to Thomas Molyneux in 1483, but this time the post was described as 'master-forester of Simonswood, Toxteth and Croxteth'.[4] The master-forestership was not merely a decorative post at this time, since this official was responsible for holding the forest courts, such as the swainmote, which has left records of sessions from 1438 to 1558.[5] In addition, he had to organise the collection of revenue from those who wished to rent grazing rights and cut hay in the three forest areas, and he had to preserve the deer.[6]

The advantage to the Molyneux family of paying £1,100 to buy Toxteth and Smithdown in 1604 is evident from their estate rentals. The first reasonably full one to survive is for 1638, when the bailiff of Toxteth, Jerehiah [sic] Aspinwall, was responsible for collecting over £200 in rent.[7] Of this, £157 10s. 8d. was payable by John Crosse (of Liverpool) as 'farmer' (i.e. lessee) of the 'demesnes' – presumably that part of the surveyed and enclosed land which still awaited tenants. Crosse, who had

---

[1] R. Sharpe France (ed.) *Lancashire Papists' Estates, 1717*, R.S.L.C., xcviii (1945), pp. 195–201.
[2] *V.C.H. Lancashire*, vol. III, p. 42.
[3] L.R.O., DDM 3/1.
[4] L.R.O., DDM 3/6.
[5] L.R.O., DDM 7/450, 452–453.
[6] L.R.O., DDM 1/14, 15, 17, 19.
[7] L.R.O., DDM 1/55.

served as one of the duchy commissioners in 1604, died a wealthy man in 1641, and left a substantial herd of cattle (worth £99) and sixty-two cheeses in his 'Cheese chamber'. This gives some idea of what he was using the demesnes at Toxteth for.[1] The tenancies had been let out as leases for three lives, with an entry fine payable on taking up possession, and a reserved annual rent. The fines could be high – John Foxe's was £90 in 1648[2] – and the rents correspondingly low. By 1655 the profits of the demesne had fallen to £30, and the annual rent was £10.[3]

This suggests that the amount of tenanted land had increased substantially as the demesne was gradually let out. The annual income from entry-fines varied, of course, depending on the number of new tenancies being taken on in a particular year. In the period from 31 January 1648 to 16 January 1649, entry fines totalled £433.[4] Revenue from the demesnes, presumably either leased for a term of years or operated as a 'home farm' by the bailiff, continued to be collected until 1679, when the demesnes were finally rented out to a Mr Garraway for three lives.[5] So, the process of leasing out the whole of Toxteth Park, following the initial survey work in 1591/92, had taken over eighty years.

What was the origin of the new inhabitants of Toxteth? There is good evidence, it is true, that some of those who came in the early years had strong connections with Bolton. Robert Marsh of Toxteth Park, whose will is dated 1625, appointed Alexander Horrocks, the puritan preacher at Deane church, as one of his executors. Marsh also left land in Deane and Atherton.[6] Horrocks had presided over the marriage of his cousin, James Horrocks, to Mary Aspinwall, at Deane in 1615, and Mary was the sister of Edward Aspinwall (to whom the earl of Derby had conveyed Toxteth Park in 1596).

Both Edward and his brother, Thomas Aspinwall, were watchmakers, as was James Horrocks. Thomas's inventory survives, dated 1624. In it is stated that Mr Hyde owed him £3 for a watch, and Mr Stanley still owed him 26s. for part of the cost of a watch and 20s. for 'a Larum'. In his work

---

[1]  L.R.O., WCW 1641 John Crosse.
[2]  L.R.O., DDM 1/57.
[3]  L.R.O., DDM 1/67.
[4]  L.R.O., DDM 1/57.
[5]  L.R.O., DDM 1/109.
[6]  L.R.O., WCW 1625 Robert Marsh. The witnesses to the will included Edward Aspinwall, William Fox, Jerehiah Aspinwall, and James Horrocks.

loft he left £10-worth of 'Tooles: Watch Worke and Watch stuffe'. He also owned property near Bolton at the time of his death.[1] A signed watch made by him (probably in about 1605) is known.[2] As we have seen, Edward was certainly living in Toxteth by 1604. Both his brother, and James Horrocks, very likely followed in his wake. Thomas was living in Toxteth by the time of his death. James Horrocks was not in Toxteth in 1604, and may not have settled there until the early 1620s. His son, the renowned astronomer, Jeremiah Horrocks, was born around 1618, but presumably moved to Toxteth when a child.[3]

Despite these Bolton connections, however, we can rule out a mass migration of puritans from that town, partly because, as has been seen, Edward Aspinwall, who was baptised in Ormskirk, lived at Scarisbrick before he came to Toxteth. In addition, there are other early residents, such as John Crosse and Richard Molyneux's cousin, William Gerrard (died 1628) – the son of Lord Gerrard of Gerrards Bromley, Staffordshire – who did not have Bolton connections.[4]

It was, rather, a small, close-knit group of relatives – the Aspinwalls and the Horrocks – united as much by their trade as by their religious beliefs, who formed the Bolton connection, and wielded an influence in their new home well beyond that which their numbers might justify. Their choice of Toxteth to settle in must have been partly economic, in that land was available to rent near to the market and port of Liverpool in what later became the watch, clock and file-making belt stretching from Warrington, through Prescot, to Liverpool itself. Liverpool was also attractive in that its corporation was inclined towards puritanism, and the extra-parochial status of Toxteth Park was a bonus.[5] Not only were residents of Toxteth free to patronise any church they liked for baptism, marriage and burial services, but their township was normally free of control by that organ of ecclesiastical discipline, the visitation of the bishop of Chester and his officials. Free, that is, until church discipline was tightened up in the early 1630s.

---

[1]  L.R.O., WCW 1624 Thomas Aspinwall.
[2]  H. O. Aspinall, *The Aspinwall and Aspinall families of Lancashire, 1189–1923* (1923); S. B. Gaythorpe, 'Jeremiah Horrocks', *T.H.S.L.C.*, cvi (1954), p. 28.
[3]  S. B. Gaythorpe, op. cit., p. 30.
[4]  L.R.O., WCW 1628 William Gerrard.
[5]  J. K. Walton, op. cit., pp. 49, 74, 114, 120–1.

The history of this puritan community is well known, largely because of the *Life and Death of Richard Mather*, written by his son Increase Mather and published the year after his death in America in 1669.[1] Although Mather's *Life*, the first biography to be published in the New World, is an important and valuable source for Toxteth's history, as with all other documents it has to be treated with critical care. It is primarily the story of Mather's conversion to the protestant form of godliness, in the context of the working out of divine providence. Not only was the later puritan divine brought up in a place of 'much Profanenesse and Popery', as he tells us in his will (and few advanced protestants would have disagreed with such a description of south-west Lancashire), but he only narrowly escaped becoming ensnared by 'popery' himself. Mather died the respected minister of the important congregational church in Dorchester, New England, but his biography makes it clear that he started his ministry at Toxteth as an ordained priest of the Church of England, albeit one of a radically protestant slant. Did the elderly New England divine and his family indulge in an element of reinterpretation of their family history, as they contemplated Richard Mather's physical and spiritual journey from godless Lancashire to the promised land of the American colonies?

Puritanism in the early seventeenth century did not necessarily imply either sectarianism or separatism. However, as a way of life and religious devotion its heart was in the family, rather than the church. When Mather was recruited to be the township's schoolmaster in 1611, it was the influence of Edward Aspinwall and his family which brought about his thorough conversion to a new way of life. Again, it must have been through this influence that he was sent to Brasenose College, Oxford, since Aspinwall had been a student there himself in the 1580s.[2] In 1618, having graduated, he was brought back to Toxteth by the community and was appointed their pastor. Apart from what the *Life* tells us, nothing else is known about his activities until his suspension by the Church authorities in 1633, and again in 1634, during the crackdown on puritan dissidents. Mather lost heart and took ship from Bristol for America the following year.

On only one occasion before 1633 did Toxteth figure in the disciplinary records of the established church.[3] This reference is particularly

---

[1]  Increase Mather, op. cit.
[2]  S. B. Gaythorpe, op. cit., p. 28.
[3]  Cheshire R.O., Diocese of Chester, Visitation Correction Books, EDV 1/26 f. 122 (see appendix 2).

eloquent because of its unique character. In 1625 the churchwardens of Walton on the Hill parish were told to hand in to the bishop's office a detailed list of all those who lived in Toxteth who did not attend Holy Communion at 'their' parish church – Walton (see appendix 2). Thomas Henshawe, the sole churchwarden of Walton parish, undertook to provide the report and, to make doubly sure, the vicar was told to do it as well. The Toxteth people were in trouble for having built a chapel and not having had it consecrated by the bishop. In addition, they did not appoint churchwardens, nor did they provide a cloth for the pulpit or for the communion table. Furthermore, they did not have a surplice or 'other ornaments', or a copy of Bishop Jewell's *Apology*, which was the standard official justification for the Church of England that was supposed to be possessed by every Anglican place of worship. In other words, they were exhibiting the external signs of a puritan congregation.

This record is the earliest official contemporary witness for the existence of the 'ancient chapel' of Toxteth. It must have been built a few years before, since Mather was not its first priest – Richard Poile had preceded him.[1] Its particular religious path, in a sense not wholly separate but semi-detached from the Church of England, was not to be challenged until the great 'clamp-down' came. Edward Aspinwall was not to see it, since he had died in 1632.

We do not know what this puritan-dominated community thought about the civil war which broke out in 1642. Whatever they might feel about the king's execution in 1649, it is unlikely that they mourned the dismantling of the Church of England and the dismissal of its bishops. The presbyterian system which resulted in Lancashire would have been much more to their liking. We can assume this because when the Church of England was re-established in 1662, after the restoration of Charles II, Toxteth chapel and its congregation refused to rejoin. In the Anglican persecution which took place in the 1660s there was, it appears, an attempt to sweep it back into the fold. A law-suit in the bishop's consistory court in 1663 tried to establish that the tithes of Toxteth Park belonged to Walton on the Hill parish, and that they could, therefore, be leased out by the rector of Walton. The minister at Toxteth since 1657, Mr Crompton, had been allowed by the Walton clergy to receive the township's

---

[1] P.R.O., Palatinate of Lancaster, Chancery Depositions, PL 10/42.

tithes for his upkeep.[1] By 1661, however, Walton was trying again to make good its long-fought claim to the control and superintendence of the religious affairs of the 'liberty of Toxteth Park'. It did not work, though. At the time of the 1689 Toleration Act, the chapel was registered as a 'dissenting meeting-house'.[2] The community continued on its singular course.

Historians of the seventeenth century tell us that it is no longer possible to make links between political views, religious beliefs and economic position in determining allegiance to king or parliament in the Civil War. If only it were, then the puritan leaders of Toxteth Park would be a textbook example. Entrepreneurial tradesmen in a new industry, they were prepared to take a risk to establish themselves in a new community. They also produced one of the most distinguished scientists of the early seventeenth century, Jeremiah Horrocks. Two of Edward Aspinwall's sons, Jerehiah and Edward, took office as JPs and committee members in the republican government set up after the king's execution.[3] John Foxe, who served as bailiff of Toxteth from 1647 to 1661, was called 'Major Foxe' from 1656, and presumably held a post in the republican militia.[4] William Fox had been one of the earliest tenants of the park, mentioned in the 1596 list.[5]

The British republic, when it came, cannot have felt unfamiliar to many of the inhabitants of Toxteth, since that was how the township had been governed since the beginning of the seventeenth century. In religious matters the community was a nominal member of the Church of England, but had been in practice self-governing for over thirty years. As far as supervision by the bench of JPs at quarter sessions was concerned, there is little evidence of it before 1649.[6] In the second half of the century, on average one and a half administrative orders a year survive in the petitions

---

[1]  Cheshire R.O.,,, Diocese of Chester, Consistory Court Cause Papers, EDC 5/1663/72. It is likely that this 'permission' was an acknowledgment of an accomplished fact.

[2]  L.R.O., QSP 669/4.

[3]  B. G. Blackwood, *The Lancashire Gentry and the Great Rebellion, 1640–60*, Chetham Society, third series, xxv (1978), pp. 86, 98–9.

[4]  L.R.O., DDM 1/56–85.

[5]  L.R.O., DDM 50/3.

[6]  L.R.O., QSB 1/158/18, 1/174/59, 1/174/60, 1/182/25, 1/182/44, 1/182/49, 1/194/52, 1/198/19, 1/198/62. These nine references between 1635 and 1638 relate to one binding-over to keep the peace, a petition for the maintenance of a bastard daughter (plus an associated cause in the ecclesiastical court about the mother's fornication) and an unlawful entry into a house.

files for Toxteth Park.[1] The supreme policy-making body for Lancashire, the Sheriff's Table, noticed Toxteth twice between 1578 and 1694. In 1621 Edward Aspinwall was sworn in as a high constable of West Derby hundred, and in 1633 Toxteth was included with the other former forest areas and made liable to pay the tax for the support of wounded soldiers.[2]

Much more, no doubt, remains to be discovered about the history of this unusual place. Of course, local communities have not normally taken much trouble to leave records for us to employ in unravelling their histories, and those we do have can prove difficult to read and interpret. From Toxteth's first century, after its resurrection in the late Tudor period, we have only Richard Mather's *Life*, written with an eye on the verdict of posterity. It suffers from distance in both space and time from the events it purports to record, and discerns an element of purpose in Mather's life, refined by hindsight, that we have rightly learned to distrust. Historical documents are fine things but, in the end, Toxteth survived as the community it became by being successful in concealing its activities from the outside world as far as possible, and so much of what we should want to know about its past may be forever lost to us.

## Appendix 1

### Report on the Disparking of Toxteth, 1604

1. WRIT of King James I to Sir William Norres, knight, John Ireland, John Crosse, and Edmund Molyneux, esquires, appointing them commissioners to go to Toxteth Park, and see whether it is still used as a park or has been disparked, whether there are any deer in it, or whether it has been converted to husbandry and tillage, and whether houses have been erected upon it, and how long ago the conversion to husbandry and tillage took place, and the tenements were built (if that be the case).

The commissioners are to make a certificate to the chancellor and council of the duchy of Lancaster in the Duchy Chamber at the palace of Westminster by the octave of Trinity next [10 June 1604].

---

[1]  There are twenty-four references in all to Toxteth Park in L.R.O., QSP, between 1652 and 1717. Fourteen of them concern poor-law matters (see the indexes in the Lancashire Record Office for details).
[2]  B. W. Quintrell (ed.), *Proceedings of the Lancashire Justices of the Peace at the Sheriff's Table during Assizes Week, 1578–1694*, R.S.L.C., cxxi (1981), pp. 79, 110.

Dated at Westminster, under the duchy seal, 24 May, 2 Jas. I [1604]

The dorse of the writ is signed: John Ireland, John Crosse, Edmond Molyneux

Title on dorse: 'Commissioners to enquire whether a parcel of ground called Toxstathe parke bee disparked'

[Summary translation from Latin]

## 2. *Certificate Of The Commissioners*

Right Honourable, our bonden dewtyes remembred. Whereas it plesed your honour to award his highnes Commissione forth of his hyghnes Court of dutchie unto us, beringe date the xxiiijth of Maye last, to enquire whether a Certeine parcell of ground called Toxtath Parck within the County of Lancaster were disparked and Converted to husbandrie or not, wee the Commissioners, according to our bounden dewtye and acording to the Commission to us dyrected, Repayred our sellves to the sayd parcell of ground called Toxtathe Parcke on Saturday being the second daie of [th]ys Instant June, and then and there did vew and survey the said parcell of grownde, and every par[t] thereof, And wee doe fynd that the same parcell of ground is disparked and not used as a Parcke, and that there is not one deare in the same grownd nor in anie p[ar]te thereof, and that the said parcell of ground is devyded and shared into severall Tenementes, whereupon severall dwelling howses are erected, and habitations and people planted; And that the ground for the most parte is Converted unto Arable and pasture grownd, and a great parte thereof marled, and now and manie yer[es] past tylled and sowen with Corne: And that there bee twentie dwelling howses and above and twoe water mylles in the severall tenures and occupacions of Alexander Molyneux, gent., Edward Aspinwall, Wylliam Foxe, Edmond Smoote, William Harrockes, Thomas Lytham, Edward Risheton, William Greene, James Risheton, Henry Fraunce, John Tennant, Edward Carter, William Gyll, Coocke's wife, Gylles Brockes, wife of Richard Hodgesone, wife of John Bird, Mylles Mather, Thomas Foxe, Robert Barrye, and dyvers others. And wee doe alsoe fynd that these persons folloing doe occupye grownd within the said parcell of grownd called Toxtath parke (but have not anye dwelling howses as yett therupon erected) Robert Bixteth, Thomas Bowlton, Raphe Gryffid, John Bannester, Evann Thomassone, William Banester, Thomas Blymston, Henry Mossock, Robert Rosse, Edward hytchyne and Thomas Lacke.

And we further fynd upon dilligent enquyrie therof, that the same parcell of grownd Called Toxtath parke hath beene Converted to husbandrye and for the space of this twellve yeres last past and above. And wee fynd the pro[ffit] of the Convercion thereof into tyllage to bee as formerly wee have downe, aswell by our owne vew and knowledge, as by reasonne of Tryalles and recoveryes which the parsone of Walton hath hadd against the Tenantes, Inhabitantes, and occupyers thereof, as well in the Ecclesyastycall Court, as before the Justyces of Assyze at Lancaster: And yt lyckewyse appereth unto us by vew [thereof] that there is not any Wooddes or underwooddes growing on any parte of the said parcell of grownd called Toxtath Parke, saving the hedge, Rough, grasses or plantes about the howses in theire Orchardes and gardenns; And that the same parcell of grownd called Toxtath Parke is usually called Toxtath, and sometymes Toxtath Parke. Of all which wee have thought meette, according to our bownden dewtyes, to Certefy your [honour] and the Councell of the said Dutchye Court of Lancaster: And so do humblye take our leaves, Toxtath, the seaconnd of June,

> Your honoures most humblye to Command
> John Ireland,    John [Crosse]    [signed]
> Edmond Molyneux

Three tags, the seals missing

(Public Record Office, Duchy of Lancaster, Special Commissions, DL 44/671: published with the permission of the chancellor and council of H.M. Duchy of Lancaster)

## *Appendix 2*

*Toxteth Park in the Diocese of Chester Visitation Correction Book, 1625*

Walton *parochia*

| | |
|---|---|
| *Officium domini merum contra Gardianos ibidem* | to give in particular the names of the inhabitants within Toxteth that doe not frequent their parish Church & Co[mmun]icate there and a surplesse & other ornaments wantinge at the saide Chappell. Thomas Henshawe apperde & hee appointed to certifye the names of all as receive nott at their owne parish church within one month nexte & to certifye by that tyme to the cons[istory]. |
| *Contra Vicarium ibidem* | doth not denounce exco[mmun]icate persons accordinge to the Canon. |
| *Contra inhabitantes ville de Toxteth* | a Chappell built & not Consecrated & want Churchwardens & wanting a pulpitt Cloth a Buckeram tablecloth & B[isho]p Jewells workes. The vicar hath [under?] taken to deliver the names of the inhabitantes & they are Called. |

(Cheshire Record Office, EDV 1/26 f. 122. Published with the permission of the Cheshire Record Office.)

# 'Serious manurers' – some comparisons between Flanders and Lancashire, 1790–1860

*Judith Swarbrick*

WASTE disposal, recycling and organic farming – those currently fashionable terms – though unfamiliar one hundred and fifty years ago, denote issues which were even then of great concern. The scientific examination of manures and their efficient commercial exploitation were of primary importance to agricultural improvers in Lancashire during the first half of the nineteenth century. The reasons are not hard to find. The population of every industrial town was growing very rapidly. It has been calculated that between 1751 and 1831 the population of Lancashire as a whole increased at twice the national rate of growth.[1]

The chief problem of Lancashire agriculture was therefore the need to produce large additional quantities of food. Furthermore, the sophisticated palates of the new merchant classes of Liverpool and Manchester demanded a more varied diet than the traditional one based on oats, barley, potatoes and pulses. By the early nineteenth century beans, which had long been a staple crop, were by some Lancastrians considered a food fit only for slaves.[2] From the late eighteenth century onwards the growing population and its demand for an ever-wider range of foodstuffs encouraged a major expansion of market gardening and arable farming, particularly in the south of the county.

---

[1] T. W. Fletcher, 'The agrarian revolution in arable Lancashire', *T.L.C.A.S.*, lxxii (1962), p. 93.
[2] W. Rollinson and B. Harrison (eds.), *The Diary of William Fisher of Barrow, 1811–59* (C.N.W.R.S., 1986), p. 2.

Existing agricultural practices, such as traditional crop rotations and the excessive use of marl and lime, were held by agricultural writers and observers to be exhausting the soil. Cattle dung was barely sufficient to maintain existing pasture lands. Manures in large quantities and of the appropriate types were needed to remedy these deficiencies and to improve many hundreds of acres of newly reclaimed mossland.[1]

At the end of the eighteenth century Lancashire already had a manurial system more varied than those of its neighbours. There are detailed, and very useful, descriptions in John Holt's *General Survey of the Agriculture of the County of Lancaster* (1795). Marl and lime and dung were supplemented by blubber in the Liverpool area and soapers' waste around Wigan, the latter becoming more widely used after the opening of the Leeds and Liverpool Canal (1774) ensured that it could be transported cheaply. Elsewhere in the county, farmyard waste was supplemented by whatever came to hand – soot, sawdust, ashes, soapsuds or even chopped-up rags.

A curious exception was found on farms in the vicinity of Morecambe Bay. Dung was hardly used, the farming practices apparently developed by the monks of Furness Abbey having – according to a local farmer – long since fallen into disuse.[2] No longer were the 'worthings' from the stables spread on the land; instead 'A great quantity of mussels are collected on the shore, for manure, the people attending when the tide serves, to secure them for all sorts of crops'. The shellfish were 'allowed to putrify in large heaps, to the great annoyance of the public and the loss of the farmer who so misapplies them'.[3] The use of shellfish had two advantages: the organic matter provided a conventional manuring, while the shells added a lime dressing to the soil.

Loss and misapplication of potentially valuable fertilisers were commonplace. Before 1840 very little was known about the properties of manures – which kinds were suitable for different crops, at what time of the year they should be applied, and the effects of fermentation on growth. Only by research, education, the dissemination of literature and a spirit of goodwill could the best practices be extended, enabling a domestic

---

[1]  G. Beesley, *Report on the State of Agriculture in Lancashire* (Preston, 1849), p. 37. He reckoned that 163,160 acres were brought into cultivation between 1795 and 1835.

[2]  W. Rollinson and B. Harrison (eds.), op. cit., pp. 2, 13.

[3]  J. Binns, *Notes on the agriculture of Lancashire with suggestions for its improvement* (1851), p. 121.

process to be transformed into the large-scale commercial venture appropriate to the needs of the expanding population.

Taking their lead from Manchester and Liverpool, the local agricultural societies formed during the 1830s and 1840s in Lancashire and other parts of the country applied themselves without delay to the question of manuring. As early as 1795 Thomas Butterworth Bayley, one of the founder members of the Manchester Agricultural Society, had published *Thoughts on the necessity and advantage of care and economy in collecting and preserving different substances for manure.*[1] The West Derby Agricultural Society (1801) studied the operation and effects of manure and the best methods of obtaining it. London followed Lancashire: at their 1839 meeting the newly formed Royal Agricultural Society promoted an investigation into the properties of 'Natural or farm-yard manure . . . compost heaps . . . liquid manures, artificial manures of a similar nature prepared in towns, refuse manure, as bones, rape-cake, rags, malt-dust, etc'.[2] The inaugural lecture in London of the Farmers' Club (1844) was on 'Manures: artificial, guano, bones; best method of application; description of crops; time of using; cost'.[3]

To improve knowledge and understanding of manuring and its potential benefits the various agricultural societies not only carried out scientific experiments but also commissioned surveys of agriculture in other European countries. In many of these the manurial practices of East and West Flanders were taken as an ideal. For example, writing in the *Journal of the Royal Agricultural Society* in 1840, Philip Pusey proclaimed that 'British husbandry cannot be considered complete until all the farms of this country, like those of Flanders, are brought into the same condition of garden-like temper and depth'.[4] The model offered by the agricultural practices and farming systems of Flanders included a strong emphasis upon the sophisticated and careful use of manures of various types, and these approaches were widely seen as applicable to English, and Lancashire, farming.

In a society where agricultural workers were often expected to labour from 5.30 a.m. to 8.00 p.m., where the pollution and health problems

---

[1] J. Bohane, 'Our county society, 1767–1917', *Jnl. Royal Lancs. Agric. Soc.* (1917), p. 26.

[2] *Jnl. Royal Agric. Soc.*, i (1840), Appendix, p. 42.

[3] D. K. Fitzgerald, *Ahead of their time: a short history of the Farmers' Club, 1842–1967* (1968), p. 202.

[4] P. Pusey, 'On the present state of agriculture in England', *Jnl. Royal Agric. Soc.*, i (1840), p. 7.

resulting from the disposal of town waste were at worst disregarded and at best imperfectly understood, and where – if we are to believe the farming writers of the early nineteenth century – rational and efficient use of agricultural resources was the exception rather than the rule, the methods obtaining in Flanders would indeed appear to have been worthy of adoption. The Flemish people were believed to be notably hard-working and frugal; they had two hundred years' experience of land reclamation; their numerous canals and smaller watercourses facilitated the transport of goods between town and country; and, like the Chinese, they had developed intensive agricultural systems to a fine art. Not only were they credited with having discovered ten sorts of manure, but they habitually conserved anything which would rot down or could be sold at a profit. It was 'an object of minute attention to the Flemish farmer to collect as much as possible and to apply it in the most advantageous manner'.[1]

The Flemish farmers had themselves published little about their own methods, or about agriculture in general, relying instead on French and German textbooks, but the English had been writing about the farming systems of their continental neighbours since the early seventeenth century. In 1818 the Board of Agriculture offered a prize for the best account, in any language, of Flemish farming. This was won by M. van Albroeck of Ghent, whose work *L'Agriculture de la Flandre* was translated and adapted by William Lewis Rham, whose unlikely background was that he was the Utrecht-born vicar of Wingfield, Berkshire. He verified Albroeck's statements by tramping from farm to farm in the Low Countries, accepting the hospitality of villagers en route. His *Outline of Flemish husbandry*, being intended for wide circulation, was published in the *Farmers' Series of Useful Knowledge*. The Royal Agricultural Society acquired a copy for its library, and then reproduced a large portion in its 1841 *Journal*.

Rham's observations are detailed, but his overall treatment of the subject is selective. When compared with the nineteenth-century reports on agriculture in Lancashire – which are highly critical – or with the contents of the later Board of Health reports on urban sanitation and public health, which give the impression that just about everything was grossly deficient and needed to be remedied, Rham's comments appear idealistic and over-praising. Nevertheless, many of the practices he

---

[1]  W. Rham, *Outlines of Flemish Husbandry* (n.d., *c.* 1838), chap. 4.

described could have been adopted, with suitable modifications, in England. There were marked similarities, at least superficially, between East and West Flanders and lowland Lancashire: they were of similar size and not dissimilar climate, their crops were alike, and in Liverpool and Antwerp each was served by a great international seaport. Flanders, like Lancashire, was noted for its textile industry.

However, nothing is more indicative of the cultural differences between the two areas than their respective systems for dealing with 'town manure' – the contents of privies, street sweepings, market refuse and other urban waste. The Flemings had, in every town, sworn brokers whose task it was to value the night-soil. They were experts, who could assess the precise quality, condition and potential application of the material and, for example, knew the exact period of fermentation proper to each stage of a crop's growth. Night-soil could be obtained wholesale and retail in Flanders, the dealers having their depots alongside the many rivers and canals. Often it was a matter of personal arrangement between the private householder and the farmer, who would call with his cart at regular intervals. Thus, in Ghent the servants could double their wages by collecting soap suds and other domestic offscourings, and in Bruges a servant could be hired for the equivalent of £3 *per annum* on the understanding that she could sell the household night-soil and refuse for £1 17s. (£1.85).[1]

In Lancashire the most effective distribution of town manure was carried out in the south of the county, mainly because the Leeds and Liverpool Canal and, later, the Liverpool and Manchester Railway gave easy and relatively cheap access to the rural areas. By the time Garnett was writing his *Prize report on the farming of Lancashire* in 1849, 20,000 tons a year were being sent by canal to the manure depots at Rufford. Farmers were able to obtain night-soil free of charge if they collected it themselves, and it was considered profitable to do this if they lived within a twenty-mile radius of a large town and the road was in reasonable condition. There were also advantageous rates for transportation by canal and railway, some canal companies even dispensing with tolls altogether by virtue of their Acts of Incorporation, which required that manure should be carried without charge. The Mersey and Irwell Navigation Companies

---

[1]  T. Radcliffe, quoted by H. Stephens, *The Book of the Farm*, vol. 1 (2nd edn, 1852), p. 484.

PLATE 1. Emptying ashcans in Back Boundary Street, Colne, in the late nineteenth century. Although by this time the equipment for the removal of night-soil had become a little more sophisticated, the basic procedure for emptying the receptacles, involving a man, a bucket and a brush, remained unaltered. In this view the movable cans, which could be pulled in and out of holes in the back wall of the property, can be seen clearly: so can the soiled state of the horse-drawn cart.
(Pendle District Library Local Studies Collection.)

charged no dues on dung, marl or manure which were used within five miles of their waterways.[1]

By 1845 Liverpool and Manchester city councils were earning £1,150 and £800 respectively *per annum* from the sale of town refuse.[2] Potentially this could have been trebled, if the system of collection had been more efficient. It was, however, the responsibility of a variety of bodies – police commissioners, improvement commissioners, town councils and private householders. Street sweepers were generally recruited from workhouses, and were often aged or feeble-bodied. Nightmen tended to be either lazy or rapacious or both; there are instances of night-soil collectors breaking

---

[1]  A. Mutch, *Rural Life in South-West Lancashire, 1840–1914* (C.N.W.R.S., 1988), p. 9.
[2]  L. Playfair, *Report on the State of Large Towns in Lancashire* (1845), p. 45.

PLATE 2. Notice prohibiting private enterprise street-cleaning in the streets of
Blackburn, 1864. In many towns the 1860s saw the introduction of regular scavenging
and street-sweeping, as local councils and Boards of Health adopted the voluntary
powers available to them under public health legislation. Blackburn Corporation
evidently wished to maximise its revenue from this source.
(Blackburn Library Local Studies Collection.)

down privy doors in search of the most lucrative ordure. More unpleasant,
physically demanding and dangerous work (there was a risk of spontaneous
combustion of, or suffocation by, noxious gases) can scarcely be imagined.
The sheer quantity of night-soil to be collected was daunting – cesspits ran
like tunnels under many of the streets of terraced houses in Liverpool. It is
not surprising that even in the 1840s the easiest solution seemed often to be
to empty privies into a huge cesspit or tip the contents into the nearest river.
Contrast the unwilling English scavengers with the orderly and industrious
Flemings who, we are told, would 'collect whatever is capable of putrefaction
and make it into composts which are laid out to dry and sold by measure.
The farmers believe its extraordinary effects are to be ascribed to a peculiar
blessing of God, as it enables the poor and destitute to gain a livelihood'.[1]

---

[1]  W. Rham, op. cit., p. 84.

Town manure also included dung which was available in the numerous piggeries, shippons and stables found in Lancashire towns. In Layton (Blackpool), for example, the Board of Health report of 1851 found that horses, ponies and donkeys from the beach were all kept in ill-drained yards.[1] Playfair discovered that in the poorer districts asses, hens and pigs were kept in houses – even in the sitting-room – for want of space elsewhere.[2] In Preston, Bolton's Court contained a row of pigsties and open dungheaps, a large trough for the storing of manure, and eight public slaughterhouses.[3] Board of Health reports for Lancashire towns and cities abound in similar examples.

The recommendations of the Nuisances Removal and Diseases Prevention Act of 1848 and the increasing realisation that such conditions were a major contributor to the appalling incidence of epidemic disease led, gradually, to a reduction in the number of animals kept in urban areas. Nevertheless, since the demand for manure was seasonal, great heaps and mounds of it could still be found in densely populated urban areas. The public depot at Saul Street, Preston, contained 2,000 tons of manure in 1851.[4] In Torrisholme (Morecambe) the village green had become a depository for manure, with the parish pump as its centrepiece.[5] As late as 1865 the Lytham nuisances inspector reported, of a property in Clifton Street, that 'in this yard several tons of manure is kept and one of the dirtiest yards I have met with pigs kept and all sorts of filth stagnant water &c &c'. The same inspector pointed to the seasonal demand for manure as a particular problem: in March 1865 he wrote that the town of Lytham had numerous overflowing ashpits and privies, 'but . . . the potato seeding is very near and I may say most of them [the cottagers] give it as a reason for having them so, on account of wanting the manure for that purpose, as is their annual custom'.[6]

In the case of Lytham the use of town manure for agriculture was purely a matter of local private enterprise. Referring to the systematic public use of this resource Playfair, writing in 1845, said that he knew of only two towns – Preston and Bury – where town refuse was used for

---

[1] *Report to the General Board of Health on . . . Layton with Warbrick [sic]* (1851), p. 11.

[2] L. Playfair, op. cit., p. 32.

[3] *Report to the General Board of Health on . . . Preston* (1849), p. 12.

[4] Ibid., p. 14.

[5] *Report to the General Board of Health on . . . Poulton, Bare and Torrisholme* (1851), p. 11.

[6] L.R.O., MBLs 3/1, Lytham Nuisance Book, 1865–8.

agricultural purposes, and he disapproved of 'the want of dilution of the refuse, which would not only prevent the escape of odour, but render the manure fit for the reception of plants'.[1] This matter of dilution had already been successfully dealt with in Flanders, but in Lancashire there had been little effort to consider it as a solution. Instead, in most Lancashire towns in the middle of the nineteenth century, the absence of comprehensive sewerage systems meant that efficient, effective and satisfactory disposal of night-soil and other organic waste was almost impossible.

It was in the conservation of liquids for manurial purposes that the farmers of Flanders showed a consummate skill. They had developed a system whereby rape-cake and the contents of privies would be added to the drainings from manure-heaps, calling the resulting compound *bons-bons* to show their high estimation of it. Urine tanks were considered to be as necessary as ploughs: they might be a simple cask sunk in the ground, or a grandiose double-chambered construction provided with a valve to separate liquids in different stages of fermentation. An adjacent *smoor hoop* held the drainage from the farm dung, which was stored in a pit rather than, as in England, a heap.

Lancashire did have its liquid manurers. Fifty years before Rham was writing, Henry Harper of Bank Hall owned a purpose-built water-cart, valued at £15 15s. in 1793, and a pump, 'for conveying water from dung-hills'.[2] He maintained a reservoir for urine from the stables and cowsheds, mixing the contents with waste water from the farmyard and the house. Harper conducted a series of experiments on different types of manure and reported an 'amazing increase' in yields when water was added to dung: 'the most clear profit I experience is from lot the 8th, water from the reservoir, which is no cost but labour, and that not so much as any other kind of manure'.[3] This must have been gratifying, since his annual expenditure on manure – £100 – was second only to the wages of his ten farm servants, £144.

Another pioneer was James Dixon of Hathershaw Lodge near Oldham, who in the 1820s provided some urine wells near the compost heap on his farm and others near his cowsheds. His home-made water cart, used for delivering liquid manure to the fields, was similar in design and

---

[1] L. Playfair, op. cit., p. 82.
[2] J. Holt, *General View of the Agriculture of the County of Lancaster* (1795), p. 31.
[3] Ibid., p. 131.

appearance to the Flemish carts. Dixon's efforts were rewarded by a prize of ten sovereigns from the Royal Agricultural Society and the publication of his essay on compost heaps in the first issue of the society's journal.[1]

The Royal Manchester Agricultural Society also offered a prize, awarded annually, for the best liquid manure system. The first winner, in 1842, was Robert Neilson of Halewood Green, an exceptionally innovative and progressive tenant of the Derby estate. In the following year Lawrence Rawstorne of Penwortham submitted a design for a clay-lined gutter and sinkhole to be used in conjunction with a reservoir. There were also liquid manurers in the north of the county. William Allen Francis Saunders of Wennington Hall in Lonsdale adapted Robert Neilson's design, constructing a tremendous tank of 50,000-gallons capacity, fed by iron pipes and guttapercha tubing, intended to hold a year's supply of urine from his cowhouses.[2] We are not told how he dealt with the problems of fermentation in such a vast quantity of liquid. William Talbot Rothwell was able to increase the yield on his farm at Foxholes, in Ellel, two-fold by using a box, in the Flemish manner, to store his manure and its constituent liquids intact. He was, said Binns with approval, 'a serious manurer'.[3]

It seems from the available evidence that the promoters of liquid manure were either gifted inventors or pioneers such as Robert Neilson, men of private means, or – occasionally – tenants on the farms of enlightened improvers such as the earls of Derby and Sefton. For example, liquid manure was used on the Clifton estates in the south Fylde. Here there were, admittedly, few suitable yards on the farms for the stacking or storage of dung, while transport of town manure was less feasible because of the absence of canals and rail links. It was, in any case, considered inferior because of the amount of ash and refuse which it contained.[4] Liquid manure tanks and water carts were therefore popular. On some farms the buildings were constructed so that the manure could be run onto the land by gutters. Henry Fisher, a tenant of the Clifton estate who gave evidence to the Board of Health, said that he had his own

---

[1] J. Dixon, 'An essay on making compost heaps from liquids and other substances, written from the evidence of many years' experience', *Jnl. Royal Agric. Soc.*, i (1840), p. 135.

[2] J. Binns, op. cit., p. 147.

[3] Ibid., pp. 59, 113.

[4] G. Rogers, 'Social and economic change in Lancashire landed estates in the nineteenth century' (Lancaster University Ph.D thesis, 1981), p. 181.

reservoir and culvert, built at a cost of £100, the liquid being taken out with scoops or buckets in spring and autumn.[1]

This enterprise seems to have been exceptional. Lancashire farmers were generally unwilling to go to such lengths to conserve waste liquids. Rothwell estimated that in 1851 half the farm rents over the county as a whole were being lost through the mismanagement of residues.[2] He saw, for example, no urine tanks in High Furness, while out of six Liverpool farms surveyed in detail only two had tanks.[3] Of Hopwood, near Rochdale, Binns noted that 'Liquid manure tanks are not very common, but highly approved of'.[4]

The average farmer was perhaps conservative by nature, but he also laboured under considerable constraints. In Flanders most of the large estates had been sold off and broken up, giving a pattern of thousands of small freehold properties, sometimes as small as fifteen acres in extent. In Lancashire, by contrast, there were many tenant farmers, on great landed estates which were as large as 20–30,000 acres. These farmers were bound by the strict procedures and regulations written into their tenancy agreements. In Parbold, for example, tenants were obliged to purchase £20 of dung per acre even if wished to experiment with other forms of fertiliser.[5] Such tenants could often not afford the additional outlay required for a urine tank unless a grant was forthcoming from an enlightened landowner.

Guano proved to be an attractive alternative to town manure or liquid manure. The first shipload, from South America, arrived at Liverpool in 1835. Nothing comparable had been available in Lancashire until that time, although in Flanders the droppings of pigeons and domestic fowls were, in powdered form, valued even more highly than animal dung. Guano had several advantages: it was relatively cheap, inoffensive, easy to transport and store, and increased yields by up to 100 per cent. It is no wonder that the amount imported rose from 1,140 tons in 1841 to 21,482 tons in 1847.[6] It use quickly spread even to the most inaccessible parts of the county, such as Bleasdale, Cartmel and the Furness Fells (where,

---

[1] *Report to the General Board of Health on . . . Kirkham* (1851), p. 19.

[2] W. Rothwell, *Report of the Agriculture of the County of Lancaster* (1850), p. 145.

[3] Ibid., p. 20.

[4] J. Binns, op. cit., p. 105.

[5] R. W. Dickinson, *General view of the agriculture of the county of Lancaster* (1850), p. 145.

[6] W. J. Garnett, *Prize Report on the Farming of Lancashire* (Preston, 1849), p. 39.

hitherto, dung had been transported by pack-horses).[1] Meanwhile, liquid manure was being allowed to drain into horseponds and watercourses, to the farmer's loss and to the detriment of the health of the population at large.

Following the cholera and typhoid epidemics of the 1830s and 1840s, and the passage of the Public Health Act in 1848, there was a growing realisation of the dangers posed by untreated sewage. Agricultural and sanitary improvements had to proceed in harmony. Benjamin Babbage expresses the view forcefully in his Board of Health report on Accrington: 'As the knowledge of the convenience of sewerage spreads through the country, large towns and populous villages will more and more adopt them; and if the sewage thus collected were turned into the watercourses and rivers . . . the courses of large rivers would be marked upon the sanitary maps as streaming with disease and death'.[2]

Partial sewerage and the re-use of industrial waste were already widespread in Flanders, where distilleries and textile mills abounded. Rham does not mention the latter, but describes how the larger distilleries maintained herds of fifty to sixty cows to consume the refuse wash, the inevitable urine tanks being built adjacent to the cowsheds. In Lancashire institutional waste was not often thought of as an agricultural resource, and instead became just another pollutant: for example, the privy waste from Hargreaves and Thompson's cotton factories at Accrington simply drained into an open ditch.[3] At Blackpool, in the township of Layton-with-Warbreck, the night-soil from a school and several boarding-houses was reported as draining into a stream and thence into the sea, whereas it could have been used for agricultural improvement on Marton Moss.[4] Very atypical is the instance of Richard Hinde of Newland Hall near Ellel, who reported in 1843 that he bought 'no heavy manure and very little guano . . . only night-soil from the factories, which nobody thought much about, when I first commenced'.[5]

The contemporary question of the possible agricultural benefits of sewerage was dominated by the thinking of Edwin Chadwick, a firm believer in the centralisation of authority and the necessity of water

---

[1] J. Binns, op. cit., pp. 16, 104, 108.
[2] *Report to the General Board of Health on . . . New and Old Accrington* (1850), p. 38.
[3] Ibid., p. 52.
[4] *Report . . . on Layton with Warbrick*, op. cit., p. 13.
[5] W. J. Garnett, op. cit., p. 32.

closets. A method of distributing liquid sewage on farmland was an essential feature in his 'unified system' of waste disposal. His ideals compelled him to try to prove that sanitation could become profitable through the sale of 'town guano' or night-soil. He had many supporters in the public health movement, including James Smith, who devoted seven pages of his report to the Board of Health on the sanitary condition of Lancaster to extolling the virtues of the liquid manure system proposed by Chadwick: 'There remains not a doubt of the propriety of its adoption'.[1]

Chadwick had conducted a series of experiments with the help of Joseph Whitworth, P. H. Holland and Robert Rawlinson. These involved the use of a canal boat on the Bridgewater Canal, delivering liquid manure onto the adjacent fields by means of a hose and jet. The local farmers were unimpressed: the anticipated crop yields did not materialise. Undeterred, in 1849 he sent a report entitled *Sewer Manure* to the Metropolitan Commission of Sewers in London. Alongside the Manchester experiment he described other – successful – uses of liquid manure in Flanders, Germany, Milan, Edinburgh and, not least, Clitheroe.[2]

The Board of Health report reveals that Clitheroe, rather unexpectedly, was very enterprising in the treatment and use of liquid manures. The landlord of the *Swan Inn*, the proprietors of Mercer and Anderson's Mill, Garnett's Mill at Low Moor, and others all maintained tanks for the reception of the contents of their privies. The liquids were either sold to local farmers, or used directly on farms attached to the mills. The scheme run by Henry Thomson of Primrose Mill was felt to be particularly suitable for national recognition. His work was also reported as an appendix to the *Minutes of information relating to the practical application of sewer water* which were presented to the General Board of Health in 1851. He explained that the privies at his factory were provided with boxes under the seat, which were exchanged fortnightly. The contents were then tipped into a storage tank capable of holding 80,000 gallons. The manure was delivered to the fields by means of hoses in 30-yard sections, made of hemp lined with cotton. Two men were needed to operate the system, one to join the lengths of hose and the other to manipulate the jet of liquid sewage. The unit cost of application was 5d. (2½p) per acre, assuming a

---

[1] *Report to the General Board of Health on . . . Lancaster* (1849), pp. 29–35, 37.
[2] E. Chadwick, *Sewer Manure* (1849), Appendix 7: Accounts of experiments . . . by H. Thompson.

horses and a watercart at an estimated cost of 4s. (20p) per acre. Thomson had apparently revised his system since 1849, when the price was given as 2s. 6d. (12½p) per acre. The resultant yield was five crops of clover and rye grass *per annum*, instead of two.[1]

Was this innovatory policy a pioneering triumph for Lancashire – an English liquid manurer taking his place alongside his illustrious Flemish counterparts? Alas! Chadwick's enthusiasm for liquid manuring systems was soon shown to be misplaced. Farmers – and other public health reformers – were becoming aware of the possibility of polluting drinking water supplies by contamination of subsoil drainage and run-off. The obnoxious vapours released into the atmosphere by the spraying of liquid sewage were increasingly unacceptable – and at a time when vapours or miasma were still held by many to be in themselves a cause of disease the practice was regarded with deep suspicion. Labour-intensive methods of manuring and of waste distribution were unpopular because of cost, and the English farmers did not strive to attain the virtue of their Flemish counterparts: 'patient industry, theme of much of the laudation which has been bestowed on them by others'.[2]

The Penwortham landowner and agriculturist, Lawrence Rawstorne, writing his *New husbandry* in 1848, ignores liquid manure, even though much of what he wrote was based on the *Journal of the Royal Agricultural Society* which promoted its use. He considered dung to be unnecessary except for use on green crops, and preferred it to be stored in heaps rather than pits or cavities. Instead, he advocated the widespread use of fertilisers unknown or rarely used in Flanders, such as bone-dust, guano, and the chemical by-products of sulphuric acid manufacture. By the middle of the century the farms in the Morecambe Bay area (still relying on seaweed and mussels) and the town-manured fields around Manchester and Liverpool, were producing abundant and varied crops;[3] but the garden-like ideal which Philip Pusey described, based on his observations of agriculture in Flanders, and which in the early years of the nineteenth century was widely suggested as a model for English farming, remained largely unfulfilled in Lancashire, despite early promise. By 1860 the engineer,

---

[1] General Board of Health, *Minutes of information relating to the practical application of sewer water and town manures to agricultural production*, vol. 19 (1852), Appendix 9, p. 149: Experiments by Henry Thompson.

[2] W. Stephens, op. cit., p. 470.

[3] See, for example, *Report on . . . Poulton, Bare and Torrisholme*, op. cit., p. 7, and A. Mutch, op. cit., p. 14.

surveyor and chemist were already starting to replace the idea of the labourer with his water-cart and ladle. The model of the Flemish system was no longer applicable, and the new order demanded the efforts of such bodies as the Liverpool Sewage Utilization Company and the Hyde Patent Eureka Sanitary Company – but that is another, and later, story!

# Healthy and Decent Dwellings – the evolution of the two-up and two-down house in nineteenth-century Lancashire

*Geoff Timmins*

I T IS WELL ESTABLISHED that working-class housing erected between the late eighteenth and early twentieth centuries showed appreciable variation in size, plan-form and provision of facilities. At the upper end of the range was 'model' housing, often associated with the more progressive amongst factory village and country estate owners. Such housing enjoyed a high reputation for the hygiene, comfort and spaciousness it offered.[1] At the opposite end was the infamous cellar dwelling. This occurred all too frequently in urban areas, being, to quote one contemporary, 'condemned by enlightened public opinion, as having less air, less light, and more of the effluvia from drains, than rooms upon or above the level of the soil'.[2]

In Lancashire a good deal of model housing consisted of well-appointed, two-up, two-down units, each having a private rear yard equipped with privy and ash-pit. Two-up, two-downs, however, were by no means confined to model housing; indeed, numerous examples were constructed as back-to-backs, a housing type rivalling the cellar dwelling with regard to the censure it received. Yet most two-up, two-down units were through houses, and these formed a substantial proportion of the country's housing stock during the nineteenth century. They may rarely

---

[1]  See, for example, J. Burnett, *A Social History of Housing, 1815–1970* (Methuen, 1978), pp. 47–53, 81–3.
[2]  G. Greaves, 'Homes for the working class', *Transactions of the Manchester Statistical Society* (1860–1), p. 83.

have achieved the standards set by model housing, but it is all too easy to assume that the opposite was true. Frequently they provided more than adequate accommodation, especially when, as was often the case, they were located beyond the squalor and congestion of urban centres.

While much has been written about the quality of two-up, two-down houses, little attention has been devoted to the ways in which their design characteristics changed. Yet this had a marked impact on the standard of accommodation they provided. Of particular importance was the way in which the plan-form of the ground-floor rooms evolved, leading to a re-allocation of room function and to the provision of that much-extolled feature of Victorian dwellings, the front parlour.

The purpose of this paper is to analyse these developments. Evidence is drawn largely from the Lancashire cotton districts, where housing of this type predominated.[1] It begins by examining the plan-form of early two-up, two-downs, demonstrating how this was adapted to meet differing needs. Consideration is then given to the way the plan-form of such houses evolved and why this evolution occurred. Emphasis is placed on the social desiderata, including high standards of privacy and morality, which, according to one strand of contemporary thought, the design of working-class housing should seek to embody.

## Early plan-form; the front living room/kitchen type

Writing about early industrial housing in urban areas, R. W. Brunskill has remarked:

> The two-storey workers' cottages which preceded the Public Health Act of 1875 usually consisted of a living kitchen and scullery/wash-house on the ground floor and two bedrooms above. Access was by a door opening directly off the street, with the living kitchen screened only by a timber 'speer'. At the rear a short yard, sometimes communal, contained earth closet and coal store.[2]

The ground-floor layout of such houses has been noted by several historians[3] and can be seen in contemporary plans prepared for Henry and

---

[1]  See M. J. Daunton, *House and Home in the Victorian City: working-class housing, 1850–1914* (1983), p. 48.
[2]  R. W. Brunskill, *Illustrated Handbook of Vernacular Architecture* (1971), p. 165.
[3]  R. Boyson, *The Ashworth Cotton Enterprise* (1970), plate VI.

Edmund Ashworth, leading cotton spinners from Egerton, near Bolton (Figure 1). The Ashworths began erecting cottages in the 1830s and those shown in the plans represent the earliest and smallest types.[1] The plans reveal that each front room, described as a living room, occupied the greater part of the available floor space – around 60 per cent. To maximise the space in the living room, the stairs were located at the back of the house. The only downstairs fireplace was in the living room, so it was here that cooking took place. In fact, the front room can best be

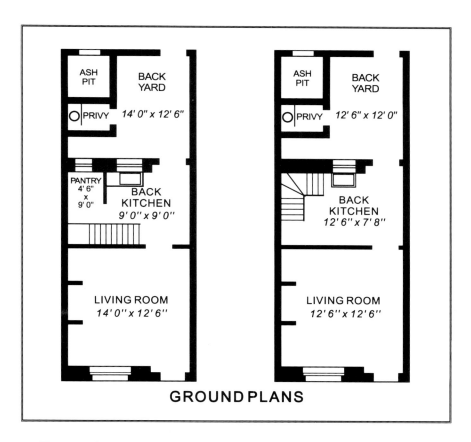

FIGURE 1. Re-drawn ground-floor plans of two cottages at Egerton, near Bolton, built by the Ashworths in the 1830s.

---

[1] Ibid., p. 118.

regarded as a living room/kitchen. It was by far the most used part of the house, providing the focus for everyday domestic life and perhaps giving sleeping space too. By contrast, the rear room was less comfortable and served a more limited range of functions, principally washing and food preparation.

Precisely when houses of this type first appeared is uncertain, though numerous examples, commonly dating from the late eighteenth and early nineteenth centuries, can still be identified. They mostly occur in short terraces and, despite modernisation, often display the vernacular qualities characteristic of this period. In Lancashire, those in the lowland zone are usually built from rough-textured, wide-jointed brick, while those in upland districts are of local stone, frequently laid as watershot coursing. As is customary with vernacular houses, decoration is minimal. Most have a two-pot chimney stack and hence two fireplaces, one in the living room/kitchen and one in the bedroom above.

These houses constitute a distinctive group, but they nonetheless show notable variation in the accommodation standards offered. Thus, in some early examples only one fireplace was provided, as single-pot chimney stacks indicate. Again, the Ashworth plans reveal that one cottage was rather larger than the other, with enough space for a pantry in the rear room. These cottages, too, were decorated at the front with Tudor-style drip mouldings above the front doors and windows.[1] Plainly, developers took account of the varying rents that families could afford and, even during the early decades of the nineteenth century, offered choice in the type and range of domestic facilities they made available.

To appreciate this point more fully, it is necessary to consider other examples of the front living room/kitchen type of dwelling, especially those built for domestic weaving and as back-to-backs. In Lancashire, both types were well represented, the former perhaps being more widespread and numerous than the latter.

The ground-floor plan of an adjoining pair of two-up, two-down cottages equipped with loomshops is shown in Figure 2.[2] It is taken from an account book compiled during the late 1790s and early 1800s by James

---

[1] Ibid., Plate VI.

[2] Small loomshops of this type would have housed two looms. For evidence on the frequency with which they are likely to have occurred, see J. G. Timmins, 'Handloom weavers' cottages in central Lancashire: some problems of recognition', *Post-Medieval Archaeology*, xiii (1979), pp. 266–7.

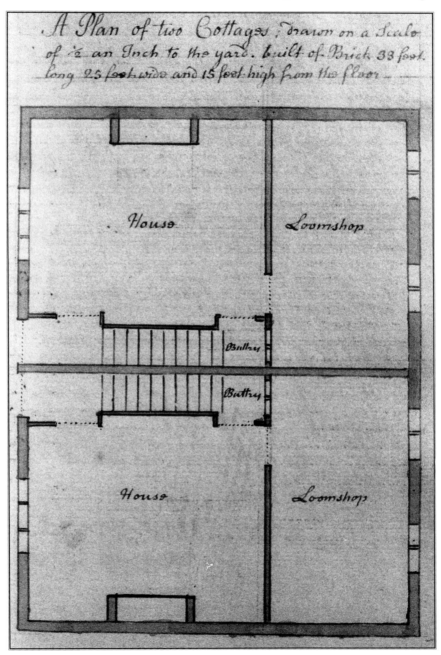

*A Plan of two Cottages; drawn on a Scale of ½ an Inch to the yard. built of Brick 33 feet long 25 feet wide and 15 feet high from the floor —*

House     Loomshop

Buttry

Buttry

House     Loomshop

FIGURE 2. Ground-floor plan of two cottages with loomshops, taken from the account book of James Brandwood of Turton, compiled in the late eighteenth/early nineteenth centuries. (Turton Tower Museum.)

Brandwood of Turton, near Bolton.[1] It can be seen that, in each cottage, the rear downstairs room was used as a loomshop, so that the front room, or 'house', had to serve as a combined kitchen, living room and scullery. Intriguingly, Brandwood does not record any sinks or slop-stones, so no indication is given as to whether the cottage was connected to mains drainage or supplied with tap water. Given the need to maintain a humid atmosphere in the loomshop to facilitate cotton weaving, no back door was provided. For the same reason, it is unlikely that the loomshop windows would have opened.[2] At least, though, space was made for a small buttery, as well as for a vestibule.

With regard to back-to-back houses, the plan of a representative four-roomed example is shown in Figure 3. Probably erected during the mid-Victorian years, its location was 8 Adelaide Street, Rochdale. Such

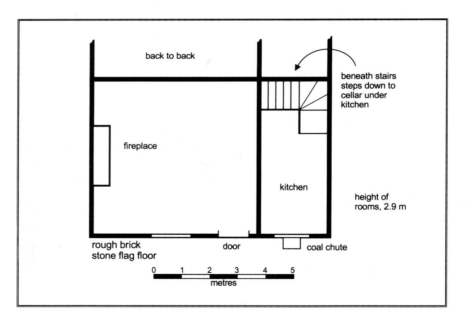

FIGURE 3. Ground-floor plan of house at 8 Adelaide Street, Rochdale
(after survey by J. G. Timmins).

---

[1]  The original is kept in Turton Tower Museum.
[2]  For further details on the importance of humidity in hand weaving, see J. G. Timmins, *Handloom Weavers' Cottages in Central Lancashire* (C.N.W.R.S., 1977), pp. 20–3.

dwellings were double-fronted, the centrally placed door giving access to the former living room/kitchen. As in the Ashworth examples, no spere or vestibule was included. However, there was a coal cellar beneath the scullery. Such back-to-backs offered more spacious accommodation than was usual with this type of dwelling, in some instances having two first-floor bedrooms and another in the attic.[1]

Although of similar size and plan-form to the Ashworth cottages, the two-up, two-downs built for hand weavers and as back-to-backs would have been viewed by contemporaries as offering accommodation of a much inferior standard. Their main concern was the absence of back doors, the consequences of which were graphically articulated by Samuel Hope Wraith, a surgeon who in 1849 reported on the sanitary condition of Darwen.[2] Given the importance domestic weaving attained in the town, he may well have been referring to cottages similar to those depicted in the Brandwood plans:[3]

> Many . . . houses have no back doors, nor any opening behind to cause a free ventilation. Many are without any back premises at all; and I frequently see the occupants emptying their chamber utensils, in those back streets, upon the surface of the streets.

Of course, concerns about deposits of filth and bad house ventilation were frequently voiced by contemporaries, amongst them that most eminent of social reformers, Edwin Chadwick. That they often held to the miasmic theory of disease – that, essentially, disease was spread by gases released from decomposing matter – helps to explain their anxiety about the problem of filth.[4] This being so, they would have seen little point in improving house ventilation if accumulations of filth were not also tackled.

In concluding this section, two main points should be emphasised. Firstly, two-up, two-down houses with living room/kitchens may well have formed the predominant house type in Lancashire, and in other parts of the country, during the late eighteenth and early nineteenth centuries, if not beyond. Usually built in terraces, they formed a cheap

---

[1]  This was certainly the case in West Yorkshire. For examples, see Lucy Caffyn, *Workers' Housing in West Yorkshire, 1750–1920* (H.M.S.O., 1986), pp. 109–12.

[2]  W. Lee, *Report to the General Board of Health on . . . the Township of Over Darwen* (1853), pp. 12–13.

[3]  Between 1813 and 1815, when hand weaving was at its height in Over Darwen, as many as 55 per cent of fathers recorded in local parish registers were described as hand weavers. For details see Darwen W.E.A. Local History Group, *The Darwen Area during the Industrial Revolution* (1987), p. 18.

[4]  See, for example, E. C. Midwinter, *Social Administration in Lancashire, 1830–60* (1969), p. 46.

and adaptable type of housing, meeting a range of accommodation requirements. Secondly, such houses showed significant variation in quality. Relatively few would have been regarded as 'model' dwellings, and far too many would have provided accommodation that was at best inconvenient and at worst downright insanitary. Yet, as Angus Reach, the contemporary journalist, was at pains to point out, they could often be made into comfortable homes, even if this was only achieved with considerable effort.

> A parlour kitchen can be made after its own fashion, a very cheerful apartment. Many a one I have recently visited, in which gleams of a good fire were playing on polished potlids and glancing crockery, arranged tidily and orderly upon the well-scoured racks, the floor either carpeted with a decent drugget, or nicely and brightly sanded: many a house of this class, I repeat, I have lately entered, in which the sensation of comfort was decidedly in the ascendant.[1]

## Developments in the front living room / kitchen type

In one respect the problems arising from building two-up, two-down houses without back doors had eased by the time Dr Wraith compiled his report. This was because cotton handloom weavers' cottages were not being built in Lancashire after the 1820s.[2] Moreover, once the loomshop in such cottages ceased to be used for hand weaving, it might be converted into a scullery, with one of the window openings being enlarged to create a back door.[3]

Despite such improvements, the absence of back doors still caused concern since, as field observation reveals, the back-to-back form of the two-up, two-down house was erected in some quantity beyond the middle of the nineteenth century. This type of dwelling was found mainly, if not exclusively, in the east and south-east of the county, perhaps reflecting the influence of Yorkshire practice.[4] Meanwhile, through-houses with

---

[1] J. Ginswick (ed.), *Labour and the poor in England and Wales, 1849–51* (1983), p. 192.

[2] J. G. Timmins, *The Last Shift: the decline of handloom weaving in nineteenth-century Lancashire* (forthcoming, 1993), p. 39.

[3] Examples can be seen at 10–24 Blackburn Road, Edgworth, near Bolton.

[4] Considerable numbers were erected in Rossendale, as field investigation reveals. For illustrations of examples in Salford, see V. I. Tomlinson, *Salford . . . in pictures* (1974), p. 38.

front living room/kitchens continued to be built. If, for the most part, they provided a fairly basic standard of accommodation, there are indications that they were becoming increasingly better-appointed as the century progressed. Thus, mid-Victorian examples at Woolwich Street, Blackburn, were equipped with speres inside the front doors;[1] at Cellini Street, Bolton with small front gardens and railed boundary walls;[2] and at Miles Street, Preston with water boilers or 'set pots', which were located in the scullery and were used for washing clothes (Figure 4).[3] These houses were also situated beyond the worst overcrowding in the town centres. They comprised part of the larger developments of grid-iron terraces, each one having its own back yard and privy.

That front living room/kitchen houses remained popular throughout the Victorian era is indicated in the writings of T. W. Cutler. As late as 1896 he was advocating that any cottage for a married couple must have 'a good living-room, and a small scullery or wash-house, in which to work, but not to live'.[4] Admittedly, he also stressed the need to have three bedrooms, so that male and female children could be separated. Even so, he saw no necessity to alter the traditional plan-form of the downstairs rooms. In his view, these could be made healthy and convenient, well suited to the needs of family life. Thus, he argues, it is

> a good plan to board the walls of the living room, and varnish, as they can then be easily kept clean, and can be disinfected and revarnished in case of illness. Dwarf cupboards should be provided in the living room, for the women's work, and the tops can be used for bookshelves, and a kitchener will provide a hot place for the kettle and saucepans, with an oven for cooking meat and baking bread.

As for the scullery, several important facilities could be provided: 'The scullery should have well-ventilated cupboards for food and stores, a good-sized copper, a large, deep, white glazed earthenware sink, with draining board and plate rack; the sink being deep it can also be used for a washing trough, and also a bath for small children'.[5]

---

[1]  They comprised nos. 65–81.
[2]  They were on the south side of the street.
[3]  N. Morgan, *An Introduction to the Social History of Housing in Victorian Preston* (n.d.), p. 50. See also A. Quiney, *House and Home* (1986), p. 106.
[4]  T. W. Cutler, *Cottages and Country Buildings* (1896), pp. 14–15.
[5]  Ibid., p. 15.

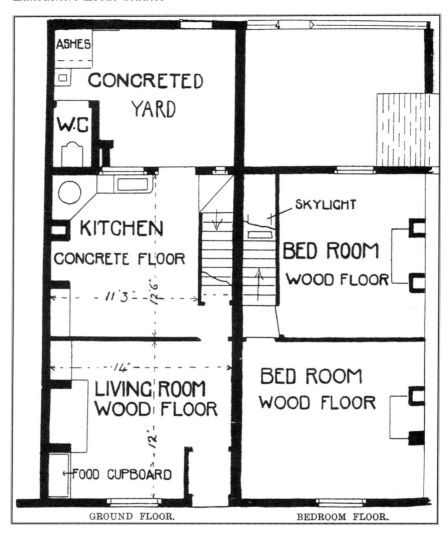

FIGURE 4. Plan of through-house with front living room:
this example is from Manchester.

Even though, as the next section will demonstrate, new types of ground-floor layout had become common in four- and five-roomed houses by the late nineteenth century, the houses described by Cutler were still regarded as model dwellings. He does not refer to any in the North West, but houses of similar design and quality were being built in

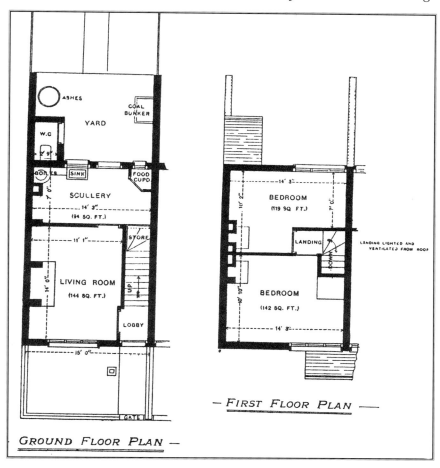

FIGURE 5. Plan of Manchester Corporation model housing of the type built on the Blackley estate in the early 1900s.

the region at this time. They include examples at the Blackley estate in Manchester (Figure 5);[1] at Fulham Street, Nelson (Figure 6);[2] and at no less a place than Port Sunlight (Figure 7).[3] Facilities and appearance

---

[1]  J. Cornes, *Modern Housing in Town and Country* (1905), p. 101.
[2]  Ibid., p. 110.
[3]  T. R. Marr, *Housing Conditions in Salford and Manchester* (1904), pp. 78–9.

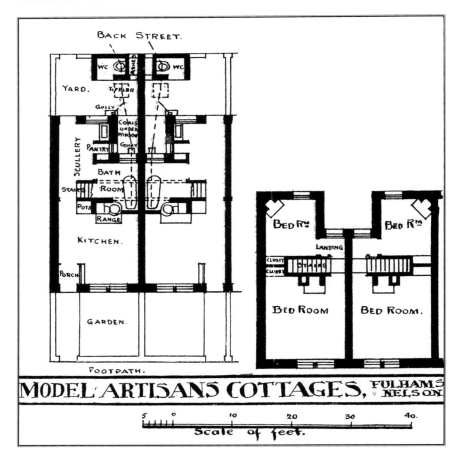

FIGURE 6. Plan of the model artisans' cottages built in the 1890s at Fulham St., Nelson.

varied somewhat, but all featured vestibules, front garden space, outside water-closets (tipplers at Nelson) and rear bedroom fireplaces.

Two major conclusions arise from this discussion. Firstly, in Lancashire as elsewhere, the two-up, two-down house with a front living room/kitchen continued to be built throughout the nineteenth century. Secondly, houses of this type could be readily upgraded to incorporate a range of improved facilities, so that the best among them could still be regarded as model dwellings. In all probability, it was the ease with which these houses could be adapted to conform to rising standards that played a major role in the longevity of their popularity.

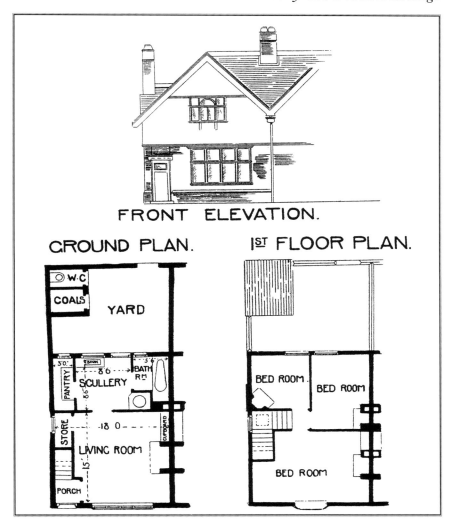

FIGURE 7. The 'Sunlight Plan' housing constructed at Port Sunlight by Lever Bros.

## *The emergence of the front parlour house*

During the middle decades of the nineteenth century, two-up, two-down houses of an improved design were becoming increasingly common in Lancashire. Essentially, the improvements stemmed from transferring cooking facilities from the front to the rear downstairs room. In this way the familiar back kitchen emerged. It is not clear when the first two-up, two-downs with back kitchens were built, but they were certainly found in some quantity by the mid-Victorian period.[1]

In moving the kitchen, space had to be found in the rear room for a fireplace substantial enough for cooking to take place. Accordingly, the size of the rear room had to be increased, either by re-allocating the available space at ground-floor level or by extending it – or a combination of both. It is plain from the Ashworth examples that both strategies were employed at an early date, the latter probably being more important than the former. Thus, in the smallest cottage (Figure 1), the rear downstairs room occupied a floor space of 94 square feet, 36 per cent of the total. In the largest (Figure 8), the figures were 135 square feet and 41 per cent.[2] The tendency may well have been for the proportionate figure to increase somewhat in later examples, though probably not to any marked degree.

No longer required as a kitchen, the front room could be used in a variety of ways. In some instances – perhaps many – it would have become a general living room as well, possibly, as providing sleeping space. It could be made more comfortable by the installation of a vestibule. Frequently, though, this was extended into a

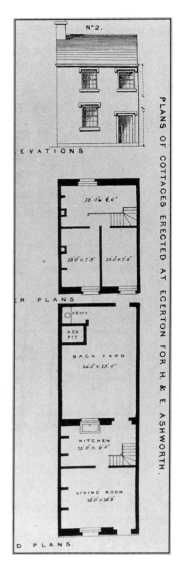

FIGURE 8. Plan and elevation of cottages built at Egerton for H. & E. Ashworth.

---

[1] This view is based largely on a survey of several hundred houses in the Hole House area of Blackburn which were demolished during the late 1970s. For details see J. G. Timmins, 'Towards a procedure for recording threatened housing', *The Local Historian*, vol. 15, no. 1 (1982), pp. 6–20.

[2] J. C. Loudon, *An Encyclopaedia of Cottage, Farm and Villa Architecture and Furniture* (1842), p. 1155.

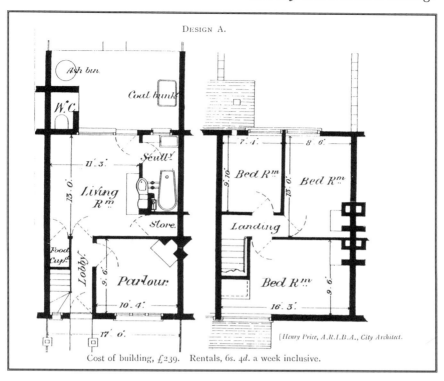

Design A.

Ash bin.

Coal bunk

W.C.

11'. 3'.

Living R<sup>m</sup>

13'. 0'.

Scull?

Store

Food Cup?

Lobby

9'. 6'.

Parlour

10'. 4'.

17'. 0'.

7'. 4'.

8'. 6'.

Bed R<sup>m</sup>

9'. 10'.

Bed R<sup>m</sup>

13'. 0'.

Landing

Bed R<sup>m</sup>

9'. 6'.

9'. 6'.

16'. 3'.

[*Henry Price, A.R.I.B.A., City Architect.*

Cost of building, £239.  Rentals, 6s. 4d. a week inclusive.

FIGURE 9. Plan of Manchester Corporation house (early 1900s) showing lobby access and separate enclosed front parlour.

lobby, which gave access to the kitchen without passing through the front room. Accordingly, an enclosed front parlour was provided, which gave a much greater degree of privacy in downstairs rooms than had hitherto been customary.[1] Figure 9 shows one example.

The way Lancashire families used front parlours varied. In the mid-nineteenth century, Reach found that an example he inspected at Hulme, Manchester, contained 'one of those nondescript pieces of furniture which play a double part in domestic economy – a bed by night, a wardrobe all day'. He noted, also, two tables and several chairs, along with cupboards containing crockery. Seemingly, therefore, the room was

---

[1]  In contemporary plans the term 'parlour' was often used when a lobby was incorporated, whilst 'living room' was used when it was absent.

used as both bedroom and dining room, thereby making full use of the available space.[1]

Not every front parlour in two-up, two-down houses, or even in larger dwellings, was so well utilised, however. From oral testimony relating to Lancaster and Barrow, Elizabeth Roberts has shown that most local families chose to restrict parlour functions, despite the pressure on space that large families inevitably brought. These functions included family parties at Christmas, laying out of bodies and, in more prosperous household, singing round the piano on Sunday.[2]

Other writers confirm the under-utilisation of the parlour, and Allan Clarke, editor of the *Northern Weekly*, was in no doubt as to the reason for it. Writing in 1899, he remarked that the parlour was unoccupied except on Sundays, being 'only kept for brag. Ostentatious superfluity in the idea of the artisan's wife is, as with those in higher grades of society, a sign of superiority'.[3] In quoting Clarke's observations, John Burnett suggests that the possession of a parlour reflected the desire to express achievement and respectability, as well as to seek identity by imitating the behaviour of social superiors.[4]

How far any 'ostentatious superfluity' really was a gender issue is not addressed by Clarke, though he might have sought to strengthen his argument by noting that numerous married women would, in their teenage years, have worked as domestic servants in households where parlours were indeed seen as 'best rooms'. And Elizabeth Roberts reports the conversion of one parlour to a workroom, a matter causing much friction between a husband and his more socially conscious wife.[5]

Whether the front room in improved houses without a lobby was also under-utilised has received less comment. However, T. R. Marr implies that this was indeed the case. Writing about the numerous two-up, two-down houses in Manchester and Salford during the early twentieth century, he remarks that 'The upstairs rooms are generally bedrooms; the back room (though sometimes the front room) downstairs is kitchen and

---

[1] J. Ginswick (ed.) op. cit., p. 30.

[2] E. Roberts. *Working-class Barrow and Lancaster* (Lancaster. 19776. p. 30.

[3] A. Clarke, *The Effects of the Factory System* (1985 reprint of 1899 edition), p. 134. A mid-nineteenth-century writer noted that Manchester parlours were reserved for holiday and festive occasions: *The Cotton Metropolis* (repr. 1972), p. 7.

[4] J. Burnett, *A Social History of Housing, 1815–1970* (1978), p. 169.

[5] E. Roberts, op. cit., p. 30.

living room, and generally some attempt is made to keep the other downstairs room as a parlour'.

The result, inevitably, was that 'the family overcrowds during the day in a room in which cooking, washing, etc., are carried on, and in which the children play, and then overcrowds two bedrooms at night'. Marr goes on to observe that the way space was allocated bore little or no relation to ordinary family life and, in more constructive vein than other commentators, proposed a solution which apparently aimed to satisfy both family needs and social aspirations: 'The living-room or kitchen, frequently too small for the many functions it had to serve in a working-class household might, with advantage, be enlarged at the expense of the seldom used front room or parlour'.[1] There is, perhaps, a hint of desperation in this, reflecting the writer's view about how entrenched the social value of maintaining a private parlour had become in working-class culture.

It only remains in this section to note how two-up, two-down houses with private front parlours, or with living rooms, differ externally from those with front living rooms. Two features can be highlighted. Firstly, the chimney stacks of the 'private parlour' types are likely to display three or more pots, revealing the increased provision of fireplaces.[2] Secondly, window lights are incorporated above the front door of both parlour and living room houses in order to illuminate the lobby or vestibule respectively. Any other differences arise from general improvements in house quality and style, rather than from changes in the downstairs plan form.

To summarise, two-up, two-down houses erected in Lancashire during the Victorian and Edwardian periods were increasingly of the rear-kitchen type. They did not by any means supersede those equipped with front living room/kitchens, and nor did they always aspire to a front enclosed parlour. Those without this facility, perhaps the most frequently occurring type, could bring considerably improved accommodation standards, since they offered the best opportunity for downstairs space to be utilised effectively. In this respect, they may have catered more adequately for family needs than two-up, two-downs with enclosed

---

[1]  T. R. Marr, op. cit., pp. 37, 94.
[2]  However, houses with three chimney stacks may have had two fireplaces in the front rooms and a set-pot in the rear downstairs room.

parlours, even if they were less successful in meeting the social aspirations of their inhabitants.

## *Reasons for the change in design*

Discussion on the improved standards of accommodation available to working-class families during the late Victorian and Edwardian era tends to emphasise the impact of bye-law regulations, along with the rise in real incomes. The former, even though they might be reluctantly implemented, raised minimum standards of hygiene and comfort in new houses, as well as ensuring better-built dwellings. At the same time, the latter created an effective demand for higher accommodation standards, which enabled a small minority of working-class families to live in the type of housing that, in no little measure, conformed to the plan-form and other design characteristics favoured by their social superiors.

Whether bye-law regulations had any influence in developing the plan-form of the two-up, two-down house is doubtful, however. This is because the type of improvements they brought could be readily incorporated into the traditional, front living room/kitchen type.[1] The resultant dwellings were less well appointed than improved two-up, two-downs, but would have been available at a lower rental. Accordingly, they would have extended the range of income levels for which improved housing could be provided. That the builders were alert to this consideration is well exemplified by the case of the Crossley's development at West Hill Park, Halifax. A product of the mid-1860s, it comprised model dwellings, some with private parlours at the front and some with living room/kitchens.[2]

As regards the impact of rising incomes on the plan-form of two-up, two-downs, a rather stronger case can be made. It is conceivable, for instance, that better-off householders could have generated a demand for houses affording a higher standard of comfort. Their needs could be met in various ways, not least by the inclusion of rear-room fireplaces. New possibilities would thereby arise with regard to the functions of the

---

[1] For a concise account, see M. Gaskell, *Building Control: National Legislation and the Introduction of Bye-laws in Victorian England* (B.A.L.H., 1983).
[2] L. Caffyn, op. cit., p. 95.

downstairs rooms. Even so, this does not explain why these rooms assumed particular uses rather than others. Further explanation is clearly needed.

In seeking it, the comments of contemporaries are particularly revealing, and none more so than those of Angus Bethune Reach. His letters to the *Morning Chronicle*, written in 1849, express profound disapproval of houses which he saw in the Ancoats district of Manchester. Most of them had living room/kitchens at the front. He wrote that 'Decidedly the worst feature of the house tenements is the . . . invariable opening of the street-door into the parlour. One step takes you from the pavement to the shrine of the Penates'. It must be appreciated that Reach consistently calls the front room the parlour, but is here referring to the usual type of two-up, two-downs in Ancoats, in which 'the front room on the ground floor is used as both parlour and kitchen'.

Reach's objections to dwellings of this type were partly on grounds of health. They tended, he maintains, to be 'a fruitful source of rheumatic and catarrh-bestowing draughts'. But he was equally, if not more, concerned about the lack of privacy they gave to those who lived in them. 'The occupant', he observes, 'cannot open his door, or stand upon his threshold, without revealing the privacy of his room to all by-passers'. In fact, he turned this to good advantage, for he found that most front doors of the Ancoats houses stood 'hospitably open', giving him 'easy opportunity of noting the interiors' as he passed along.[1]

Other contemporaries raised different objections. For instance, G. T. Robinson noted in 1872 that the houses of the poor, which had one general room for cooking, washing and 'all the daily needs of life', opened directly into the 'uncleanly streets'. Presumably he feared that the dirt they contained was all too easily transferred to the living room. Nor, he thought, was this type of accommodation conducive to family morality, since 'all those functions of life are performed in public which decency compels all those who can do so to discharge in private'.[2] Unfortunately, he gives no further details. Doubtless, though, he would have felt that weight was added to his argument with regard to those households containing non-family members, particularly lodgers.

---

[1] J. Ginswick (ed.), op. cit., pp. 21–2.
[2] G. T. Robinson, 'On town dwellings for the working classes', *Transactions of the Manchester Statistical Society* (1871–2), pp. 71–2.

Also noteworthy are the comments of James Hole. He was actually writing about back-to-back houses, but his reference to a single fire suggests that his remarks could apply with equal force to dwellings with front living room/kitchens: 'The reeking clothes round the one fire, and the general sense of discomfort caused by the whole family "pigging" together in one small room, tend to lessen tidiness in women, and to destroy the attractiveness of home'.[1]

The same theme was rehearsed by Allan Clarke, from an equally male-orientated perspective. This time referring to two-up, two-downs with front living room/kitchens, he remarked that 'on wet days, the clothes are dried in the living room, to the discomfort of the husband, when he comes home from the factory'.[2] It was left to T. R. Marr to take this line of argument to its logical conclusion: 'When the home is over-crowded, dull and dismal, and where there are few or no opportunities for wholesome recreation, the public-house is the only place to turn to'.[3]

Having articulated the drawbacks of the front living room/kitchen houses, solutions were required. As far as Angus Reach was concerned, much could be achieved by providing houses in which 'the street door . . . opens into a narrow passage, from which the stairs to the bedrooms also ascend'.[4] This lobby or hallway, he maintained, by itself placed houses 'fifty per cent above those built after the old fashion'.[5] It clearly helped to counter anxieties about screening family living from the view of the passers-by and reducing health hazards from front-door draughts. To a degree the same effects could be achieved by installing a vestibule or porch, field work suggesting that the former expedient was frequently adopted.[6] Even so, these measures could not eliminate the other concerns expressed by contemporaries and a more radical solution was obviously required.

It was achieved by transferring cooking facilities to the rear downstairs room. Apart from meeting Reach's concerns about privacy and health, this arrangement had several other advantages. Firstly, the house water

---

[1] J. Hole, *Houses of the Working Classes with Suggestions for their Improvement* (1866), p. 11.

[2] A. Clarke, op. cit., p. 133.

[3] T. R. Marr, op. cit., pp. 26–7.

[4] J. Ginswick (ed.), op. cit., p. 19.

[5] Ibid., p. 22.

[6] Loudon favoured porches because he, too, objected to front doors opening directly into the living room and because he thought they would 'take away from the full uniformity of the exteriors'. See J. C. Loudon, op. cit., p. 1154.

supply and cooking facilities could be brought together, an arrangement which added so much to the convenience of running the household that it eventually became the norm. Secondly, with two downstairs rooms available, different functions could be ascribed to each, thereby reducing the discomfort, if not lessening the untidiness to which James Hole referred. It could also go a long way towards alleviating Robinson's concerns about family decency. Lastly, the front room, screened from the rest of the house by a lobby, could be used as a private parlour. Its attractiveness and superiority could be enhanced in various ways, especially by providing a bay window, a small front garden and architectural embellishment, both inside and out. Indeed, it was suggested, the possession of such a room could do much to inculcate habits of self-respect, as well as promoting a 'degree of laudable ambition' through maintaining it 'in the handsomest manner possible'.[1]

It can be seen, then, that contemporary concerns about the inadequacies of two-up, two-down houses with front living room/kitchens ranged widely. Such dwellings, it was argued, not only lacked privacy from the prying eyes of outsiders, but could do much to harm the health, comfort and morality of their inhabitants. In part, these anxieties could be met by the relatively simple expedient of adding lobbies or vestibules behind the front door. However, to alleviate the 'problems' more fully, it was necessary to go further and to alter the downstairs layout of the houses. Accordingly, the rear room was converted into a kitchen and, depending upon whether a lobby was preferred to a vestibule, the front room came to be used either as a private parlour or as a living room, which might still be regarded as a 'best room'. It was a transformation that, in Lancashire at least, proved extremely popular.

## Conclusion

Much of the improvement which took place in working-class housing during the nineteenth century, particularly from the mid-Victorian years, arose from the type of requirements that bye-law legislation imposed. They brought more spacious street layouts; lower housing densities; airier

---

[1]  *The Cotton Metropolis* (repr. 1972), p. 7.

and lighter houses; and private rear yards with individual privies. Sounder constructional techniques were also fostered, not least with regard to drains and foundations. Since they only applied to new houses the bye-laws had a muted impact on improving overall housing quality, but given the large volume of domestic building which took place in Lancashire during the late nineteenth and early twentieth centuries, their importance should not be understated.

Meanwhile, well before bye-laws were being enacted, considerable numbers of improved working-class houses were being built in the county. Mostly of the two-up and two-down type, though increasingly with rear extensions,[1] they were characterised by a back kitchen rather than a front living room/kitchen. Some, though probably a relatively small proportion, could boast an enclosed front parlour. These improved houses were erected partly in response to varied and, over the long term, rising working-class incomes. But the plan-forms they adopted owed much to the attitudes embodied in one line of contemporary thought, regarding the manner in which working-class people should live. This condemned the front living room/kitchen on a variety of grounds, including the lack of privacy it brought both within the household and from outsiders.

Despite such concerns, houses with front living room/kitchens continued to be built during the later decades of the nineteenth century, some even attaining the status of model dwellings. In general, they offered a relatively cheap form of accommodation, being smaller and less well appointed than the back-kitchen type of house. Quite possibly, too, the families which occupied them made better use of the available space than did those living in front-parlour houses. Even so, there can be no doubt that back-kitchen houses grew to prominence. Those with an enclosed front parlour could be of especial help in meeting the needs of families with social aspirations, even if, within the home, day-to-day living was still largely confined to a single room. Those with an unenclosed front living-room could more clearly differentiate their various household activities, while at the same time meeting many of the contemporary objections to front living room/kitchens. For these reasons, this type was particularly popular, and it may well have outnumbered the 'enclosed parlour' type by a large margin.

---

[1]  S. Muthesius, *The English Terraced House* (1982), p. 123.

# Wheels Within Wheels – the Lancashire Cycling Clubs of the 1880s and '90s

*Zoë Lawson*

URING THE LAST TWO DECADES of the nineteenth century the improved design and greater availability of cycles produced a cycling craze which it seemed would last for ever. Beginning as a London fashion in the 1870s, the popularity of cycling quickly spread throughout the country, but its greatest stronghold was in the industrial towns of the Midlands and the North. Lancashire, in particular, was at the forefront of the cycling boom. Already a mature industrial society, it readily assimilated new ideas and inventions, while the rising living standards, increasing leisure time and a growing appetite for consumer goods of its people ensured the cycle's success. The cycle represented the dawn of a new era of social freedom and equality. Anyone could travel anywhere at any time, unhampered by horse and carriage or railway timetables. For cyclists from the industrial towns it meant perhaps a greater freedom – escape from the grime and noise into the peaceful and, as it seemed to them, idyllic countryside.

Cycling clubs were at the very heart of the cycling boom, giving it life and structure. They made cycling a social as well as a physical activity and provided the impetus for its further expansion and diversification. In Lancashire the clubs can be seen as evolving in three separate stages, as new designs, cheaper models and changes in society's attitude to cycling altered their social composition and consequently their activities. The first clubs accompanied the rise in popularity of cycling, with the development of the ordinary bicycle (commonly known as the penny farthing), and their members were almost exclusively young men from the middle classes. Then, the advent of the 'safety' bicycle in 1885, combined with the development of the pneumatic tyre two years later, led to a renewed interest in cycling in the late 1880s. New clubs were established with a wider social class of membership, though still confined to men. Finally, from the early 1890s onwards there was an even greater cycling craze as it became increasingly fashionable for all, and in particular for women. This was to have a significant impact on the clubs. The development of the clubs in Lancashire is, to a large extent, a mirror of the national scene but there is a local flavour.

## 1: Early cycling clubs

The development of the ordinary bicycle in the early 1870s signalled the start of cycling as a popular sport and pastime, for it was the first really efficient and practical design of bicycle. Nevertheless, riding these high bicycles required considerable agility and they soon became a cult for athletic and adventurous young men; the higher the wheel the greater the prowess. Riding at such a height, with inadequate brakes or no brakes at all, involved enormous risk and accidents were a frequent occurrence. Apart from the physical dangers of riding the 'ordinary', the early cyclists also had to contend with ridicule, verbal abuse and outright hostility both from passers-by and, in particular, from the drivers of horse-drawn vehicles, who were not averse to forcing cyclists off the road. To some extent the cyclists were to blame, for a few riders took delight in racing other vehicles and speeding down on unsuspecting pedestrians, which often resulted in collision. The cyclists were also subject to malicious practical jokes, such as sticks poked in their wheels or wires stretched across the road causing them to be pitched forward.

Such factors were partly responsible for the establishment of clubs, where cycling with fellow clubmen combined comradeship with an element of protection. Clubs were founded in Lancashire from the late 1870s onwards and by 1882 there were over thirty in existence, with eight in Liverpool alone. Members of these early clubs were exclusively young men; Henry J. Whitworth was, at the age of twenty-three, the oldest member of the Rossendale Bicycle and Tricycle Club when it was founded in 1878.[1] They were also

---

[1] *Rossendale Free Press*, 29 July 1899.

PLATE 1. Entrants for the one-mile tricycle race held by the Rossendale Bicycle and Tricycle Club on the Whitworth track in July 1898. The winner was A. J. Whitworth (second from right), a founder member of the club.

predominantly from the middle classes: cycling was too controversial for the upper classes and beyond the means of the working classes. The better quality bicycles cost upwards of £30, while even second-hand ones were around £4 (equivalent to about three weeks' wages for a skilled worker). The expense of joining a club was also prohibitive for working people, for apart from the annual subscription of around 7s. 6d. there was the club uniform to buy. Uniforms were compulsory when riding out with the club, and they were not cheap. The Blackburn C. C. uniform cost 32s. in the early 1880s, while the grey stockings of the Vale of Lune Cycling Club alone cost 7s. 6d.

Clubs took to wearing uniforms not only to give themselves a sense of identity and (they hoped) respectability, but also to enable them to give a show of solidarity against any antagonism. The uniforms were usually dark, to conceal the dust and dirt of the roads; black, brown, green or blue were especially favoured. The Anfield Cycling Club (established in 1879) wore a black uniform 'decent, sober and correct',[1] with a little hussar black braiding on the jacket, and a huntsman cap; Blackburn (established in 1880) wore a blue Norfolk coat and knee breeches, and a blue helmet. Preston Cycling Club was an exception and must have cut a dashing scene in their ruby red cord breeches, brown jackets, hose and jockey caps.

The uniforms were indicative of an almost military discipline evident in the early clubs. The clubs rode in formation with their captain at the front and a sub-captain at the rear, and the rules dictated that the captain's orders were to be obeyed at all times while out riding with the club. Most clubs had a bugler who signalled commands to mount, dismount, ride slower, faster and so on. The bugler also warned the cyclists of dangers ahead and passers-by of the cyclists' approach. A somewhat farcical episode surrounded the attempt by Preston C. C. to sport a bugle. It seems that, having bought the bugle for the princely sum of 22s., there was no member 'sufficiently musical to master it'[2] in spite of the purchase of an instruction book and subsequently lessons from a teacher. Eventually the instrument was sold, and Preston suffered the embarrassment of being without a bugler.

The cycle runs were the clubs' *raison d'être*. Most rode out on Saturday afternoons and some on mid-week evenings as well. Sunday cycling was generally frowned upon and although individual members did cycle on Sundays, the clubs prohibited the wearing of uniforms on such occasions so that such cyclists could not be associated with a particular club. A Blackburn C. C. rule stated that: 'No member be allowed to wear the Club hat on Sundays. Any member offending this rule will be liable to a fine of 2s. 6d.'.[3] Fixtures were set by each club for the cycling season, which generally lasted from early April to October, and runs invariably went to places of local interest or scenic beauty: Blackburn C. C. went to Mellor Brook, Clitheroe, Ribchester and Whittle Springs for their

---

[1]  F. Marriott, *The Anfielders: being the story of the Anfield Bicycle Club, 1879–1955* (A.B.C., 1956), p. 2.
[2]  W. Pilkington, *The History of Preston Cycling Club and Longridge Cycling Club: Jubilee, 1878–1938* (Preston Guardian, 1928), p. 11.
[3]  Blackburn Library Local Studies Collection, *Blackburn Cycling Club Rule Book* (n.d., c. 1885), p. 61.

Saturday club runs in May 1885. The club runs were, for many, a ticket to freedom. Anxious to escape their grey grim towns, the members cycled through the surrounding countryside like an invading army, stealing precious breaths of fresh air and capturing scenes of beauty to take back home with them.

The runs also gave members the chance to try out new cycling skills, to experience the exhilaration of speeding downhill with feet over their handle-bars, and the thrill of the ever-present danger of being pitched forward. However, 'scorchers', a term used for cyclists who went at excessive speeds, were not usually tolerated because they gave the clubs a bad name. Even so, the rural areas at first took exception to these town people intruding upon their villages on strange contraptions – hence the practical jokes. In contrast, the country innkeepers welcomed the cyclists for they brought lucrative trade which they had not seen since the mail-coach days. In fact so eager were the innkeepers for their custom that the Cyclists' Touring Club and the National Cyclists' Union (two national cycling bodies) were able to negotiate lower tariffs for their members with many hotels and inns. Calling at inns and tea-rooms *en route* became part of the tradition of the club runs, and they inevitably ended up at an inn in the evenings where impromptu concerts of singing and playing, known as 'smokers', took place.

Some clubs, such as the Anfield C. C., specialised in long distance runs, and members were awarded stars and medals for distances cycled. The greatest feat was the all-night twenty-four hour ride, known as the '24', for which members received a silver star for cycling 100 miles and a gold star for 200 miles. In 1885 a member of the Anfield Club, named Fell, was the first person to ride from Liverpool to London in twenty-four hours.

Apart from club runs, which were generally leisurely affairs, all clubs at this time went in for racing. The annual club races were a key feature in every club calendar. These were commonly held on cricket fields or similar grounds temporarily marked out for the occasion. In its early days, the Rossendale club held its races at Ramsbottom cricket field and both Preston and Blackburn C. C.s held their races at Preston Pleasure Gardens. The races covered a range of distances, from the five- or ten-mile championship to the one-, two- or three-mile handicap race. Road racing was also common in the 1880s. Blackburn C. C. had an annual fifty-mile (handicap) race, the route of which went from Blackburn to Lancaster via Preston and back again.

Cycle racing was inextricably bound up with the Victorian enthusiasm for athletic sports, which emanated from the public schools in the mid-nineteenth century and filtered downwards. The Victorians sought to rationalise sport, and rules and regulations were soon laid down for cycle racing. To the clubs racing was strictly for the 'gentleman amateur' and the National Cyclists' Union (the national sporting body) barred 'mechanics, artisans and labourers' as, according to *The Times* in April 1880, 'their muscular practice is held to give unfair advantage over more delicately nurtured competitors'.[1] The extent to which these regulations were put into practice in Lancashire in the early 1880s is not known, but certainly by the end of the decade the cycling champions came from varied backgrounds. John Clegg, the winner of the Blackburn C. C. fifty-mile road race, was a leather currier, while the famous Haslingden racing cyclist, Jack Cordingley, started his working life as a half-timer in a cotton

PLATE 2. Burnley C. C. in the 1880s: the military-style uniforms and helmets were characteristic of the early clubs.

---

[1] *The Times*, 26 April 1880, quoted in J. McGurn, *On Your Bicycle: an Illustrated History of Cycling* (1987), p. 61.

mill, and later joined his father in the furniture trade before setting up his own business as cycle manufacturer and shopkeeper.

Although the races were strictly for the amateur, and no money prizes were given, they could, nevertheless, be extremely lucrative for the successful winner. A cup valued at fifty guineas was the prize for the two-mile bicycle race held at Preston Guild in 1882. Apart from cups and medals, others prizes offered at races included such valuable items as clocks, dinner services and bicycles. Mr Calverly, a founder member of Burnley C. C., was a very successful racing cyclist and won between £300 and £400 in prizes during the 1880s.

The highlight of the year was the annual meet, when a cycling club invited neighbouring clubs to gather for a parade through the streets of its particular town. This was usually followed by a formal reception at an inn and a 'smoking' concert. The meets had a regimental air about them, each club riding in strict formation wearing their uniforms with pride. Their popularity is indicated by the 'Monstre Meet'[1] of cyclists at the Preston Guild held in 1882. This was attended by forty-one clubs from all over the north of England, and cyclists arrived from as far afield as Bradford, Cockermouth, and Newcastle. These were prestigious occasions for the clubs and the number of cyclists each club could muster was a matter of honour. Silver-plated bugles were commonly presented to the club with the greatest number in uniform in a parade. Such parades had dignity and showed to the world that the cycle was not just a fashionable toy but a machine which heralded a new age; it symbolised man and machine in harmony.

The cycling season ended in October, when the inclement weather and impassable roads made riding impossible to all but the most hardy of individuals. Clubs offered non-cycling activities in the winter months to retain members' interest. This was the time of year for the annual dinner, grand soirées, and the ever popular 'smoking' concerts. Blackburn C. C. actually offered weekly quadrille classes on a Thursday nights for its members. Clubs held 'Monstre' socials, in contrast to the 'Monstre' meets, when local clubs were invited for a get-together. Fifty members of surrounding clubs attended one such social held by Pendle C. C. in December 1882. After tea at the Swan Hotel in Whalley, there was the

---

[1] The word 'monstre' was commonly used in the late nineteenth century for cycling events: it is presumably just a variant spelling of 'monster'.

PLATE 3. A programme from a smoking concert held by Blackburn C. C. in February 1891. 'Smokers' were commonly impromptu concerts of singing (usually adaptations of music hall songs) and playing which took place in inns after club runs. However, some were more organised and formed part of a club's social events during the winter months.

inevitable 'smoker' which, as well as including the usual singing and piano-playing, had some unique turns as the *Blackburn Standard* records: 'Mr Railton (Blackburn) made some splendid sketches in charcoal and Mr Vipond gave some masterly performances on an instrument called the "fairy bells". This was the most entertaining part of the evening, as the instrument was one which probably had been heard but by few of those who were present'.[1]

Such social activities became more important than cycling for some clubs, and as the popularity of the ordinary bicycle dwindled in the mid-1880s these ended up as little more than gentlemen's social clubs. Fewer members turned out for club runs: in 1885, of Blackburn C. C.'s twenty-four members, at most only three went out on the Saturday runs in July, and one meeting was cancelled through lack of support. In an attempt to revive the spirit of the club, Blackburn offered prizes for the best attendance on club runs. It is probable that cycling might have declined into a minority sport for enthusiasts, had it not been for the invention in 1885 of a new design of bicycle, the 'safety'. This, accompanied by the development of the pneumatic tyre in 1887, created an upsurge in interest in cycling.

## 2: *Clubs in transition*

The safety bicycle is of crucial importance in cycling history, for it opened up the activity to a wider range of people, not only by making the bicycle relatively easy and safe to ride but also by putting cycling within the price range of the lower middle classes, the clerks and shop-assistants, and to some extent the skilled workers. All took to cycling with an unparalleled enthusiasm. As a result there was an enormous growth in membership of cycling clubs from the late 1880s onwards. Membership of Blackburn C. C. increased more than 50 per cent in 1889 alone, to over forty members. Many new clubs appeared on the scene, among them Lancaster, Burnley Victoria and Nelson Star C. C.s, all of which were established in 1887. These new clubs attracted a different class of member. Burnley Victoria C. C. offered its members 'advantageous terms enabling them

---

[1] *Blackburn Standard*, 2 Dec. 1882.

PLATE 4. Nelson Star Cycling Club, *c.* 1890. This was one of the new clubs established in the 1880s. The military-style uniforms of the early clubs were no longer in fashion, and nore were bugles. The members are all wearing whistles round their hats.

to acquire machines and accessories by payment of weekly subscriptions',[1] and was clearly aiming to attract those previously prevented from cycling because of the cost. It was a very successful club, and had over seventy members in its first year. Similarly, the Nelson Star C. C. had working-class members. James Duerden, for example, was a tackler in Hartley Nelson's Mill when he joined the club in 1888 at the age of eighteen.[2] Other clubs, like Blackburn, were concerned to retain their middle-class image and only gentlemen who were 'fit and proper persons'[3] could be elected members. Nevertheless, its list of members for 1889 included a boot- and shoe-maker and a leather currier, so even Blackburn was not totally exclusive.

---

[1] *Burnley Mid-Week Gazette*, 6 June 1888.
[2] *Nelson Leader*, 16 Mar. 1951.
[3] Blackburn Library Local Studies Collection, *Blackburn Cycling Club Minutes*, vol. 2.

The fact that the clubs had a wider class of membership indicates that more people were able to own bicycles. Historians of cycling have attributed this to the rising living standards of the late-nineteenth century combined with a lowering of the prices of bicycles, which put them within reach of the lower middle classes and skilled workers. In 1893 the price of a Rossendale Model C Roadster built by Jack Cordingley, a racing cyclist and manufacturer in Haslingden, was £12 10s. According to *The Wheeler* this 'price is well within the reach of the artisan class, who doubtless form the great bulk of Mr Cordingley's patrons'.[1] However, the price of a Model C was equivalent to at least seven weeks' wages for a skilled worker. It was a cost prohibitive to all but the most thrifty bachelor. Yet the skilled working class did have bicycles from the 1880s. How can these apparent contradictions be reconciled? As we have seen, some cycling clubs helped members to buy bicycles by weekly subscriptions and shops also offered hire-purchase schemes. In addition, there was an abundance of cheap second-hand ordinaries on the market in the late 1880s as wealthier cyclists bought new safety models.

The clubs were still exclusively male preserves, and there was little change in their activities except that the meets and races increased in popularity with both cyclists and the general public from the late 1880s. The new clubs, such as Burnley Victoria, surpassed the older clubs in enthusiasm. In 1888 Burnley Victoria won the much sought after silver cup at the North East Lancashire C. C. meet by having no fewer than fifty-six members in uniform — nearly half the total number attending the parade. Similarly, nearly 2,000 spectators attended the Burnley Victoria C. C.'s sports day in 1891, in spite of bad weather, and cyclists had come from as far away as Hull and Southport to compete. Rivalry between clubs was intense on these occasions. It was during this period that Jack Cordingley, the Haslingden racing cyclist, won the Rossendale championship for seven consecutive years between 1886 and 1892, an amazing feat. Road racing, however, ceased from 1890 because it was condemned by the National Cyclists' Union as a danger to the public. Thereafter, until 1940, racing was confined to field tracks and time-trials.

---

[1] *The Wheeler*, March 1893.

## 3: *Women and cycling*

The development of the safety bicycle opened up the world of cycling to women. A few women had ridden tricycles and sociables (a kind of side-by-side tandem) in the early days but the machines were heavy and impractical. The ordinary was, of course, too dangerous for women in long dresses to ride. The safety, on the other hand, was relatively easy and safe to ride, and middle-class women were eager to try out this new mode of transport. Yet in the 1880s women who cycled 'were regarded with a kind of pious horror'[1] and were considered socially unacceptable. According to Lillian Davidson, 'It was openly said that a woman who mounted a bicycle hopelessly unsexed herself'.[2] She was ridiculed and taunted wherever she went, and it was a brave women who subjected herself to such torment in the name of pleasure. A few persevered and by the mid-1890s attitudes to women cyclists had generally relaxed. Nevertheless, the *Clarion* maintained in 1895 that lady cyclists riding through Lancashire towns 'create quite a sensation'.[3]

Retaining feminine charm was the key to acceptability, and numerous handbooks were published to give advice on how this was to be accomplished. Dress was of paramount importance. To cycle in the contemporary fashion of voluminous skirts and large sleeves would court disaster, and alternative styles of dress were sought to meet the needs of the 'new woman'. The Rational Dress Society endeavoured to make full knickerbockers the accepted costume for lady cyclists, which, although ideal, was received with horror by the scandalized Victorian public. A few brave women did adopt this 'Rational Dress' but at best were treated with contempt, at worst with outright hostility. Edith Rigby, the Preston suffragette, was one of the first ladies to be seen riding in such garb in the locality and 'the boys pelted her with vegetables and eggs and the girls booed and hooted as she went by'.[4] 'Swiftsure', the cycling correspondent in the *Clarion*, wrote in September 1895: 'Few would believe how insulting

---

[1]  L. C. Davidson, *Handbook for the Lady Cyclist* (Hay Nisbet, 1896), p. 10.
[2]  Ibid.
[3]  *The Clarion*, 6 July 1895, p. 215.
[4]  P. Hesketh, *My Aunt Edith* (1966, repr. Lancashire County Books, 1992), p. 8.

and coarse the British public could be unless they had ridden through a populated district with a lady dressed in Rationals'.[1]

Rational dress did not conform to the Victorian idea of femininity. Lillian Davidson in her handbook stressed, that the lady cyclist 'should not dress in a style to excite undue notice or make her pastime unattractive to the eyes of the outsider'.[2] The widely accepted cycling attire was, in fact, a compromise: a narrower, shorter skirt (an inch or two above the ankle) with knickerbockers underneath to replace the layers of petticoats. It was far from perfect, for the long skirt was inhibiting and prone to take off in the wind. Women resorted to keeping their skirts down by sewing lead shot into the hems or by attaching elastic straps to the inside of the skirt to act like stirrups, holding the skirt down by the feet as they pedalled. Nets were designed for bicycle wheels to prevent skirts getting tangled. Lillian Davidson gave advice on the art of riding elegantly in a long skirt: 'I cannot too strongly insist upon the importance of having it [the skirt] hang evenly and nicely in the saddle. Not only does one's whole appearance depend on this point but comfort in riding is increased or diminished by the way in which the draperies conduct themselves'.[3]

The style of riding was as important as dress. Cycling for women was to be a graceful activity, as Fanny Erskine elucidates: 'The rider and her machine move as one, fast or slow, rough or smooth, apparently effortless as a hawk on the wing'.[4] Cycling too low in the saddle was inelegant and riding excessively fast was frowned upon for 'lovely womanhood is anything but lovely under these circumstances'.[5] For the lady cyclists the art was to remain neat, tidy and cool, even after a day's cycle ride. Hints on how to achieve this were numerous. A Lancashire cyclists' road book advised 'Overnight, when intending to ride the next day, damp your hair with the following: one lump of sugar dissolved in a tablespoon of cold tea. Wear a fringe net and your hair will be kept in perfect order.'[6]

Learning to ride a bicycle was, therefore, much more difficult for women, for they not only had to cope with unsuitable clothing but also

---

[1] *The Clarion*, 7 Sept. 1895, p. 215.
[2] L. C. Davidson, op. cit., p. 115.
[3] Ibid., p. 17.
[4] F. J. Erskine, *Lady cycling* (Walter Scott, 1897), p. 52.
[5] L. C. Davidson, op. cit., p. 68.
[6] *The Lancashire Cyclist's Road Book and Guide to over 100 Routes and Tours* (T. Johnson, printer, n.d.). – the Victorian version of hair lacquer, in fact!

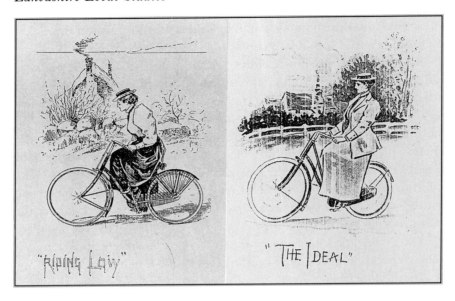

PLATES 5 and 6. Illustrations from *Bicycling for Ladies* by Fanny Erskine, showing the 'right' and 'wrong' ways to cycle. The art was to ride high in the saddle: riding low was considered a 'hideous fashion' and frowned upon as inelegant and ugly.

with the Victorian demand for elegance. As a result, many women practised in private before appearing on the roads. Manchester Athletics Club, for example, allowed them to practise on its track at certain times during the week. In spite of the limitations society laid upon women cyclists, many were able to ride most successfully. S. Dawson, from the Lancaster C. C., remembered that 'we had some splendid lady riders, as I have known a few of them reach Windermere in three hours, Sedbergh in two and a quarter, and Blackpool in two hours and ten minutes, without any trouble'.[1]

The bicycle was, indeed, an important factor in the liberation of women. In 1895 Louise Jeye wrote in the *Lady Cyclist*: 'There is a new dawn, a dawn of emancipation, and it is brought about by the cycle'.[2] Women could travel independently, unhampered by chaperones, giving

---

[1]  S. Dawson, *Incidents in the course of a long cycling career* (author, n.d.), p. 13.
[2]  *Lady Cyclist*, August 1895, p. 224, quoted in D. Rubinstein, 'Cycling in the 1890s', *Victorian Studies* (Autumn, 1977), pp. 47–71.

them a real taste of freedom and a chance to be self-reliant. Women formed their own cycling clubs at, for example, Manchester and Burnley, because many existing clubs refused to allow them as members. Even in mixed clubs, women often had their own captains, and separate club runs in addition to the established ones. The ladies' section of the Lancaster C. C. visited a wide variety of places, from sedate Silverdale where 'they got stranded in the woods in looking for the much prized lilies-of-the-valley'[1] – to the more *risqué* Blackpool, where 'in the afternoon bathing was indulged in'.[2] The appearance of a group of women riding out together for an afternoon or evening shook Victorian sensibilities, and brought conventional opinions of femininity under attack. Cycling in a mixed group caused a similar controversy, for here women were able to meet men on equal terms.

For women, therefore, the bicycle offered the potential not only of greater freedom of travel but also social liberation. The bicycle was used as a weapon of rebellion in the fight for emancipation.

## 4: Clubs of the '90s.

The upsurge in interest in cycling during the late 1880s was insignificant compared with the craze which developed in the mid-1890s. Suddenly, cycling became fashionable in society and even the aristocracy flirted with the idea for a time. It seemed that everyone wanted to ride a bicycle, and all who could afford one did so. The Lancashire cycling clubs flourished and many new ones were established. The Burnley Wheelers was founded in 1895 and within a year had seventy-one members, eight of whom were women. There were cycling clubs attached to churches and temperance societies; there was even a police cycling club in Burnley. The clubs now had a wider social composition in terms of class, age and sex, and as a consequence a distinct change in their emphasis and character is evident from this time. The uniforms became less military in style: Blackburn C. C. now wore straw hats with a black and white band in place of their original blue helmets, and in some clubs uniforms disappeared altogether.

---

[1] Morecambe Library Local Studies Collection, newspaper cutting from manuscript notebook concerning Lancaster Cycling Club, 1891–1910.
[2] Ibid.

PLATE 7. A group of cyclists in front of Stirzaker's Tea-rooms, Brock, *c.* 1904. Brock, near Goosnragh, was a popular destination for club runs and the tea-rooms, opened in 1898, were a great attraction. As the sign outside indicates, they catered particularly for cyclists, and offered reduced tariffs for members of the Clarion Cyclists Union and the Cyclists Touring Club.

Bugles, so proudly displayed in the early clubs, gave way to whistles. In general, a more relaxed social atmosphere can be discerned. Some of the more traditional clubs, such as Anfield, Rossendale, and Preston, refused to admit lady members and so retained their gentlemen's club image, but even some of these dispensed with their uniforms and bugles in the later 1890s.

Club runs now included picnics and games at the destination. Teas at country inns formed a prominent part of the expeditions. The sheer pleasure of cycling on club runs is evident from the evocative passages written in the cycling columns in the local newspapers. The Secretary of Lancaster C. C. wrote of one such run to Kirkby Lonsdale in 1899 that: 'It was a real treat to be out on the roads with a nice refreshing breeze in our faces and long-lost-found-again prodigal sun throwing his warm rays upon our backs. It made us feel as if we were in another world'.[1]

The contrast between industrial town and countryside was so great that the cyclists would indeed seem to be in a different world. Cycles

---

[1]  Ibid.

enabled ordinary town people to rediscover the countryside. The image-makers of Victorian England had for years idealised the countryside in art and poetry: now more humble folk could see for themselves, and discover the truth of the image. So vivid were the descriptions of the cycle runs that it was almost as if the cyclists were seeing the world for the first time in colour. Flowers, birds and the passing of the seasons were portrayed with idyllic sentimentality.

It is surprising how much these runs were enjoyed considering the state of the roads with which the cyclists of the 1880s and '90s had to contend. Many of the main rural highways had been left to decay after the development of the railways, and they were in a deplorable condition, deeply rutted with numerous pot-holes. Cycling under these conditions, on the heavy machines of the time, with their solid tyres, must have been excessively uncomfortable. Pneumatic tyres when they became widely available in the 1890s, gave a softer ride but did not survive long on such rough roads. Cycling in the winter months was almost impossible and even in summer was weather-dependent. Wet weather meant large quantities of mud which got under the chains and caused them to break, and the riders themselves were frequently plastered from head to foot. Dry weather was equally daunting, for the cyclists raised clouds of choking dust as they rode along, and were compelled to cycle in small detachments in an attempt to allay the dust. The description of the Lancaster C. C. run to Grange in 1899 illustrates the problem vividly: 'Dust in front of you, dust behind, dust all around and looking at the foliage of the hedgerows you could scarcely distinguish the blossom from the leaves'.[1]

Many clubs hired out country cottages for the benefit of their members, who could cycle out and find every home comfort awaiting them. Burnley Victoria C. C. had a cottage at Hurst Green and spent over £20 furnishing and decorating it. Sixpence was charged for overnight accommodation and the lady in the adjoining cottage prepared meals for visiting cyclists at a reasonable price. Similarly, Preston C. C. had a house at Scorton for its members. Less affluent clubs went camping: Darwen C. C. bought tents and camping equipment and had a permanent summer camp near the Guide's House at Warton.

---

[1]  Ibid.

PLATE 8. Three generations of the Cordingley family at the Haslingden Wheelers' Fancy Dress Carnival Parade, 1899. Jack Cordingley, the famous racing cyclist, is fourth from the right, with his wife and children. His father is next to him. The children depicted England, Ireland, Scotland and Wales. Ireland (first from the left) actually carried a piglet during the parade!

The great cycle parades of this era had a festive air. Gone were the regimental lines and smart uniforms. In their place were fancy dress and lantern parades. The latter were a particular favourite with clubs and public alike. A description of one such parade by Blackburn C. C. serves to illustrate the magic of these occasions:

> about 150 Japanese lanterns were distributed: these were fastened to the machine in every possible manner, some being only a few inches from the ground and others as high as 8 ft . . . the effect was charming and a large crowd gathered . . . to witness the sight.[1]

The fancy-dress cycle parades of the 1890s were amazing sights, with hundreds of riders wearing elaborate costumes. Even tableaux depicting various scenes were erected on cycles. Manchester hosted some of the

---

[1] Blackburn Library Local Studies Collection, newspaper cutting from Blackburn Cycling Club Minutes, March 1890.

most spectacular cycle parades of the time. At their annual life-boat cycle parade in October 1895 more than 2,000 cyclists rode in a procession which was a mile long. They were

> dressed in a variety of costumes, both serious and burlesque, from a collier to a duke, from Columbine to Richard III. The tableaux were both pretty and vulgar, one being a representation of the 'New Man' in contradistinction to the 'New Woman' rigged up on a tricycle, New man sitting up in bed with a dummy baby and the wife (also a dummy) laid beside him snugly asleep.[1]

Such fancy dress parades were frequently held in aid of a charity and collecting boxes were carried *en route*. Lancaster C. C. had an annual parade for the infirmary and in 1893 they collected over £30 in two days.

Similarly, many of the annual club sports were involved with fundraising for local charities, and they became more of a family affair. The proceeds of the annual Blackburn C. C. sports day in the 1890s went to the infirmary and the programme of events included not only cycle races but also athletics, including a tug of war; the local brass band was usually asked to perform.

The clubs of the 1890s changed to meet the needs of their new memberships. Cycling was no longer an élitist activity but was now widely accepted and avidly pursued. The clubs' social events reflected these changes, and became an increasingly popular source of entertainment.


## 5: *Clarion cycling clubs*

In the mid-1890s a different type of cycling club arose, which combined the pleasure of cycling with socialist propaganda. These were the Clarion Cycling Clubs. The first one was established in Birmingham in early 1894 and it was soon emulated all over Lancashire. In fact, the north of England was soon the stronghold of the movement. Allied to the *Clarion* newspaper, from which they acquired their name, and like the paper's readership, the club members were essentially skilled workers, and members of the lower middle classes, with a few wealthier people such as the Pankhursts. The subscriptions were much lower (2s. 6d.) than those of

---

[1] *The Clarion*, 19 Oct. 1895, p. 335.

other clubs, in order to attract working-class members. From the beginning these were mixed clubs and, in particular, they aimed to persuade
women to join by making their membership free. They also actively
encouraged Rational Dress. The movement emphasised outdoor pursuits
combined with fellowship. Its philosophy was to show the working classes
a better way of life by introducing them to socialist ideas within a friendly
and informal atmosphere. A typical club run consisted not only of a ride
out into the country but the delivery of socialist tracts as well. The
Liverpool C. C. C. recorded its run to Knowsley in 1894 as follows:

> First to Knowsley where His Lordship the Earl of Derby did <u>not</u> invite us
> to dinner, but his tenants were supplied with Clarions and Clarion
> leaflets. We also called at the police station and left some tracts for the
> edification of the gentlemen in blue.[1]

The Clarion cycling clubs were also involved in electioneering and the
women members were active in the women's suffrage movement, delivering tracts to promote their cause. In spite of their serious outlook, the
Clarion cycling clubs were full of joviality and comradeship, and they
were immensely popular with both men and women. Club runs were
enlivened by a special language, 'Clarionese'; for example, 'Boots' was
shouted on meeting a fellow Clarion cyclist on the road, and the reply
'Spurs' was returned if all was well.[2] Such rituals helped to increase the
sense of solidarity and no doubt added to the enjoyment of cycling.

In common with other cycling clubs, the Clarion clubs held meets
where hundreds of members gathered together, but theirs included socialist talks as well as the usual festivities of a meet. Because of this the
large Clarion meetings were treated with a deal of caution by the authorities: some, for example at the Chester meet in 1898, actually called the
police out for fear of revolution. Their fears were groundless, for the meets
were very light-hearted affairs, the members more intent on enjoying
themselves in like-minded company than planning the overthrow of the
government.

Lancashire was the pioneer of the Clarion club houses, which could
be seen as forerunners of the youth hostel movement. These houses
offered Clarion members simple and cheap accommodation, enabling

---

[1]  Ibid., 6 Oct. 1894, p. 7.
[2]  J. McGurn, op. cit., p. 135.

working people to have a holiday. The first club house was opened by the Manchester Clarionettes at Bucklow Hill, Knutsford, in 1897 and soon a chain of such houses were established around the country; for example, there was one at Clayton-le-Dale near Ribchester. Some houses also provided evening entertainment for their guests, in the form of concerts and lectures.

The Clarion cycling clubs were probably the first to realise the potential importance of the bicycle for the dissemination of information and they used it to great advantage in promoting the socialist cause. Never before had it been possible to reach such vast numbers of people, especially those in the outlying rural areas, with relative ease and be able personally to communicate the message to them. Other political parties soon emulated such activities, but they were never to have the same impact as the Clarion clubs.

## 6: *Economic and social impact*

Bicycles and their offspring, the cycling clubs, had a significant impact on the economy of the country as a whole and Lancashire was no exception. Shops selling cycles increased rapidly in number in the last decade of the nineteenth century. In Preston there were twelve cycle shops in 1895. This figure had doubled by 1898, and by 1904 there were no fewer than thirty-eight cycle shops in the town. Similar increases were recorded in other Lancashire towns. To keep pace with the apparently insatiable demand for cycles in the 1890s many local small-scale manufacturers developed, some branching out from established businesses – commonly plumbing and ironmongery, as with T. M. Schofield of Southport. Others, like Jack Cordingley, turned a hobby into a very successful business and his cycles were exported all over the world.

Tailors and clothes shops also benefited from the cycling craze. Specially designed costumes, raincoats, gloves and shoes were marketed for and eagerly purchased by cyclists, while the demand for club uniforms kept the tailors busy. In fact all manner of goods were affected by the upsurge in cycling. The sales of bugles, bells, badges and whistles rose many-fold, as did those of lamps, oil, lubricants and other cycling accessories. Books, journals and maps for cyclists proliferated. Between 1895 and 1899 at least fifty-five books were published on the subject (excluding

PLATE 9. The Burnley Clarion Cycling Club was founded in 1898 and was one of the many clubs established all over Lancashire in the early years of the movement. From the beginning the Clarions were mixed clubs, and in fact positively encouraged women to join by offering them free membership.

travel guides), while in 1897 there were over thirty different journals for sale. The market for goods associated with the cycling trend seemed endless and Lancashire commerce took advantage of it.

The social impact of cycling was more subtle. There is no doubt that the cycling clubs created the right conditions for a greater mingling both between the middle and working classes and between the sexes, although to what extent it is difficult to determine. Similarly, the gathering of cyclists from different towns at club meets would inevitably create greater social awareness as information and ideas were exchanged. For women, cycling certainly meant increased social freedom as Victorian conventions were eroded by it.

Perhaps the greatest impact was in the sphere of improved communication. Both urban and rural cyclists were able to visit friends and relatives in distant towns and villages more frequently and with greater ease. The increased mobility afforded by the bicycle promoted greater socialisation. Perry noted the decrease in intra-parochial working-class marriages in rural Dorset from the late 1880s and attributed this to the advent of the bicycle making possible marriages to partners living some distance away.[1] This could be equally applicable to Lancashire marriage partners, living within both a rural and urban context.

At the dawning of the new century the bicycle was heralded as the universal mode of transport. Within the next decade the greater availability and lower prices of the bicycle were to open up cycling to all but the poorest. In Lancashire the working classes were to take up cycling with great enthusiasm and the clubs, in particular the Clarion cycling clubs, were to play an important role in working-class leisure activities, especially before the First World War. For many these were seen as the halcyon days of cycling. Alice Foley remembers with great joy her outings with the Bolton Clarion Cycling Club: 'In merry company we slogged up long hills and free-wheeled joyously down them, thrilling to the beauty and excitement of a countryside as yet unspoiled by the advent of motor transport'.[2] It was not until after the Second World War that the motor car was to eclipse the bicycle as the main form of personal transport. Up to that time the bicycle was king of the road.

## Acknowledgments

I wish to thank all the local studies librarians for their help in providing me with such a wide range of information for this study. In particular, I am grateful to Mr Ken Bowden for allowing me to see his research on Jack Cordingley. Many thanks also to Cath Rees for her work on the photographs. The illustrations in this paper are from the following sources: Burnley Library local studies collection (nos. 1 and 9); Blackburn Library local studies collection (no. 2, which is taken from a Blackburn C. C. Minute Book); Nelson Library local studies collection (no. 3); Rawtenstall Library local studies collection (no. 4); private collection of Mr Albert Clayton, with his kind permission (no. 7); and private collection of Mr J. Cordingley, with his kind permission (no. 8).

---

[1]  P. J. Perry, 'Working-class isolation and mobility in rural Dorset, 1837–1936: a study in marriage distances', *Transactions of the Institute of British Geographers*, xlvi (March 1969), pp. 121–41.

[2]  A. Foley, *A Bolton Childhood* (Manchester University Extra-Mural Department, 1973), p. 72.

# List of subscribers

Mr J. P. Ashton, Bury
C. W. & M. A. Atkin, Levens, Kendal
J. O. Baehren, Blackpool
Miss Angela Barlow, Surbiton
W. Bee, Urmston, Manchester
Birkdale & Ainsdale H. & R.S. Southport
George L. Bolton, Leyland, Preston
Mr & Mrs C. L. Brancker, Knutsford
Stanley Brown, Lytham-St-Annes
Tom F. Charnley, Preston
Mrs J. Clarke, Yealand Redmayne
Mr Douglas Clements, Withington, Manchester
Audrey Coney, Aughton, Ormskirk
Michael P. Conroy, Bury
Mrs Jacquie Crosby, Preston
Dr Alan G. Crosby, Preston
Mona Duggan, Haskayne, Ormskirk
John Exley, Cleveleys
Gillian Fellows-Jensen, Denmark
R. N. & E. S. Finch, Lowton
Mr E. Foster, Shaw, Oldham
Brenda M. Fox, Garstang, Preston
Mr D. J. French, San Francisco
Miss D. A. French, Gravesend
Mr & Mrs H. R. French, St Ives, Huntingdon
Morris Garratt, Cheadle
A. D. George, Manchester
Mrs Josie R. Green, Accrington
James A. Grimshaw, Pendleton, Salford
Brian Hall, Burnley
Mrs B. A. Hayes, Preston
Marian Hesketh, Lostock Hall, Preston
Eric & Mary Higham, Clitheroe
Mrs Lyn Hitch, Wray, Lancaster
Alistair Hodge and Anna Goddard, Preston
R. E. Huddleston, Lancaster

Betty Lee Jackson, Garstang, Preston
Jean Jolly, Westhill, Skene
Lancashire County Library HQ, Preston
Lancashire Record Office, Preston
Mrs Margaret Lancaster, Lancaster
Michael G. Leigh, Barnoldswick
Longridge Local History Society, Longridge, Preston
L. R. Lubbock, New Longton, Preston
C. E. Makepeace, Disley
Miss E. H. Marsland, Normoss, Blackpool
Mere Brow Local History Society, Preston
Mr Geoffrey P. Morries, Bamber Bridge, Preston
Raymond J. Pilkington, Blackburn
Sheila Powell, Lydiate
Mary Presland, Eccleston, St. Helens
Don Rainger, Pendleton, Salford
Martin Ramsbottom, Kirkham, Preston
Derek G. Richbell, Sale
David Rushton, Blackburn
Miss Barbara E. Sharp, Preston
Miss J. Siddall, Burnley
Mr Ronald Smith, Bolton
Jennifer E. Stanistreet, Crosby, Liverpool
Mrs Christine Storey, Poulton-le-Fylde
Alan Stott, Blackpoool
Stretford Local History Society, Stretford, Manchester
Frank Sunderland, Starling, Bury
Andrew B. Thynne, Lancaster
Joseph M. Till, Longridge, Preston
M. C. Turner, Fulwood, Preston
Mr N. Tyson, Ainsworth, Bury
David A. Whalley, Blackburn
Miss Doreen Williamson, Prestwich
John Wilson, Lancaster
Janet Withersby, Aughton, Ormskirk
Dr J. R. & Mrs G. M. Wolfenden, Marchington, Staffs.